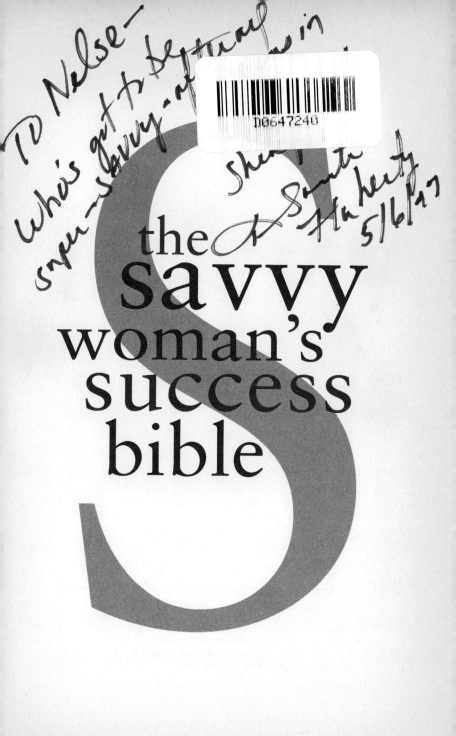

the
savvy
woman's
success
bible

tina santi flaherty • kay iselin gilman

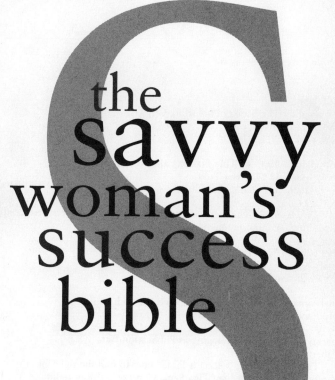

the savvy woman's success bible

how to find the right job,
the right man,
the right life

a perigee book

A Perigee Book
Published by The Berkley Publishing Group
200 Madison Avenue
New York, NY 10016

Copyright © 1997 by Tina Flaherty and Kay Gilman
Book design by Maureen Troy
Cover design by Charles Björklund

First edition: May 1997

Published simultaneously in Canada.

The Putnam Berkley World Wide Web site address is
http://www.berkley.com/berkley

Library of Congress Cataloging-in-Publication Data
Flaherty, Tina Santi.
    The savvy woman's success bible : how to find the right job, the
right man, the right life / Tina Santi Flaherty and Kay Iselin
Gilman.
       x.   cm.
    "A Perigee book."
    ISBN 0-399-52299-9
    1. Single women—United States—Life skills guides.   I. Gilman,
Kay Iselin.   II. Title.
HQ800.2.F53   1997
646.7'008'652—dc20   96-38803
                                                                CIP

Printed in the United States of America

10   9   8   7   6   5   4   3   2   1

With perpetual thanks to my grandmother, Mrs. Vattie Velma Headrick, whose voice and wisdom permeate this book.
Although no longer with us, she remains forever alive in my heart and continues to inspire me.

To my husband and soul mate, Bill Flaherty, for putting up with endless days of papers spread out all over the apartment, and the lights burning in the bedroom until 3:00 A.M., while I wrote and rewrote yet another chapter.

—TSF

To my mother, Betty Iselin, who really *did* know best, although I may not have realized it at the time.

To my super-supportive husband, Bjorn Ahlstrom, who helped me keep my eye on the ball and my perspective in kilter.

—KIG

Contents

Acknowledgments   ix

Why Read This Book?   1

PART ONE

The Right Job   9

Chapter 1   Help! Who Am I?   11

Chapter 2   The Right Job   25

Chapter 3   The Mental Machete: Self-Esteem
Whacking Your Way Through the Job Jungle   49

Chapter 4   Keeping It: How to Make Yourself
Indispensable   64

Chapter 5   Losing It: How to Get Fired   77

Chapter 6   Getting Back on Track   82

Chapter 7   The Romance and Business Merger   84

Chapter 8   Business Myths and Realities   98

Chapter 9   Tales from the Top   103

Chapter 10   The Ten Commandments of Business
Success   126

Part Two

The Right Man   133

Chapter 11   The Pleasures and Pitfalls of the Single Life   135

Chapter 12   Good Sex, Bad Sex, Safe Sex, and No Thanks   157

Chapter 13   Thirteen Ways to Lose Your Man   170

Chapter 14   Ten Terrific Turn-Ons
What Men Really Want from Women   176

Chapter 15   How to Keep Your Man Forever
What the Guys Told Us   182

Chapter 16   Breaking Up   189

Part Three

The Right Life   199

Chapter 17   Creating Your Style
The Bridge to the Right Life   201

Chapter 18   Looking Good: Dressing for the Office   205

Chapter 19   Tips from Your Courtesy Coach   220

Chapter 20   The Female Lair   233

Chapter 21   Solo or Share?   250

Chapter 22   The Care and Feeding of Your Social Life
Hitting the Party Circuit   258

Chapter 23   Max-ing Your Money
How Not to Get Shortchanged   276

Chapter 24   Psyching Yourself Up: Crisis Time   295

Chapter 25   What's Up, Doc?
The Care and Comfort of Your Bod   302

Chapter 26   The Good Life Express   314

Acknowledgments

These are the people whose contributions were the key to the birth of this book:

Connie Meehan—*The Savvy Woman's Success Bible* would never have been born without Connie Meehan, our in-house Executive Editor, who worked with us every step of the way. She invested her time, talent, heart and soul, dotting every "i" and crossing every "t." She saw to it that this book was the very best effort each of us could possibly make, separately and together.

And Special Thanks to:

Hank Baer of Skadden, Arps, Slate, Meagher & Flom—A wonderful attorney and friend, he greatly increased our knowledge of the issues and legalities surrounding sexual harassment. He reviewed and refined our text until we got it right.

Suzanne Bober, our editor at Perigee Books—A savvy woman and role model for our readers, she edited our "Bible" with exquisite sensitivity and finesse, always tuned in to both of us and, more important, kept us tuned in to our potential readers.

Helen Gurley Brown—The original savvy woman who has never received the credit due her for liberating millions of us. Her books helped women realize that a career could lead to "Having It All." Helen, we're in your debt more than you know!

Cathy Cash-Spellman—The bestselling author who not only generously shared her contacts and wealth of experience in the publishing world, but also made possible a superlative match between us and the William Morris Agency.

Debra Goldstein, our agent at William Morris—As savvy as they come, her belief in this book from the get-go provided a healthy dose of moral support and enthusiasm when we needed it the most.

Stedman Graham—The super-smart marketing entrepreneur who really opened our eyes to the business benefits women can enjoy if they're sports participants, not just spectators.

Dr. Clarice Kestenbaum—This eminent psychiatrist provided us with valuable insights and a wealth of information for our Crisis Time chapter.

We also want to recognize and warmly thank the following people who shared their expertise, told their stories, or just generally gave us their time and considerable caring:

Stefanie Antoine, Jack Atkinson, Letitia Baldrige, Marilyn Boll, Mario Buatta, Adrienne Colgate, Kitty D'Alessio, Ada and Danny DeMaurier, Sandra Derickson, Duane Garrison Elliot, Susan Falk, Annemarie Flaherty, Christina and Brian Flaherty, Ena Francis, Patricia Francy, Anne Sutherland Fuchs, Phyllis George, Al Goldstein, Mary Louise Guertler, James B. Hayes, Gary Hickman, Josie Kenin, Elsa Klensch, Beth Kobliner, Ron Konecky, Kay Koplovitz, Petrushka Kreitman, Ann Landers, Nancy Lane, Regina Leon, Trip Leon, Dale Leon, Felice and Al Lippert, Susan Lucci, Bea Lund, Marina Maher, Josie Natori, Lars Nilsen, Johnson O'Connor Foundation, Wendy Pantone, Judith Price, Vicki and Dr. Stuart Quan, William M. Quirk, Kate Roberts, June Rooney, James Rosenfield,

Steve Schaeffer, Ralph Schultz, Fritz Selby, Lynda Meade Shea, Martin Shea, Victoria Shepherd, Betty Sherrill, Muriel Siebert, Donald G. Saftness, Roula Stephanides, Barbara Tober, Dr. John Walsh, Sara Hanson Walsh, Kelly Weems, Dr. John Whelton, and Terri Williams.

Lastly—a forever thanks to David R. Foster, former CEO of Colgate-Palmolive, whose belief in me so many years ago changed the course of my career and my life.

—TSF

P.S. Special kisses to Liam & Ashleen, our beloved fur persons, who contentedly slept at our feet as we wrote every word of this book.

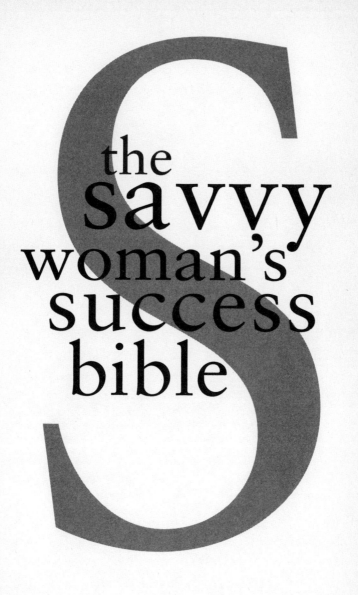

the
savvy
woman's
success
bible

Why Read This Book?

Why, Dear Reader, is it worth your time and money to bother with this book? Do you actually need someone to tell you how to lead the Good Life? Can't you do it on your own? Don't they teach that stuff in college? Can't you pick it up from your parents? Won't your company give you a few on-the-job training lessons that guarantee success?

Guess again! Granted, you can pick up a lot of know-how over the years, but who wants to wait? Unfortunately, there's no single font of knowledge you can drink from that will magically make you a success. You have to work at it as you go along. *The Savvy Woman's Success Bible*, however, is designed to help you get there faster. Starting now!

This book is a uniquely personal, yet practical, guide to work, life, and love. It will give you a lot of simple shortcuts to follow, whether you're about to enter the job market, are stuck in a dead-end job, or just generally want to restructure your career and love life. Even if one of your main goals is to cozy-on-down with your man in a rose-covered cottage, this book should be your personal bible. After all, you have to know how to *find* him before you can *get* him! And while you're looking for him, you've got your nine-to-five life to think about—to say nothing of learning how to soothe your psyche, the deep-down spirit that makes you tick.

But this isn't just another business book or catchy guide to finding a man. Nor is this a self-help opus on nurturing your Inner Child. It's all of these and more.

Your appropriately grateful authors *did* find the Right Job, the Right Man and the Right Life. Although we didn't have a handy guidebook to follow, we certainly would have welcomed one. Happily, our search for three of life's most important elements was very successful. We want to share with you our combined experience, as well as that of other top professional women, to make sure you hit the bull's-eye in every aspect of your life.

Our Story

As bona fide career women, with the track records to prove it, we've been in the trenches and know from the bottom up what it takes to find the Right Job, the Right Man and the Right Life. Here's our story:

Tina Santi Flaherty arrived in New York at age twenty-four. She didn't know a single soul, except her cousin, Mary, who came with her. So how did a relatively green, down-home girl, from Memphis, Tennessee, with no special contacts, and one hundred dollars in her pocketbook, climb up the career ladder to become the first female vice president at three of America's largest corporations? Quick Answer: The hard way! She learned by plunging headlong into life, which isn't always the easiest education.

There were plenty of failures, along with sweet successes. Coming from a family of strong southern women helped a lot. Persistence was in her genes. Equally valuable was a determination to be the best, no matter how many times life kicked her in the teeth. She lost her mother at age fourteen—the first big blow. Her self-confidence was shaken and she was without a mother's guidance at a critical time in her life. She weathered the hard times, however,

and eventually her inner strength and relentless determination to succeed paid off. Firmly entrenched in the business world, as the first
female corporate vice president in the history of the giant Colgate-
Palmolive Company, Tina took the leap at age thirty-five and married her soul mate, another self-made, highly successful executive.
Her achievements became legendary to the people who watched her
climb so far, so fast, at a time when most women didn't even dare
to *try*.

Kay Iselin Gilman, who grew up in a small town on the New
Jersey shore, took a slightly different life course. Buying into the
''Better Marry Than Tarry'' ethos of the sixties, she became a bride
between her junior and senior years of college. Immediately after
earning her B.A., she had two babies.

Kay's early marriage was an emotionally abusive one that trampled her spirit and sense of self-worth. The attempt to survive her
situation, along with raising two small children, effectively quashed
her lifelong dream of being a writer. She divorced, subsequently
remarried, and had a third baby. When her children were old enough,
she revived her goal and landed a job as a reporter for a local newspaper. Within a year, she became the first woman sports columnist
in the history of the *New York Daily News*, one of the country's
biggest newspapers. She also wrote a book about professional football.

After her second marriage ended in divorce, Kay was ready to
broaden her career horizons and became a partner in a major New
York special events firm. Along the way, she found the right man
the third time around. She's living proof that a late start out of the
gate doesn't mean you can't win it all at the wire.

This book is partially a step-by-step re-creation of what your
authors experienced—the good, the bad, and the ugly. It's also
chock-full of practical advice from leading experts on everything
from managerial maneuvers and life-style issues, to tips on cement-
ing a romance.

Sweeping Sea Changes

Unless you've been living in a cave, you have to know about the changes over the past thirty years that have forever altered the lives and destinies of American women. Before the mid-sixties, the typical girl-child was programmed from the cradle on to fill the traditional role of wife and mother—and *always* in that order.

Like her mother and grandmother before her, she followed a predictable road map—get some education and find a husband. If Mr. Right didn't show up immediately, she just took a nice little job—any job—that would support her while she did her real work: looking for Prince Charming. Once she found him, her happiness quotient supposedly was complete. At last, society told her, she'd reached Nirvana. To stay there, all she had to do was be a good wife to the Prince, and Supermom to the little Charmlets who eventually came along.

Wave good-bye to her. She's been gone since the early eighties, when large numbers of women began scaling the corporate ladder. At that time, many of those early executive women mistakenly felt they had to be male clones in order to succeed. So, they adapted everything they could from their male counterparts, right down to the power suit, bow tie, and big black briefcase. Ten years later, a new wave of career women began to challenge that concept. They refused to bury their femininity, even in the most high-powered business environments. Instead, they saw their womanliness as a definite asset, *not* a liability.

Naturally, this Generation Xer has the same ambitions, drive, and dreams as any man. Call her the "I want-it-all-*too* female." She expects her equal share of the good things in life: money, power, satisfaction, recognition, love, friendships, and control of her destiny. And she's willing to make the same sacrifices a man would.

The contemporary woman's wants and needs have taken a sharp turn over the past three decades. Yes, indeed—she's determined to have it all, but the "it" has changed. Sure, the Gen X woman still wants marriage, but not necessarily tomorrow. If you suggested that she should go husband-hunting "before it's too late," she'd think you were quaint. After all, she's probably had one or two live-in relationships with men she had no intention of marrying. When she *does* decide to marry, motherhood is no longer a constant. She decides if, when, and how many children she'll have. An instant family is no longer automatic. If she does decide to have children, she'll either opt for maternity leave or take a few years' sabbatical. But don't count her out. Once she's had the taste of honey that a career provides, it's the rare woman who's willing to give it up entirely. That's the big difference of the nineties and beyond.

Breaking the Barriers

Take it from us, as late as the swinging seventies, the single businesswoman over thirty was considered practically an "old maid." The common wisdom was that she was only working because she couldn't find a man, poor dear. If and when she finally did marry, her family and friends were pleasantly surprised. Of course, they didn't realize that she'd planned it that way on purpose—to get her career moving and not settle for any man just to add *Mrs.* to her name.

Today, those few ambitious women who went the job-first-marriage-later route in the sixties and seventies are now considered pioneers. Just what made those few late-marriage rebels smart enough to realize that a New Age for women was dawning? It was a combination of things. Title VII, guaranteeing women equal opportunity in the workplace, was passed in 1964. Corporations co-operated reluctantly, cracked the door open a bit, and promoted a few token women to managerial positions.

The hardy handful who managed to climb the Corporate Alps in the seventies found out really quickly that the air up there is positively exhilarating. Other women took heart and carved their own path to the top. Today, a woman who isn't highly career conscious is in the minority.

None of us is born knowing how to scale those slippery slopes of success. Getting there, not falling off, and enjoying the view are talents that don't come naturally. But if we did it, you can, too! And we're going to show you how.

Life's Different Now

Achieving success in business, finding our soul mates, and living a satisfying life, take planning and know-how. They usually come with long years of experience, not to mention a few bumps and bruises. This book will share with you the secrets of success of those women who did it—and are still doing it—*their* way.

Life now is vastly different from the way things were even a scant ten years ago. How?

- ✔ Competition is fierce; only the candidate with the edge gets hired.

- ✔ College graduates can no longer automatically expect to slide right into a job.

- ✔ No matter how capable you are, job security is a thing of the past.

- ✔ Your apartment or house takes a bigger bite out of your income.

✔ In your love life, you're equal partners—or should be.

✔ You're not alone if you seek therapeutic help.

✔ You can retaliate against unwanted sexual advances.

✔ Since nearly 50 percent of today's labor force is female, it's obvious that most women now regard work as an economic and/or emotional necessity.

Your job should be a springboard to all the things you're looking for: a mental challenge, a terrific social life, a better bank balance, a great wardrobe, or maybe even a BMW! And most certainly, your job should be a daily learning experience, preparing you for bigger and better things.

To get there, you need a proven success formula that tells you how to combine your job with the right advice and the right attitude. When you put it all together, you can turn your job into a career—and stake your claim to the top, too.

Must Reads

Here are just a few of the highlights you'll find in this book. Like all the chapters, they're designed to give you a leg up in every important aspect of your life. Read on:

"How to Make Yourself Indispensable" tells you how to become such an invaluable asset to your boss—whether you're a junior executive or a manager—that company layoffs and down-sizing won't give you a permanent migraine. We'll teach you the street-smart way to cement relationships with your employer, not the heavy-handed stuff you'll find in conventional business books.

"The Romance and Business Merger" helps you choose the kind of job that not only is right for you, but also offers the sort of super-scintillating social life you want as well. It illustrates why, if the job isn't satisfactory, chances are your male co-workers won't be your type either.

"The Female Lair" gives inside tips on how to provide the proper setting for your glamorous life-to-be. We'll show you how to decorate rich without spending mountains of money. You'll learn how to create surroundings that'll make you feel good and, in the process, help you seduce *him*—and the rest of the world—at the same time.

"Psyching Yourself Up: Crisis Time" gives you some invaluable mental insights—whether for love or work—that will help you achieve your goals, no matter how distant. You'll learn how to recognize if and when you need a shrink, how to find the right one, and the therapy no-no's to avoid.

"The Care and Feeding of Your Social Life: Hitting the Party Circuit" tells you how to entertain with wit and style, and why it's worth your while. The savvy, ambitious woman works almost as hard at being a successful hostess as she does at her job.

"Max-ing Your Money" shows you how to be a super-savvy shopper, and how to keep from being taken when your wallet's at stake.

In short, *The Savvy Woman's Success Bible* is designed to tell you everything you need to know to get there, stay there, and be incredibly successful in all aspects of your life!

Part One

The Right Job

one

Help! Who Am I?

So—you've finished high school, college, or grad school. Now you're about to embark on the vast, murky sea of careerdom. Or maybe you're past that, but stuck in a job you hate. You want to do something else—but what?

Before we tell you how to get your dream job, you've got to do a little research on yourself—like finding out what you want to do with the rest of your life.

It's not exactly a piece of cake to find a job that's 100 percent right for you—whether you're a beginner or have a few years of working under your belt. Most of us know what we *don't* want to do. It's much harder to determine what we *do* want. And, in these days of corporate downsizing, choices are more limited than ever.

Wish Upon a Star

Too many people entering the job market for the first time are so eager to land a job, *any* job, that they skip the basic exercise that can mean the difference between a successful career or just a ho-hum job. Before you even think about looking for a position, you need to do a self-assessment survey to determine your strengths and weaknesses. This single exercise can be the most important part of your job hunt. It will tell you what kind of business environment you're best suited for, where you'll flourish and feel most at home. If you avoid this self-examination, you could easily shortchange yourself for life.

Your objective is to decide what kind of work would make you happy. Why? Because if you enjoy your job, you're much more likely to succeed at it. Work isn't supposed to hurt. Ask yourself what you really want—beyond the basics of salary and job type. Reach deep inside yourself and pull out your hidden dreams. Don't hold back. Feed your fantasies! Let them run riot! Who would you want to be if you could wish upon a star? Don't be embarrassed if your vision of you is different from the way others perceive you. No one, except you, knows what you're really capable of. Don't allow anyone to trample on your dreams.

So what if you see yourself as rich, famous, and courted by kings? There's nothing wrong with that. What qualities do you have that might get you there?

There Are Two Parts of You

Who are you *really*? This is a question that will take time to answer. Who you are and what you're all about has dual components: personality style and aptitude. Personality style, by the way, has nothing to do with being the life of the party. It has everything to do with the way you naturally act and function. The second part of who you are is defined by your aptitudes. Aptitudes are inborn talents—special abilities for doing, or learning to do, certain kinds of things easily and quickly. They have nothing to do with your IQ, education, or even interests. They have to do with heredity. Aptitudes are in the genes, just like the color of your eyes, hair, and skin. Musical talent and artistic ability are some examples of gifts that are passed down to you. Because your aptitudes are so much a part of you, it's only human to take them for granted. People wrongly assume their talents are no big deal when something comes easily to them.

Career Guidance Specialists

There are a number of tests available that provide guidance and clues as to what fields are best suited to your special abilities and personality type. (Look in the Yellow Pages under Career and Vocational Counseling.) These are *not* IQ tests—they measure aptitude, not intelligence. When you're setting out to sea, they can be lifesavers.

We've recommended the Johnson O'Connor Research Foundation (JO'C), a nonprofit educational organization, to many of our friends. It's one of the oldest career guidance services in the business, with centers in eleven cities across the country. Although their fees aren't low, many people consider it one of the best investments they've ever made. JO'C's premise is: "Everyone finds that some things seem to come more easily than others. For example, some people can easily learn a new language but find it difficult to program a VCR; others are great at talking to people but find paperwork tedious. The work you're most likely to enjoy and be successful in is a job that uses your aptitudes." Less expensive testing is also offered at most high schools, colleges, and possibly at your local church/synagogue/community center.

Square Pegs in Round Holes

According to JO'C, there are basic aptitude and personality differences among people that help determine career choices. That's what makes one person suited to be a journalist, another a sales executive, still another an engineer.

Tricia S., a communications executive at a huge hi-tech corporation, came to JO'C because she was dissatisfied with her job and didn't quite know why. After she took the Foundation's personality and aptitude tests, JO'C informed her that she scored extremely high on "ideaphoria," their term for the ability to generate new ideas. Someone with a vivid imagination, for example, would qualify as an "ideaphorist." Tricia always assumed everyone had this ability and was amazed to learn they didn't. It was one of the reasons why she excelled in communications, a field that demands a steady flow of fresh, creative ideas. In Tricia's present job, she had little opportunity to use this talent, since the company's culture was very structured and bureaucratic and operated on the theory that "we do it this way because that's the way we've *always* done it."

Equally important to Tricia, JO'C defined her as a "subjective" personality type, an individualist who's happiest working in an unstructured environment that encourages personal creativity. Individualists are people who like to come up with their own ideas and implement them from start to finish, with little or no interference from anyone else. Individualists see the job as an extension of their very essence. They don't blossom in a regimented environment, where others call the shots. Art directors, actors, film directors, fashion designers, architects, photographers, painters, journalists, copywriters, and musicians are usually categorized as individualists. People in these fields feel strongly about bringing their personal interpretation to the job and aren't very tolerant of interference. As they feel they must preserve their artistic integrity, they rarely like to compromise.

Why does all this matter? Think about it for a second. If it's important to you that the job at hand bear your personal stamp, you'll most likely be frustrated working in a group and having your ideas watered down. People who prefer to create their own road map don't work well in an environment where others totally dictate the direction.

The polar opposite, according to JO'C, is the objective personality. Objective types are described as generalists, consensus-oriented people who have no burning need to make each and every project uniquely their own. They have no problem working with, around, or through others. Ideas are pooled and decisions reached by a consensus. No single individual gets the credit; instead, it's a team effort.

JO'C cautioned Tricia that her corporation's bureaucratic style was definitely not suited to her personality type and would ultimately stifle her creative ability. "For you," they explained, "it's like being a bird in a gilded cage." What the "little bird" story told her was to get out of her corporate confines into a more free-flowing environment. She resigned and hooked up with a medium-sized production company that specialized in TV documentaries. There she was able to concentrate on her lifelong love of writing and her talent for sparking new ideas. Plus, the atmosphere—less structured and formal—was far better suited to her creative personality. The moral of the story is, once you discover what you're all about, don't ignore it. Remember, a square peg can't fit in a round hole!

Be advised, however: career counseling is not a magic pill you can pop and suddenly discover what to do with the rest of your life. Instead, look at it as part of the ongoing process of examining your goals and finding out how to adapt your inborn abilities to them.

This whole concept of what your aptitudes and personality profiles are, and where they best fit, may not be immediately clear until you have a job or two under your belt. However, if you're at least aware that these differences in personality styles exist, you'll soon be able to determine what your type is.

Analyzing Your Personality Type

To start, try this do-it-yourself quiz that'll help you assess your personality profile. It may not be 100 percent perfect, but it will give you some obvious clues. Ask yourself if you are:

• Outgoing and good at convincing people to see things your way, versus a shy soul who shrinks at the very thought of pushing people to buy into your ideas?

• A "people person" who likes lots of interaction with others, or more of a loner, who'd rather work solo on a project and plug away until it's finished?

• Someone who likes being in a formal and structured environment with definite rules and regulations, versus an individual who'd rather work in a freewheeling, casual atmosphere where people do their own thing?

• Someone who prefers to keep regular work hours, or the type who's willing to put in whatever time it takes?

• The kind of person who's prepared to make your own decisions and take the heat if something goes wrong, versus someone who needs the safety net of group input and consensus instead of solving problems on your own?

• Someone who thrives in a high-pressure environment, with constant deadlines, and a thousand things to do at once, or a person who functions better when given one assignment at a time, with a long lead time?

• A person whose identity is so closely tied to the job that you look on most suggestions as interference, rather than a consensus kind of individual who accepts other points of view and compromises when necessary?

There's no right or wrong answer to any of these questions. Instead, they should give you some insights as to where your personality style fits best. Think carefully about your answers. An honest self-evaluation can save you a lot of grief and point you in the right job direction that much sooner.

What Am I Good At?

As stated earlier, the second part of what you're all about has to do with your God-given aptitudes, your innate abilities. If you do what comes naturally to you, you're bound to succeed. Here's an easy way to analyze your talents. You may think it sounds obvious, but writing down your "Likes" and "Dislikes" on a big yellow pad can help you decide which way you want to go. Under each heading, list everything that tickles your fancy, no matter how minor. Do the same for areas you tend to avoid whenever possible.

Putting your preferences and aversions on paper makes them real. It doesn't matter how long your list is or how trivial it appears to you. Anything goes. If you love to bake brownies, work every crossword puzzle you can get your hands on, or "perform" before a group, list it under "Likes." These abilities and interests are tip-offs to career niches. Connie, our co-worker, is mad for crossword puzzles, which is not surprising, given her gift for learning new words. The fact that Connie edits her company's newsletter meshes perfectly with her natural aptitudes.

On the other hand, if you hate to write letters, reports, etc., put that under "Dislikes." Obviously, you should avoid professions that demand strong writing ability, such as public relations, publishing, and journalism. (Even lawyers are required to write lengthy documents. Their command of grammar, syntax, and punctuation is critical to their work.) If geometry made you gag, put the fact that you hate working with numbers under "Dislikes." Obviously, you're not cut out to be a wiz on Wall Street.

We advised our friend Valerie to try this Like/Dislike exercise. She wanted to change jobs but couldn't decide what to try for. At the top of her list of "Likes" she wrote: Scuba diving and photography. It didn't dawn on her that something fun like scuba diving could ever be translated into a career until someone suggested she combine it with her other favorite hobby, photography. Valerie was fortunate enough to be able to put some of her "Likes" together and turn them into a job. Today, she's a successful, well-paid underwater photographer.

Our pal Jim was a struggling actor who happened to be a passionate animal-lover. Hoping to assemble an attention-getting portfolio, he asked a friend to photograph him with his dog in a variety of different wardrobes and settings, which he planned to send out to theatrical agents. Jim used his inherent artistic ability and imagination to make the photos unique. When he saw the finished pictures, he realized he had a real flair for photo design. He decided to go into animal photography. Today, his successful company, Petography, has published two books, and Jim is much in demand as a photostylist.

Not everyone has clear-cut, marketable hobbies like Valerie, Connie, and Jim. But most of us can manage to incorporate *some* aspect of our genuine interests into our jobs. For instance, if you like sports or are into physical fitness, a career in sports marketing or working with a professional sports organization or franchise is one of the many possibilities you can pursue. If you love to cook, clip every recipe you read, entertain as often as you can, and even relish the zillions of details involved in putting a successful party together—consider becoming a conference planner, or working for a special-events firm, or a big company that does a lot of customer entertaining.

But don't confuse your interests with the talents and aptitudes you were born with. Interests change with experience; aptitudes do not. They're with you for life.

Ask Others About Your Talents

Ask those closest to you—family members, a few trusted friends—what they think you do well. If you've been blessed with wise parents and pals who have your best interests at heart, take advantage of their opinions. Think carefully about what they have to say. They may spot a marketable talent you take for granted. Also, listen objectively to feedback from your bosses and peers— the good, the bad, and the ugly. Weigh the merits, discard the junk, and learn from their observations.

If Uncle Fred, the accountant, tells you you're not so hot with numbers, listen to him. Don't waste your time trying to be a mega-dealer on Wall Street—or an accountant, engineer, or tax expert.

On the other hand, Patricia Francy, now the treasurer of Columbia University in New York, was told by a boss early in her career that he thought she had a head for figures. She was working as an administrative assistant at the time, and finance was the furthest thought from her mind. Like so many others, she'd bought into the myth that women and numbers don't go together. As Patty says, "Sometimes, it takes someone else to spot a talent you didn't even know you had. As it happens, my boss was absolutely right! I listened to him and took a chance at switching careers. It was a smart move for me. I really like my job and I do it well." (Patty's story is detailed in chapter 9.)

Dig into the Past

To find your niche, think back. What were your best—and worst—subjects in school? This can give you a classic clue as to where your talents lie. Were you a whiz in English lit.? Did biology give you the willies? Were you always chosen for the lead in the school play? TV soap star Susan Lucci, of *All My Children* fame, was—and look at her now! (The story of Susan's blockbuster career appears in chapter 9.) Did your leadership abilities get you elected class president? Executive talent has to start somewhere. Did you finesse French or sail through Spanish? Foreign language skills can open a lot of corporate doors. School, whether it's kindergarten or postgrad, is the dress rehearsal for life. It gives you bona fide feedback as to what you should do later on.

Suppose you're like Stefanie, who was born with a lifelong passion for the printed word. Her dream was to leave her hometown in the Midwest and head for New York City, the heart of the publishing world. The fact that entry-level jobs in publishing pay a pittance didn't matter. Ever since she wrote a prize-winning essay, "Mikey, the Mouse," in first grade, Stefanie knew she wanted to work in a world of writers and editors, manuscripts and books. As a child, there was nothing she liked better than to curl up with a good book. She still feels the same way, but now she's getting paid for it.

Stefanie chose her work environment over salary. She opted for the chance to plant her feet firmly in the field she really wanted to be a part of. She wakes up happy and goes to sleep the same way, because she's doing what she always dreamed about. As an editorial assistant for a large, prestigious publishing house, she's learning, making contacts, and creating her own opportunities to become a full-fledged editor one day.

More importantly, Stefanie feels comfortable in her environment because it's right for her. She's surrounded by people she admires, respects, and wants to be like.

If you find yourself in the opposite situation, working with people whose jobs you would never want, and whose goals, interests, and values have nothing to do with yours, it's probably time to split.

Amelia, a friend of ours, was a successful advertising sales executive for a popular women's magazine. The atmosphere was friendly, and everyone was willing to help one another. She heard about an opening at an internationally famous fashion publication. Although she genuinely liked her job, the new one would pay twice the salary she was currently making. It also had all the elements of a dream job—money, prestige, and lots of clout. Amelia knew that her ability to sell was top-notch, so she felt she could easily handle the job. She interviewed, was offered the position, and happily accepted it.

Unfortunately, after only a month, the dream turned into a nightmare. Unlike her former co-workers, her new associates were uncooperative, secretive, and unwilling to help her in any way. Instead of getting the accounts she was promised, Amelia's boss gave her an inferior list to sell to. The place gave off such bad vibes that she was genuinely miserable.

While others advised her to stick it out ("It'll look bad on your résumé if you leave so soon"), we told her to call it quits, based on our own similar experience. We've found it's best to cut your losses as quickly as possible if you're absolutely, positively certain that things won't work out. However, it's always wise to line up another job *before* you quit your present one.

That's just what Amelia did. Realizing that prospective employers would find her much more desirable if she was currently working, she didn't leave the job-from-hell until she found a new one. She learned from her previous mistake and this time made sure that her personality style matched with her co-workers' and the office environment. She was extra-observant during her interviews and talked to everybody she could who either worked there or had friends who did. It paid off. As was not the case in her previous position, her new bosses love her work, her co-workers are friendly, and her account list is terrific, to boot.

Amelia's mistake in taking the so-called dream job was that she was more in love with her fantasy vision of *where* she would be working than in touch with the reality of *what* working there would actually be like. Although her aptitudes meshed with the job, her personality style clashed with that particular corporate culture and environment. Sometimes, the problem with a job isn't what you're doing but where you're doing it.

So even after you've evaluated yourself and isolated what you're most passionate about, you can still make mistakes and bad decisions. As we've illustrated, Amelia learned from her bad experience and didn't make the same mistake twice.

School Days

A lot of people are hung up on where they went to school, especially if they didn't graduate from an Ivy League university. If you went to an obscure college, will it put the kibosh on your career? The answer: yes, no, and maybe. True, Harvard, Yale, and Princeton graduates often get preferential treatment, particularly on the first go-around. Companies tend to assume that you must be bright if you were able to get through four years of college under some of the best professors in the country. But beyond that, Ivy Leaguers also have the advantage of being a close-knit family. Those who've made it through the hallowed halls usually will offer a helping hand to their buddies who passed through with them. That's what "old school tie" means—it has nothing to do with neckwear!

Non–Ivy Leaguers will be glad to know that sometimes there's reverse discrimination when it comes to hiring people who attended the "right" school. Some interviewers have a heavy chip on their shoulders if they themselves didn't go to a top university and take a jaundiced view of any candidates who did. One really smart, successful friend of ours, who attended a state college, says she'd never hire someone who went to an Ivy League school because she feels their education is too elitist.

There are many people in top management who went to small or little-known colleges. We worked for two CEOs of *Fortune* 100 companies who didn't go to college at all! Obviously it's not just your education that gets you the job. You've also got to stand out with that extra something—like enthusiasm and energy, along with a can-do attitude. If you combine your aptitudes and the knowledge of where your personality style best fits with the basics of a career plan, you can get and keep the job you want no matter where you went to school.

Now, What's Next?

You've done your homework, psyched out your personality, made your lists, gotten feedback on your abilities—now some solid ideas should pop out about the fields that interest you. Compile a list of the companies where you think you'd like to work, and then plot and plan until you get your foot in the door (more about plotting and planning in chapter 2). If you have to mark time for a while, that's okay. Remember, Rome wasn't built in a day. Just don't give up!

Here are a few reminders that'll help you find the answer to that eternal question: "What should I do with the rest of my life?"

- If you could imagine a dream job, what would it be? Heed your hidden dreams and talents.

- Don't be flustered if others think you're aiming too high.

- Only ask people you respect to help you tally up your talents.

- List your "Likes" and "Dislikes" to pinpoint your aptitudes.

- Discover your personality style and go with it.

- Get professional aptitude guidance, if needed.

- Don't get hung up on where you *didn't* go to school.

- If you're in the wrong job, cut your losses.

The preceding list is just to get your thinking processes started. You may be enthusiastic about one career direction but, after having been exposed to it, decide to switch in midstream. That's perfectly natural. In fact, all of us should reassess ourselves periodically, because our interests and needs evolve over time. For now, if you can zero in on what you think you want to do, you've got a leg up on the competition, even if you change your mind later. There's nothing more appealing to a potential employer than a candidate who obviously really wants the job and has the right personality and skills to do it well.

Chart your career campaign like a four-star general. Finding a job that's right for you takes organization, determination, and, most of all, self-awareness of your natural talents and abilities. If you follow the steps we've outlined, you'll be able to conquer your world and find your place in it.

two

The Right Job

The economy is on the upturn, stores are crowded, the stock market is climbing—so why haven't you found the job you want?

It may have something to do with downsizing, the current business buzzword. You know *that* dirty word, don't you? During the recession of the eighties, corporations found they could operate just as well with far fewer employees, and make more money. Mergers and acquisitions are eliminating people and their jobs, too. There's no sign on the horizon that any of these policies will change.

Nonetheless, there still are jobs out there to be had. Thousands of them open up every day. So how do you go about getting the one you want? You've got to get real, get organized, and get going.

Whether it's your first job or a career switch, you have to decide which field dovetails best with your talents, interests, and personality. If that statement seems obvious, you'd be amazed at how many first-time jobhunters have hardly a notion of what they'd *like* to do, much less what they're *suited* for. With barely a moment's thought, they blithely walk into personnel departments asking, in effect: Can you tell me what kind of job I'd like?

The Right Stuff

As we pointed out in chapter 1, friends and relatives who care about you can give you valuable advice. But to presume that anyone else can determine your career path is asking a bit much. Sure, you can profit from well-meaning counsel, but the final decision is yours, and yours alone. Ultimately, only you can figure out which way you want to go, what your real strengths and weaknesses are, and what you can bring to a prospective employer's table.

Once you've decided on a career direction, go for it. Let's say you think broadcasting could be right up your alley. The glamour, excitement and the chance to meet interesting people really appeal to you. But can you offer what they need? Whether it's broadcasting, beauty and fashion, law, medicine, Wall Street, whatever—be sure you're selling what they're buying.

And remember, every business is made up of various components: sales, advertising, public relations, finance, marketing, purchasing, research, etc. Could you fit comfortably into one of those areas, even if it's only a door-opener to what you really want? If your answer is yes, then you've got to dream and scheme for a way to get on the company payroll.

Ask anyone and everyone you know if they have any connections with the companies you're interested in. Don't be shy! According to Kelly Barrington, a top recruiting manager, "The average adult is in touch with three hundred other people you don't know. You should never assume that because someone isn't in your field, he or she can't help you."

Forget about thinking you have to find a job all by your lonesome. Consultants estimate that over 70 percent of jobs are obtained by word of mouth. We know we don't have to tell you this, but it's called *networking*.

For starters, try something as simple as talking to friends and relatives. Just ask them straight out if they know anybody at a TV station, for example, or in whatever field interests you. If the reply is affirmative, that could be your ''in,'' especially if they're willing to pave the way for you by writing or phoning. If they hesitate, don't give up. Keep bugging them until they say okay—just to get rid of you.

Network Yourself Around-the-Clock

The opposite of networking is not working. Networking is your life's blood when you're career shopping. If someone offers to personally recommend you, be sure to mention his or her name when you call to arrange your interview. It's highly possible Ron Recruiter won't recognize *your* name. (Miranda who? Do I know you?) You'll get a far better reaction to your first phone call if you mention that your mutual friend, Ludlow Hance, suggested that you call. It doesn't matter if you met Ludlow just last week at the neighborhood bar. People help people they know, like, and trust. Ron doesn't know you, but he does know, like, and trust Ludlow. *A contact is a contact is a contact.*

When you look for a job, don't be shy. Tell everyone—the mail carrier, your friendly pharmacist, and even the guy who cuts your hair. You never know—you could be networking and not even realize it.

Take Dale, for example. Newly engaged and flying to Florida to join her fiancé, she struck up a conversation with her seat mate, Peter G. She mentioned to him that she had recently left her job in Dallas as a computer sales executive and was relocating to be with her future husband. Peter listened up immediately. He had a software company based in Florida and just happened to be looking for someone with Dale's qualifications. By the time the plane landed, Dale had herself a new job.

So—networking can happen when you least expect it. Our friend Petrushka, sans job and eager to do *anything* to get out of the apartment, offered to walk the dogs for her roommate's boss. It didn't matter that the pay was minimal. It was better than sitting home feeding her face. One day, she offered to do double duty; while dog walking, she dropped off a package at a chic jewelry boutique. Petrushka started chatting up the owner, a Mr. de Maurier. In the midst of telling him the story of her life (Petrushka likes to talk), she mentioned that she was looking for a job. Guess what? Mr. D. needed a new assistant and hired her on the spot. Now Petrushka is learning all about jewelry design, and she's one of the company's most valued employees.

Another out-of-the-blue job offer happened to our friend Tara. While traveling on the Metroliner from New York City to Washington, D.C., she was busy putting the finishing touches on a speech she was going to give. Unbeknownst to Tara, her Metro seat mate was slyly reading over her shoulder. When he finally asked what business she was in, she told him she conducted motivational seminars for corporations. He beamed and exclaimed, ''Wow, could our company use you!'' Tara waltzed off the train with the promise of a year's contract.

The moral of these stories is: *Do* talk to strangers, network shamelessly, and always take a dog for a walk.

And now to the next part of your career plan.

The All-Important Résumé

The first step in getting organized is to plot your résumé. It's literally your life story, and it should sing your praises, but in a businesslike and subtle way. It's the primary tool for marketing yourself, so give it your best.

There are dozens of books on the nitty-gritty of writing a résumé. We've skimmed the fat to extract the really important points you should remember. So, here are some clues:

A Few Résumé Yes-Yesses

1. Prepare this document as if your life depended on it—because, in a sense, it does. Spell-check all company names, as well as every single word on the page. If prospective employers notice you can't spell simple words, how bright can you look to them?

2. Keep it succinct—on one page, if possible. Prospective employers' attention spans are short. According to *Money* magazine, interviewers spend an average of thirty seconds reading a résumé. So it shouldn't be surprising to learn they won't take the time to plow through three or four pages crowded with superfluous detail. Even senior managers, with years of experience to list, keep their résumés brief. If you're a junior executive, you'll look pretentious to people if your résumé is overly long.

3. Remember, there are umpteen ways to write a résumé. Everyone you show it to will have a different suggestion. You could spend your life rewriting your résumé if you take everyone's advice. What most people do agree on, however, is that it must be brief, easy to follow, and written in businesslike language. If the style makes it confus-

ing and difficult to read, a prospective employer may get the impression that logical thinking isn't your strong suit. This could get you rejected before you even have a chance to sell yourself! Make absolutely certain the key elements pop out.

There are various résumé formats, but we strongly recommend that you use the chronological style (see page 35). This form lists your previous jobs according to date, beginning with the most recent or present position. (If you're just out of college, summer jobs count. So do extracurricular activities like working on the school newspaper, participating in the drama club, volunteer projects, etc.)

4. Use acceptable businesslike language and style. Don't start every line with "I did," "I wrote," etc. Your résumé is not a letter to a friend. For example, if you're referring to a previous job, don't say, "I managed four people and I developed a new method for taking inventory." Take the "I's" out. Just say, "Managed a staff of four and developed new methods for taking inventory." Got it? Good!

5. Put a job objective on your résumé if you want to define the kind of job you're looking for; e.g., a marketing position in a consumer products company with high growth potential. A job objective also allows you to briefly describe some special advantage that you bring to the table (e.g., "experienced marketing specialist.")

6. Focus on your ability to solve problems and find solutions. Pick a problem you resolved in a previous job and describe in as few words as possible how you did it. What action did you take that demonstrated your managerial skills? Companies seek problem solvers who can grow with the corporation.

7. When you list previous experience on your résumé, include only those areas that are pertinent to your job objective. Make sure you describe your management capabilities, not the day-to-day minutiae that are part of every company's routine. And, by the way, virtually every

job requires some management skill, whether you're managing your boss's appointment schedule or a departmentful of people.

8. *Quantify! Quantify! Quantify!* Always use percentages or numbers when you can. If you claim you helped build sales, list the percentage of increase. *Numbers sing out to the reader.*

9. When you've got it all down on paper, ask a couple of business friends who have good writing skills to evaluate your résumé for grammar, style, and clarity.

10. Spend a few extra dollars to have it offset on good-quality paper, or print it out on a high-quality laser printer. This will give it a crisp, executive look that stands out in the pack. Don't use a standard photocopier; you'll get a far less professional look. It's like wearing a dress that screams Bargain Basement. Some prospective employers might think you have little or no idea of acceptable business standards, and your résumé could end up in the "dead" file.

11. If teachers or past employers have given you letters of recommendation or character references, have copies made and bring them along to the interview. They can be valuable endorsements, especially when you're a young professional and don't have much, or any, previous job experience to fall back on.

12. If you don't have such references, get some. How? It's fairly easy. Ask someone who has an upper-level job, knows your capabilities, and is willing to put it in writing. We'll bet there are lots of people who think you're great! Just make sure the reference is bona fide—remember, employers *do* check them.

    HINT: Put your résumé and letter(s) of reference in an executive-style notebook. Cover them with plastic sheet protectors. You'd be surprised how much more professional you'll appear than if you just handed out a batch of papers.

13. Don't ever mail a résumé without a carefully thought-out cover letter. You'll just be wasting paper and postage. The letter should state your reason for writing, who (if anyone) referred you, and why you think you're qualified for the job. Go easy here. No unnecessary back-patting, please. It's too transparent.

   More important, if you're answering an ad, be sure you try to match your qualifications with the job's requirements. In other words, tell them you've got exactly what they said they're looking for.

   HINT: Your cover letters should be typed, but never on personal stationery. Spend a few bucks and have business-type letterheads printed. Or, they can be thermographed (lots cheaper than engraving). You can always do it yourself on the computer, too. White, gray, or ecru stock is preferable; no rainbow colors or cutesy patterns. Of course, you'll have your name, address, and phone number printed on the stationery, and your return address on the envelope, to make it easy for people to contact you.

   This stationery can also be used for the post-interview thank-you notes (again, typed) you'll undoubtedly be writing. More about the necessity of this later.

It's obvious how important résumés are to the job hunter. Since it's your calling card in the wide world of business, you should avoid the pitfalls that could make you appear to be an amateur. So here's a zap list of what *not* to do.

A Few Résumé No-No's

1. **Never forget to check each and every word.**
   Many a résumé has been trashed simply because of typos, misspellings, and grammatical errors. They can kill your chances for an interview before you even get your foot in the door. A sloppily done résumé gives the impression of overall carelessness, which no employer wants.

2. **Never include a photo with your résumé.**

   No matter how fetching, photos give potential employers a chance to nix you before they even meet you. ("She looks like an airhead to me.") Besides, it makes you seem "show-offy." And don't *dream* of listing your vital statistics—age, height, weight, etc. Who cares?

3. **Never, but *never*, falsify facts in your résumé.**

   If you didn't graduate from MIT with a degree in nuclear fission, don't say you did. People who lie on résumés invariably get caught. (Employee information is checked and double-checked these days. Computers make it a snap).

4. **Don't hand out messy résumés.**

   If your address and phone number have changed, don't cross out the old ones and scribble in the new. Get the résumé reprinted instead.

5. **Don't try to razzle-dazzle!**

   In an effort to get an interview, some people have been known to send their résumés in offbeat ways—attached to

---

RÉSUMÉ DISASTERS

Our friend Marina, who heads up a leading public relations firm, receives dozens of résumés every week. Once, when she had a specific spot to fill, she started plowing through the current pile of résumés. Because she's inundated with applications, she's only able to give each one a quick glance. In this particular batch, there was one that really caught her eye. Right at the top of the page, under Job Objective, the candidate stated her desire to work in a top *pubic* relations firm. That missing *l* gave everyone a good laugh—and the boot to the careless candidate. Marina reasoned that if the would-be hiree was so blatantly sloppy with her own résumé, what catastrophe could she create with client material?

helium balloons, boxes of candy, or bouquets of flowers. One enterprising young woman sent hers in a shoe with the message attached, "I'd like to get my foot in the door." She didn't. While we get a kick out of these creative efforts, business people are pretty serious and rarely respond to silly shenanigans.

On the following page is a sample of the hard-to-beat chronological résumé that demonstrates our Yes-yesses and can help you get the job you want.

The Big Interview

You've finally scheduled your first interview with Company A on your wish list! Don't rush in where angels fear to tread. Remember, you've got competition—others who are trying for the same job. How do you beat them out? By having a Game Plan. That starts with proper preparation, both mental and physical.

Mental preparation means doing your homework before the appointed day arrives. Learn everything you can about the company. If it's a public corporation, start by getting your hands on its annual report. Companies are required by law to make this information available to shareholders. You aren't a shareholder? Not to worry. Corporations pass out these reports like peanuts because they think you might be interested in buying stock or its products/services. Just call their public affairs department. If that doesn't work, try asking a friendly stockbroker who wants your future business to send you a copy.

Annual reports contain a lot of valuable information about a company *if* you read between the lines. You'll get an idea of its overall financial health as well as the general direction in which it's moving. Plus, you'll learn about its product lines, what countries it does business in, and who the top staff people are, as well as its

MARY LOUISE GAINES
55 East 89th Street, Apt. 2B
New York, New York 10128
Home: (212) 555-7674
Office: (212) 555-3563

SUMMARY

Five years of communications experience in major marketing companies.Strong progressive record of achievement in all areas of communications. Unique ability to sell concepts, products, and people.

JOB OBJECTIVE

Opportunity to contribute significantly to marketing communications and image developments in a creative environment.

PROFESSIONAL EXPERIENCE

Great Big Company, New York, N.Y.   1996–present
   Public Relations Manager

Help develop campaigns for worldwide media relations. Created the "Love Our Rivers" campaign, featured on three major TV networks. Responsible for supervising new campaign expenditures; saved 11% over previous year's budget. Manage staff of three.

Large PR Agency, New York, N.Y.   1992–1996
   Deputy Director, Corporate Relations

Assisted in the development of publicity campaigns for agency's leadingclients. Created media vehicles which successfully revitalized formerly failing brands. Strategy achieved a 3% increase in market share.

EDUCATION

Duke University, B.A., 1992, magna cum laude

EXTRACURRICULAR ACTIVITIES

- Editor of college newspaper, responsible for all editorial content and layout.
- Member of college Debating Society.
- Winner of statewide essay contest "Making the Most of Living in North Carolina."

SUMMER EMPLOYMENT

- Apprentice in summer stock, between freshman and sophomore years.
- Editorial assistant for suburban newspaper, the *Fox Glen Gazette*.

VOLUNTEER ACTIVITIES

Currently weekend volunteer for The Children's Fund.

REFERENCES: Attached.

board of directors. Here's where you just might strike pay dirt! Maybe you'll discover that your boyfriend's uncle—or some such connection—is an executive with the company, a board member, or even its outside legal, accounting, or communications consultant. In any case, now you've got a real bigwig to endorse you. Believe us, it doesn't get any better than that!

If the company you're interested in is privately owned (this means the public can't buy stock in it), you'll have to scratch around a bit for information. Go to the library and try to find out if there's been any recent publicity, such as newspaper or magazine articles. Failing that, when you set up your interview, ask if there are any company brochures.

Also, make it a habit to read business publications. While you're sipping your morning coffee, you also should be drinking in the "Business Bible," the *Wall Street Journal*. Ditto for the business section of your local newspaper. And don't forget the major business magazines—*Fortune*, *Forbes*, and *Business Week*—for further news about the company. Look for specific information that will tell you if they're hiring (or firing). Are they downsizing or beefing up their staff? Are they a takeover target, planning an acquisition, or perhaps undergoing corporate turmoil?

Knowledge is power, and this kind of knowledge, used judiciously, can be helpful beyond belief. Just imagine what a positive impression you'd make on the recruiter for Wilson's Widgets, for example, if you could tell him you just read in *Business Week* that their new branch in Britain was voted "Widget Maker of the Year."

Beauty Is in the Eye of the Recruiter

Physical preparation is the second part of your Game Plan.

Start thinking well in advance about the way you're going to look when you have your interview. This is not the time to frizz your hair à la the Bride of Frankenstein. Your nails must be clean and neatly manicured. Believe it or not, people *do* notice dirty fingernails or chipped polish. Your makeup should be subtle and natural. This is not the time to experiment with black lipstick and matching nail polish—and exposing your pierced body parts is not recommended. We'll delve deeper into your business wardrobe "musts" in a subsequent chapter.

How should you dress? If you're just beginning your career, stay on the safe side. Your all-important first interview with a company is not the time to try to wear the latest fad outfit. On the other hand, we're not saying that you should look as if you're going to a funeral. The ideal outfit is a tailored suit or dress in a flattering shade, preferably a solid color. Wear simple, closed-toe pumps (no sexy red toenails peeking through), a matching handbag, and minimal jewelry. Boring—but businesslike—is the idea. Long, dangling earrings and clanking bracelets communicate the wrong message here. And, even if your breath isn't kissing sweet, don't even *think* about chewing gum. You're a businesswoman, not a bimbo.

Once you've got a year or two of working under your belt, you'll be a better judge of what clothing is acceptable in a particular industry. In publishing, advertising, or the music business, for example, more casual dress is generally all right, depending on the type of job you're looking for within the company. Once you're on the payroll, you can always dress down if that's their look.

HINT: It's always a good idea to stash an extra pair of panty hose in your bag in case you get a run en route to your interview. Why let something so simple spoil your carefully planned appearance?

So, you've dressed for the interview, you look in the mirror, and you like what you see. Now, walk out the door with plenty of time to spare. You *never* want to be late. In this situation, where every impression counts, it's better to be thirty minutes early than three minutes late. No excuses are acceptable. Besides, waiting in the reception room gives you a great opportunity to spy.

This is usually where the company puts its best foot forward. If the area is shabby or haphazardly run, that says something about the company. Is the receptionist who takes your name ditzy or is she competent? Well-run companies make sure outsiders are greeted politely and efficiently. Is the carpet dirty and worn? (Uh-oh—watch out. Sales may be down, which means they probably won't pay as much as you want.)

Also notice how people look and dress. If you don't see people whose style you admire, do you think you'd be happy working with them? It may sound trivial, but these are bona fide clues to the company culture.

As you walk into the office of your prospective employer, what do you do if your hands are shaking, your mouth is dry, and your stomach is doing flip-flops? Nothing! Just remember, these are normal reactions to stress. To counteract the queasies, reach deep down inside yourself and pull out your self-confidence. In other

---

HINT: Be careful not to drink too much coffee before or during the interview. It makes your energy level and mood go up and down just when you need to have all your wits about you. Also eat ''smart'' beforehand. Choose foods that will give you a mental edge, like protein—eggs, lean meat, or poultry. Eating carbs only, like a big bagel, a sugary Danish, or a huge plate of pasta can make you less alert.

words—*psych yourself up*. Remember—you're an intelligent person with good qualifications and no weird habits—at least none that show.

A few words about self-confidence: Everyone you'll meet on your interview path had to start somewhere. Once upon a time, they had cotton mouth before going through the same screening process. They've been rejected and disappointed, too. The trick is to look and act calm and confident. It'll convince you and them that you can handle the job.

To help calm yourself, put people in perspective. You're not some tiny little bug hoping not to be squashed. The interviewer is not inherently superior to you. He or she has just been around longer. Try to realize, they're only human, no matter how intimidating they seem. They may be in the driver's seat today and job hunting tomorrow.

Focus on your positives—visualize yourself in the job you're going for and act as if you have every confidence that it *can* and *will* be yours—if you want it.

When you sit down with the interviewer, all the homework you've done should start to pay off. If you can subtly show your

---

HINT: Avoid the "résumé scramble." When you interview, always have extra copies on hand, even if you've sent one in advance. You'd be surprised how often interviewers seem to misplace them. Sometimes another company co-worker will sit in on the interview; he or she will also need a copy, along with your letters of recommendation. There's nothing worse than losing valuable time looking for a lost résumé. It gets the meeting off to a bad start, creating a sense of disorganization. It's not your fault, of course, but you'll look far more professional if you bring extra copies.

knowledge of the company without sounding like a showboat, this is the time to do it. Don't be a know-it-all, but don't be too passive, either. Initiate as much conversation as you can without seeming to take over the interview.

Be conscious of your body language. Always look your interviewer directly in the eye. Never stare down at the floor; it conveys a lack of confidence. Answer everything you're asked as concisely as possible. Don't ramble but make sure to ask your fair share of questions, too. Human Resources Directors consider the interview process to be a two-way street. Your chances of getting the job depend as much on what you ask as on how well you answer their questions. Some of the right things to ask, if these issues haven't surfaced, are:

1. "Is there a written job description listing the responsibilities?" A printed description usually demonstrates that the company has carefully thought out what is expected from the job candidate. If no such position outline is available, ask for a verbal rundown. And we think it's perfectly okay to take detailed notes of your conversation. It can be very helpful later, when you're reviewing the meeting in your mind.

2. "What are the most important things you'd want me to accomplish in the first six months?"

3. "Whom would I report to?"

4. "How much on-the-job training would I get?" (In the case of your first job, this is especially important.)

5. "How long has the position been open?"

6. "May I ask who held it before?"

7. "Is he or she still with the company? If not, what happened?"

8. "When do you expect to conclude the search?"

How Much?

In the course of the average interview, company recruiters will either give you the salary range or ask you what you have in mind. In the latter case, play it cagey! Don't be tempted to answer immediately. Instead, ask them: "What are you offering?" If they still insist that you answer first, go ahead, but just give them a rough, rather than a set, figure. Something like "I'm looking for between $25,000 and $30,000, depending on the responsibilities of the job." Make sure you've done some preliminary research to determine a realistic amount. You can get a ballpark figure by looking at the classified ads in the business section of your newspaper. Also, ask friends who work in similar positions what they think this kind of job should pay.

Always put your salary request in terms of a year, never weekly. Do *not* go into your personal financial needs—rent, etc. No one's interested. Obviously, if you can't make it on the salary they're offering, you'll politely decline your interest in the job. As a general rule, the interviewer will tell you what benefits the company offers. If he/she doesn't, it's perfectly okay to ask if there's a company health plan. Just make sure it's toward the end of the interview, not the beginning. Otherwise you'll sound as if you're more interested in perks than performance. Once you've gotten past the critical first interview, you can feel free to think about your upcoming root canal and ask if the company has a dental plan.

Invariably, during the course of an interview, you'll be asked what your current salary is. Some people tend to exaggerate this with the expectation that the prospective employer will make a better offer. Be careful! Some companies will ask to see your W-2 tax form to prove that your information is accurate.

However, you do have an edge if you state your yearly income in terms of total compensation. This could include a 401(k) plan, use of a company car, expense account, medical and dental plans, etc.

Speak the Queen's English

In an interview, what you say and how you say it have major impact. You don't have to speak like a professor, but even some college graduates sound like functional illiterates. We once overheard an interviewee who sounded like this: "I was like—you know—basically happy at my last job when my boss and me started to disagree. And then he and myself just, like, had a personality clash, you know?"

Be honest—is this the way you speak? If so, you've got a serious problem. To solve it, try the following:

1. Tape-record yourself talking on the telephone—just your end of the conversation. If every other word is "like" or "you know," you'll know you're not speaking decent English.

2. Be careful with your use of pronouns. Look up those boring, but important, rules of grammar you learned back in the fourth grade, especially pronouns. "He took Mary and I to dinner"—ugh! (It's "Mary and me"—of course.)

3. Also, drop the collegiate/beach/bar expressions. They just don't work in a business setting.

If you can't get your thoughts across during the interview because you're too nervous, consider a course in communications training. Learning to express yourself better not only can help you get the job, it'll boost your self-confidence as well.

One job candidate promptly wrote the requisite post-interview thank-you note to a potential employer. Nice try, but the letter was so full of incomplete sentences and misused verbs, it defeated its purpose. If you find it difficult to write a business letter, it could be well worth your while to take a refresher course in basic English. Don't sneer! Brushing up on your sentence structure and correct use of the language can make a big difference, both in getting the job and in paving the way to future promotions. At the very least, you should get a friend who knows how to write a decent letter to review yours.

Making the Interview Count

What you do after the interview is almost as important as what you did before and during it!

Within twenty-four hours of your initial meeting, type a thank-you note to the interviewer. Do not underestimate the importance of this gesture! It will send an even stronger signal if your letter arrives the next day. Always restate your interest in the company (assuming, of course, this is the case). If a second meeting hasn't been proposed, mention in your letter that you'll be calling about the status of the search. Confirm you'll be phoning on a specific date. Then, make sure you do.

The obligatory business thank-you letter is nothing to be sneezed at. A successful New York events manager, who was a stickler for manners, told us about her experience with a wannabe hiree who failed to write a note. Her reaction was that anyone who didn't know enough to thank her for her time and interest wasn't her kind of person.

If someone outside the company set up the interview for you, that person, too, should be written (or phoned) and thanked. This is not only polite, it also keeps the other person involved. Never, ever forget to say "thank you" to people who help you in your job hunt. It's common courtesy—and let's face it, who knows when you'll need them again? Everyone appreciates—and expects to be— thanked for doing you a favor. People always remember those who take the time to thank them, and you can be sure they never forget those who don't.

Send a recruiter a "thank you for your time" note, even if you think the job isn't right for you or you didn't get it. You never know to whom your interviewer might mention your name. The same applies to contacting everyone you know. Case in point: Kate literally pushed her way in to see her old friend Jim, who told her he had no openings but reluctantly agreed to meet with her anyway. As luck would have it, that very night Jim had drinks with a colleague who was looking for a PR executive but couldn't find anyone suitable. Jim mentioned Kate, passed on her phone number, and voilà! She got the job, at twice the salary she'd been making.

The importance of thank-you notes and the acknowledgment of favors cannot be overemphasized. This applies from the beginning of your career to the end.

Closing the Deal

So, you got the job offer. What's next? Now here's the tricky part. After all, if you want the job, you expect to be paid fairly for it. During the interview process, you've probably discussed salary, at least a ballpark figure. Now's the time to firm it up and try for other goodies as well.

Negotiating salary isn't easy. It's embarrassing for most people to discuss money and to be firm about what they want. How do you do it? For lots of entry-level jobs, it's nonnegotiable. For more senior jobs, there's usually a wider range of salary potential. At the higher levels, most employers expect you to ask for more than their initial offer. How far do you go?

This depends on how much the company wants you. It can also turn on whether they've got other qualified candidates, and how your credentials stack up against the competition. You'd better get some good advice—fast—from a colleague who knows both the market and something about the company you're dealing with. Armed with that ammunition, you can decide how best to proceed.

Once you think the salary is right, all things being equal, take the job! Why play games when you've got a solid offer? Make a list of the other things that you feel are important and that weren't covered in the interview. Health benefits, vacation, profit-sharing, 401(k) Plans, whom you'll report to, frequency of performance reviews, and salary evaluations are all valid questions. Maybe you'll be willing to ''sacrifice'' one benefit to gain another. For instance, our friend Lauren was willing to take less money in exchange for a full-time assistant.

Another word of caution: In today's marketplace, jobs are getting scarcer and scarcer. If there aren't any other promising prospects on the horizon, don't play too hard to get. While you're weighing your options, someone else could come along who's ready to commit then and there, leaving you out in the cold.

Now what if the job you're offered at Company X isn't at the level or in the area you anticipated? Let's say you're asked to be the receptionist and general gofer, rather than being offered the more substantive—and glamorous—position you really wanted.

Don't storm off in a snit. Think about it. If this is a company you're really interested in, sometimes it's worth it to take the job— any job—just to get your foot in the company door. *Many moguls have been hatched in the mailroom.* Also, if it's taking three to six months to land your first job, sometimes it's crucial just to get in motion. In other words, do something—anything—rather than nothing. It will help build your self-confidence. Once you're in, you can plot your next move.

Always bear in mind, your first job is just that: it's only the beginning. You won't be handcuffed to the desk and forced to spend your whole life there. Remember, if after a reasonable amount of time you feel certain the company or job isn't right for you, you can always move on. You sometimes have to experience firsthand what you *don't* like before you find out what you *do*. And having at least one job notch on your belt is helpful when you're looking for another.

Having said all of the above, there is one exception. If your gut feeling tells you that the person interviewing you (*not* the personnel executive, but your prospective boss) is a nerd, dud, or bore, pay attention to it. Don't lull yourself into thinking that because this person seems wimpy and complacent, you'll have carte blanche to make the job anything you want. Duds can be as devious as anyone else.

We know of one executive who was lured from her big job to an even bigger one with promises of more money, prestige, and responsibility. The company was jumping up and down to get her. "We'll make you a star; the sky's the limit," they promised passionately. A little voice inside her kept warning, "Don't!" She knew in her heart of hearts that the culture and chemistry were wrong. It was a huge, bureaucratic company, highly regimented, and managed by people who had little appreciation for individual creativity. It was the kind of environment she'd avoided all her life. She didn't listen to her inner voice, the job was a nightmare, and she wanted to quit the first week. After a few miserable months, she did just that. If the job starts out wrong, it usually doesn't get any better.

Washout!

You had all the qualifications. You looked great, you said all the right things, and they hired somebody else! Don't despair. It happens all the time. It's called chemistry—that indefinable something between you and the interviewer. Good chemistry creates an immediate bond. Bad chemistry causes the interview to fall apart. Sometimes it can't be helped. You may just have rubbed someone the wrong way, no matter how hard you tried to ingratiate yourself. Chances are you may even have felt the same toward the interviewer. If, despite these negative vibes, you're offered the job and accept it, it probably won't work out in the long run.

The interview process can be incredibly subjective. What fizzles with one person can sizzle with another. Some job candidates, in their efforts to please, talk too much and can't seem to manage to say the right thing. Others know just which buttons to push.

Good example: Thea had to hire a sports promotion manager. She interviewed eight candidates and narrowed them down to two, both of whom were equally qualified. She finally chose Joe because, at the end of the interview, he said, with great sincerity, a few magic words: "If I get the job, *I won't let you down.*"

This little off-the-cuff remark, however simple, was just what Thea needed to hear. It reassured her that Joe was the right candidate.

Wrap-Up

We're not trying to tell you that finding the right job is a piece of cake. But if you follow our Game Plan, you'll make it a lot easier on yourself. Every single one of the items we've covered is crucial to your success—networking, the right résumé, style/presence, interviewing skills, follow-up, and that elusive compound, chemistry. Put them all together and they spell J-O-B!

The Job Run-Through

- It's *your* job to decide which field dovetails with your talents.

- Make sure you're *selling* what the company's *buying*.

- Ask anyone and everyone if they have any contacts.

- Personnel experts estimate that over 70 percent of jobs are obtained by word of mouth.

- Network around the clock.

- Write your résumé as if your life depended on it.

- You'll be twice as impressive if you do your homework on the company *before* the interview.

- Dress in a businesslike way.

- Always bring extra copies of your résumé.

- Watch your body language: make eye contact with the interviewer.

- Don't be afraid to ask questions.

- When it comes to salary, try to get the interviewer to mention a figure first.

- Always send a thank-you note, even if you don't want the job.

- If you lose out, don't despair; it could just have been a case of bad chemistry.

three

The Mental Machete: Self-Esteem

Whacking Your Way Through the Job Jungle

When a woman sets out on her great adventure into the jungle of life and work, she needs a mental machete called self-esteem. Some people have more than their fair share. Most don't have enough. But self-esteem and confidence will help you sail through the interview, land the job, and solve the other daily crises of life, including problems with personal relationships. If you think you have enough of that magic elixir, skip this chapter. However, very few of us—male or female, successful or not—feel we have sufficient self-confidence flowing through our veins.

No one is born with it. True, family relationships can build up—or tear down—your self-esteem. (But you can't use an unhappy childhood as a lifelong crutch.) Naysayers to the contrary, feelings of self-worth can be developed. A lot of us whose self-confidence was almost nil *learned* to believe in ourselves. When you know way down deep that you really have value, that you're inferior to no one, you'll be amazed at how your life changes.

What Is It?

Just what is self-esteem? How can you get it and make it work for you?

Before we say what self-esteem *is*, let's discuss what it's *not*. As writer Judith Stone explained in a recent magazine article, "It isn't self-absorption, arrogance, conceit, or incessant high-decibel horn-tooting."

Boiled down, here's what it is: self-esteem is knowing that you have value and ability. And even if you mess up now and then, you still keep that good feeling about yourself. In other words, your sense of self remains relatively intact, not smashed to smithereens. You don't have to be perfect to feel good about who you are. You just have to accept yourself, warts and all, and give yourself a little wiggle room to make mistakes. When you respect yourself, you enhance your relationships because it's that much easier for you to appreciate others.

Self-esteem is as fragile as spun glass for most of us. To quote Woody Allen, "Self-esteem is that thing with feathers, often ready to fly away at the newest puff of cold air from the outside world." So a little self-esteem touch-up now and then never hurt anyone. Hey, we all have our down days, when everything seems to go wrong. But the trick is not to be too hard on yourself. Everyone makes mistakes occasionally.

Take a tip from the male species. Many psychologists theorize that when guys goof, they don't beat themselves up to the degree women do. Instead of personalizing failure—i.e., "it's all *my* fault"—men are generally more objective and find ways to gently let themselves off the hook, if not totally, at least in part. In other words, they're able to understand if the problem was simply beyond their control.

On the other hand, we women sometimes see our mistakes as the end of the world. We not only take total responsibility for our goof-ups, we hold on to them for dear life. Instead of letting failure fly off into the wild blue yonder, we keep it alive by berating ourselves: "If only I had done this, that, or the other thing," we wail.

This constant worrying chips away at self-esteem. There are a million reasons why we tend to second-guess ourselves. To pick one, women are nurturing creatures; we want our decisions to make everyone happy. Remember, it's hard to please everyone. If you did what you did for a good reason, don't lose sight of that fact. Why jump to the conclusion that you're wrong?

But pumping up your self-esteem can change the way you handle all of this. You'll not only learn to forgive and forget your failures, you'll actually start to take credit for your successes. No more attributing your achievements to accident, good timing, or other people's help. Forget that! You'll be able to look yourself in the mirror and give yourself a (gentle) high five. And when you get a good shot of self-esteem, you'll find it easier to make decisions and stand by them. The real secret of self-esteem is to see setbacks—whether they were your fault or not—as temporary glitches that can be fixed for the future.

Word to the Wise

For most of us, positive self-esteem revolves around such things as how likeable, loveable, attractive, or intelligent we think we are—or aren't. Most of those qualities can be upgraded, even intelligence. If your grades in school weren't all that great, don't lose heart. School smarts are just one kind of intelligence. Technical ability, artistic talent, or a natural ability with people are just as valuable.

For example, our friend Patty, who is plenty smart herself, grew up with an older sister who was even brainier. Instead of holding it over Patty's head, her sister always pointed out all the things that Patty could do better. As a result, Patty didn't feel in the least inferior to her talented sister and, in fact, has the kind of self-esteem we could all use. She was fortunate to have the sort of sibling who told her she was fine just the way she was and didn't try to demean her abilities.

One quick tip: If you want to keep, protect, and nurture your self-worth, spend as much time as possible with people who make you feel good about yourself just as you are. If you hang out with someone who's always putting you down, you'll soon start to think negatively yourself. Nothing erases your self-esteem faster. This applies to both the workplace and the outside world. So for heaven's sake, spend your precious leisure hours with only positive people—co-workers, boyfriends, girlfriends, etc.—who aren't out to change the real you. If they make you feel inferior, blow them off!

Repeat twenty times to yourself that your *real* friends don't try to hurt you in any way, even indirectly. Think about that! Hidden insults are just as unfriendly as any other kind. A so-called girlfriend once told one of her nearest-and-dearest pals, ''Dennis said that you'd be so pretty if you'd only learn to do something with your hair!'' Huh? It took a while for this to sink in, but true friends don't repeat hurtful remarks under the guise of trying to be ''helpful.''

Self-Esteem and Your Job

A great job, or even a not-so-great one, feeds your self-esteem faster than a flying Frisbee. If you really want to feel good about yourself, go to work and knock yourself out to do your very best. Working will lift your ego higher than practically anything. Just getting hired these days—with all the competition out there—gives you a heck of an ego boost. It's a seal of approval. You beat out the others!

Besides, work is a place where you can get positive feedback on your abilities. Doing your job well, and getting recognized for it, can be heady stuff. Compliments like "Your sales presentation was right on the mark," or "Your solution to that problem was awesome," often are the sweetest pick-me-ups.

Work also offers the chance to meet and get to know new people, which can work wonders for your morale. In the overall scheme of things, your job is one of the most important parts of your life. It provides structure and routine to daily living. It doesn't leave you much time to feel sorry for yourself. Besides, knowing you're capable of earning a living is something no one can ever take away from you.

Self-Esteem Under Attack

Unfortunately, there are beasts in the business underbrush. We're not promoting paranoia, but in today's supercompetitive environment, you need to know how to protect yourself. It's devastating when your job hurts, rather than helps, your self-esteem. Whether it's the boss who puts you down, the colleague, or even someone lower down the ladder who tries to do you in, don't just ignore them and hope they'll go away. When you feel your self-worth is under attack, it's WAR! Let's face it, half your life is work. The rest is everything else.

The current dog-eat-dog climate in corporate America seems to bring out the worst in some people, especially those insecure insects who try to build themselves up by knocking you down. Fearful of losing their jobs in an ever-shrinking market, they will stoop to any means short of murder to protect their turf. As deviously clever as these lowlifes may be, don't make it easy for them to jeopardize your job or zonk your self-esteem. Here's how to use your Mental Machete to whack your way through the corporate zoo and keep your confidence from crumpling:

1. **Never let others steal your thunder**. Always make sure you get the credit due you. If you come up with a good idea, don't hesitate to remind everyone it was yours in the first place. You'd be surprised how easily people forget, or even try to take the credit for themselves. Don't let them! Find a way to work your ideas into the conversation whenever appropriate. And immediately follow up with a memo: "As I suggested at the meeting today, etc." Save it, along with every single scrap of paper that proves it was your concept to begin with.

2. **Watch out for conniving co-workers**. There are people out there who, due to their own shaky self-image, jealousy, or blind ambition, will resort to anything to get what they want. They'll access your computer for confidential information or rummage through your papers while you're out. Always keep your desk drawers and briefcase locked, and don't give your voice mail code to anyone. Even a quick trip to the rest room can give someone the chance to get your customer list or status reports.

    Here's one case history of a sneak at work. Our friend Donna typed her résumé on her office computer. Okay, she didn't like her job all that much, but she didn't want to leave until she found something else. Unbeknownst to Donna, a co-worker wanted her axed so he could bring in one of his buddies. While she was at lunch, he decided to cruise on her computer. Lo and behold, he spotted her résumé and promptly turned it in to the boss.

    He confronted her with "You can't be happy here, Donna, if you're sending out your résumé." Guess what? He let her "resign" and hired her co-worker's friend. True, Donna was looking for another job, but she wanted to leave in her own time, and certainly not before year-end bonuses were passed out.

Moral of the story: Don't leave anything around that you don't want someone else to see.

3. **Be prepared for liars and troublemakers**. There might be someone in your office who doesn't like you, for no special reason you can figure out. And that person could try to convince others to feel the same way. Invariably, they'll put out bits of misinformation about you and your work. Be prepared to prove them wrong! Always hold on to memos, presentation material, or complimentary letters from clients, bosses, or co-workers. You never know when you might need them.

4. **Recognize classic office put-downs**. One nasty example is the co-worker who contradicts you in front of others. If you're caught off guard, it's easy to get confused. Understand that the other person is trying to take control. Don't let her get away with it. Tell her you don't agree and explain why, very briefly. If at all possible, defer a controversial comment. It's a lot smarter than responding to it and engaging in a lengthy discussion in front of others. This forces you to lose momentum, creative energy, and the opportunity to strut your stuff. Stick to your guns when you feel you're right, but do it unemotionally. Don't raise your voice or wrinkle up your face. Doing so lessens your authority by making you seem overly dramatic. Conversely, if you *are* wrong, don't be defensive and too apologetic! You can admit you made a mistake without beating your breast. Just say something like "Okay, your point is well taken." Be businesslike, not contrite.

5. **Control "co-worker interruptus."** We've all met the type. You're making a point and he cuts you off in mid-sentence. How do you deal with such bald-faced bad manners? You could try a line like "Excuse me. If you'll just be a little patient, I'll get to that," (even if you weren't planning to). Or, "George, I'm almost finished, then the floor is all yours." You could even try to keep on talking as if you didn't hear him. Personally, we find this tough to do, and wouldn't. However, one woman we worked with

used this trick over and over. She just kept on talking and wouldn't back down until she finished what she had to say. It was a duel of words, but she usually won because everyone else gave up in exasperation.

6. **Beware of associates who are out to get your job or just plain resent your success.** How do you recognize such snakes? They're the kind who always find ways to make you defend your decisions and are ever ready to stick-it-to-ya. And, whenever they have the opportunity, they'll dis you to the boss or your colleagues. What to do about it? The first step is to recognize the game they're playing, and it isn't Hearts. Once you've identified the ruse, call them on it. Confrontation can be unpleasant, but in the long run, backing down will only damage your self-esteem. Try something like "Mary, do you have a problem with . . . ?" Then just bring up whatever you think is bugging her. The mere fact that you did it can make you feel awfully proud of yourself.

TIP TIME: Not everything that happens in the office should be taken personally. Learn to know the difference between what's important and what isn't. Don't sweat the small stuff. So what if Ms. or Mr. Senior Executive never says "please" or "thank you," and is inclined to bark on occasion? Just try to remember that it's their problem, not yours. Probably they're that way with everyone except their own head honcho. It doesn't lessen the amount of your paycheck, does it? Well, then, it shouldn't lower your self-esteem either. Remember, you're not married to the monster. Someday you'll leave, and he'll be just a remote and laughable memory. He'll probably get his just desserts before it's all over. You've heard that the mighty do fall, haven't you? We've met a lot of skunks in business who, today, are either out of a job or whose careers have been completely derailed. Time wounds all heels!

Quick Fixes

So that's the downside: the nasty ways others can pick and chip at your confidence. But there are other people and situations that can put you on top, if you let them. We're not trying to sound like pop psychologists, but there are some steps you can take to lighten your mood. Admittedly, they're quick fixes, but they're easy-to-do things that should make you feel as though you're floating in a warm bubble bath instead of drowning in a pool of self-doubt.

Pamper Yourself

Bridget, a friend of ours, says whenever she's upset about work (which isn't too often) she goes for a massage. She finds that these healing touches not only lift her mood but also soothe her psyche. Susan gets a new haircut and adds more blond streaks. And yet another friend, Victoria, shops till she drops, even if she doesn't buy a thing. She says just looking at all that fashion creativity and color makes her feel better and gets her mind off her troubles.

One of the least expensive pickups you can give yourself is music. If you live alone, sometimes the sound of silence gets to you. Trust us, music heals the soul and can be great company. And anything that makes you feel better can't help but raise your self-esteem.

Take a Break

If something upsets you at the office, do whatever's necessary to calm your nerves. There's no law that says you must keep on working through an upset. When you're so shook up that you can't think straight, it's better to break away from whatever you're doing. Some women call a good friend and share the problem. Others find that leaving their desk and doing anything else helps. Try slipping out for a breath of fresh air to clear your head.

Look for a "Laugh-In"

When you've got the business blues, there's nothing better than a dose of humor to lift you up. Sure, it's easier to cry, but force yourself to find some way to laugh. Try any of these activities: Run, don't walk, to the nearest friend who's tons of fun. Sharing a few giggles with someone you genuinely like is great for lifting your mood. Also try watching the funniest sitcom you can find on TV. Or rent a silly video. Anything that genuinely tickles your funny bone and gets your mind off your troubles is a great antidote to work-induced depression.

Working Out

As hard as it can be to "just do it," there's nothing like working out if you're feeling low. We've all heard that exercise releases endorphins, little "happiness pills" that can lift your spirits and make you feel all's right with the world. And, when you're physically fit, you obviously feel and look better. Positive self-esteem is essential if you want to keep success in your corner. So—force yourself to take a half-hour walk when your mood needs a happiness jolt. Or hop on the treadmill, climb some stairs, or bike around the block. Move it!

Looking Good

When you're down, it's easy to let your appearance go. You figure, if nobody else cares, why should you? Marching orders: Wash your hair, put on a little makeup, then get into something zippy. A little spritz of perfume makes you think pretty thoughts, too. All of this will provide a quick pickup when you most need it. Believe us!

Lighten Up

Why do you think birds fly south for the winter? The last one we talked to said it was for the sunshine. Seriously, light—or the lack of it—can bring your mood up or down. There's even a medical term for it—SAD, or Seasonal Affective Disorder. If you can't afford to jet off to the Caribbean, do the next best thing. Put some sunshine in your personal environment, both office and home. Hang a big colorful poster that you love on your office wall. Get a brighter bulb for your desk lamp. On the way home, buy a bunch of tulips or a flowering plant. Turn on the lights. And when it's gray and gloomy outside, wear colorful clothes. Save fashionable black for when you're feeling more positive. In other words, lighten up your life!

Admittedly, the above are just short-term solutions to self-esteem problems. To get a longer-lasting lift, here are some things you can do that'll have a more permanent effect on your self-confidence:

Find an Activity to Succeed in Outside of Your Job

You can find success and get that good feeling about yourself in a dozen different ways. One method we found that always seems to work is to look for a volunteer project that appeals to you. Whether it's reading to inner-city kids or walking dogs for an animal shelter, your extracurriculars will prove to you that there's a world beyond your workplace.

To begin with, doing for others always makes you feel good.

Beyond that, being successful at any job, even if you're not getting paid for it, will make you realize how worthwhile you are. Once, when we were down in the dumps, we threw ourselves into some serious social work. Because we did a good job, everyone thought we were terrific and said so.

Another way to build self-esteem outside the office is to find a new evening or weekend activity you'd enjoy doing. It could be anything from taking a course in jewelry design to learning how to scuba dive. Some women are taking karate or boxercise. This not only gives them a sense of empowerment, it also makes them feel more physically secure. Any activity that allows you to gauge your abilities and see tangible results can provide the "upper" you need.

Become an Expert

Find some area at work that you can specialize in. This way, everyone will automatically turn to you for the answers. After all, you're the expert. Few will question your authority, because they simply don't have the knowledge base that you do.

We know one male executive who's invaluable to his boss because he's not only smart but intensely organized. He's masterminded a filing system that enables him to locate any piece of paper that ever was stored, no matter when. This guy winds up getting bonus points because whenever he says something, everyone assumes he's right because he's so organized.

So, look for some area *you* can become the expert in. It's a great feeling when you hear yourself referred to as a specialist.

Don't Just Slap It Together

If you're feeling insecure, being handed a really tough assignment can be terrifying. That's when it's easy to shrug your shoulders and say, "Why bother breaking my back to do this right? It doesn't matter anyway!'' Force yourself to tackle the project with everything you've got, and make it the best job you've ever done. When you're filled with self-doubt, it's simple to conclude you're probably not up to the task at hand. Assuming that kind of negative attitude is just selling yourself short. Plus, you're surrendering your self-esteem to potential enemies on a silver platter. Prove to the bastards, and more importantly to yourself, that you're worth something, whether they realize it or not!

Set a Time Limit

When your self-confidence is crumbling at work, set a time limit for turning your emotional state around. Tell yourself that within three weeks (or however long you think is practical), things will get better. Now's the time to take out that yellow pad and make a list of all the things you can do within that period to give your self-confidence a shot in the arm. You could try to land a new account, finish a project before it's due, or even straighten out your desk if it's messy—anything that gives you a feeling of accomplishment.

Whatever makes you feel more in control is fair game. Here's a possible regimen: Work out at the gym three times a week, have dinner with two co-workers you genuinely like and respect, or make weekly lunch dates with friends who not only believe in you but also willingly share ideas that'll help you do your job better.

Allowing yourself a set time to climb out of a deep, dark hole usually works. It's only when you're miserable and think things will never get any better that the problem seems insurmountable. Instead, if you tell yourself the sun will shine tomorrow (or in three weeks), it usually does. By the very act of viewing setbacks or misery as temporary, you'll put a halt to them. We kid you not. It works.

Keep Your Perspective

A job needn't be a lifelong commitment. After all, nothing is forever. If your boss and co-workers don't recognize your worth, after you've given your all, it's probably time to move on. That's easier said than done when you need the money. But if you're in a really negative situation, the chances are that if you don't leave, they'll make the decision for you. It's much better for your self-esteem if you're the one who says good-bye first.

Wrap-Up

This chapter is really the most important one in the book. Every good thing in life springs from a positive self-image. Protect it and nourish it!

Self-Esteem Roundup

- You have to *work* at building self-esteem.

- You don't have to be perfect to like yourself.

- Respecting yourself makes it easier to respect others.

- Look at mistakes as temporary glitches that you can fix.

- If you stumble, don't wallow in self-blame.

- Self-esteem allows you to take credit for your successes.

- Hang out with people who make you feel good about yourself.

- Doing your job well is a self-esteem enhancer.

- Don't let the beasts in the business underbrush undo your self-respect.

- When you're in the dumps, try any of these solutions:

    - Find an activity to succeed in outside your job.

    - Become an expert in a special area.

    - Tackle tough tasks with everything you've got.

    - Set a time limit to turn around your emotional state.

    - Keep your job in perspective.

four

Keeping It: How to Make Yourself Indispensable

~~

Once you've landed the job, how do you make yourself so indispensable they'll never want to let you go? It's easy. Just make impressions so favorable the company will feel it's impossible to do without you. In business, as in life, perception becomes reality. You may be as brilliant as Einstein, as creative as Steven Spielberg, but if you can't organize and complete your projects on time, you'll look confused and unfocused. It's how people see you that counts. Everything matters—the time you get to the office, the way you speak and dress, or even how you react to assignments. The list is endless. To help you solidify your job, here are your Lucky 14—the most positive impressions you can create.

1. **Get Up with the Birds**

   Getting to work on time is no big deal. That goes with the territory. But, arriving early gets you positive points across the board. Don't think no one notices. When you're an early bird, it's like wearing a neon sign around your neck that blinks: "I'm serious about my job." Spending this extra time has to show up in your performance. *Fortune* magazine once surveyed the habits of some of the country's most successful executives. No matter how diverse their careers, they all had one thing in common— they got started early in the morning. And, invariably, they stayed late. As top business schools preach, beat your colleagues to work. Over time, this gives you an edge, making it difficult for the drones in your department to catch up with you.

Conversely, your boss and colleagues can't fail to notice if you habitually come in late, drag out your lunch "hour," and take advantage of the company's time. Eventually, they'll clock-watch your comings and goings like hawks—how often you're late, how early you leave at night, and how many times you disappear from your desk and no one can find you. Co-workers will resent your unorthodox work hours and be the first to squawk when you goof.

2. Be As Flexible As an Acrobat

Jobs unfold slowly. They may not always turn out to be "exactly as advertised." Delete "That's not part of my job" from your vocabulary. Always be ready to shift gears. Take it as a compliment when you're asked to handle an additional function. This just might be a little test to see if you're ready for more responsibility. The businesswoman who gives the impression that she's not willing to go beyond her specific duties will either be stuck on the shelf or eliminated in favor of an eager beaver who's willing to do it all—and more!

3. Sing in the Rain

Whenever you're handed a tough task, bend over backwards to do it well. Never act as if it can't be done or you don't know where to start. Just find a way to do it. Your boss knows when he is asking you to go above and beyond. The way you react gives you a golden opportunity to create a positive impression. Companies keep and promote people who act as if no assignment is too much. Conversely, they weed out the complainers, the naysayers, the whiners.

Case in Point: Terri, a marketing director for a *Fortune* 100 company in New York, was approached by her CEO to handle a complicated assignment with an almost impossible deadline. He asked her to set up a last-minute meeting of security analysts in London with only a week's notice. He also wanted full press coverage. Her reaction? She silently gulped, marshaled her forces, worked around the clock, and got it done. It was one of the company's most successful conferences ever, which sent its stock soaring.

Terri always accepted a challenge without hesitation. It never crossed her mind that anything was impossible. Her positive attitude quickly earned her a solid reputation around the company. It surprised no one when she was made the first woman vice president in the corporation's history. Later, her CEO mentioned that the ease with which she had handled the London assignment was one of the things that convinced him she was VP material.

4. **Speed It Up**
   The way to get yourself noticed fast—is to be fast. When your boss gives you a job to do, move on it immediately. Fast, but factual, is in tune with the times. A quick-response individual makes an impression money can't buy. Patricia Francy, the treasurer of a leading university, said that once she learned what fast really meant (she had an even faster boss), she found she could finish in a day what used to take her a week. But take note, speedy doesn't make up for sloppy.

5. **Button Your Lip**
   Be known as someone who can be told anything in confidence and would rather be tortured than tell. If you think you're impressing people when you share hot inside information, you're wrong. You'll just look untrustworthy. Corporate confidences are meant to be honored, not betrayed. There's often a lot at stake, including people's jobs and the company's financial health. Why do you think the wartime slogan ''Loose lips sink ships'' resonates in the corporate vocabulary?

6. **Walk in Lockstep with Your Boss**
   Never forget that your boss's time is more valuable than yours. Whenever she or he gives you a specific assign-

ment, always assume it's more important than what you're working on at the moment. Put that job aside. What if it, too, was assigned by your boss? Easy enough. Just ask, "What would you like me to do first?" Speaking of the boss's time, if you're on the phone when she or he walks by, find a way to hang up—fast. Tanya said her boss sometimes came by her desk unexpectedly to talk. Once, after waiting a few minutes for her to get off the phone, he turned around and left. The next time he walked up to her when she was on the phone, she knew better and concluded her conversation immediately. You should do the same. Just say, "I'm awfully sorry, my boss needs to speak to me. Can I call you back?" Don't ever keep your boss waiting even for a minute! It shows a lack of respect for the person and the position.

Obviously, there are exceptions to this. If you're in a service business and you're talking to a client, you can't very well hang up abruptly. You just need to acknowledge your boss's presence. Catch his or her eye and mouth out c-l-i-e-n-t or scribble a quick note.

7. Put Your Boss in the Best Possible Light
Simply translated, this means always make your boss look good. Why? If you make your bosses look good, you'll look just as good in return. Your job is to enhance their job. For example, if your supervisor is giving a presentation, prepare for it thoroughly. Make sure every fact is accurate, that the audio-visual equipment was checked and double-checked, and that the audience is ready and waiting.

See yourself as a mirror image of your boss. The way you interact with other people, dress, and handle a problem are a direct reflection of her. If others react negatively to you, it puts your boss in a bad light too. After all, she hired you. You can be sure she won't let this go on forever.

8. Keep Your Cool
The cool cucumber, who remains unflappable in any circumstance, gets the kudos. Bosses, clients, and others ad-

mire the person who not only doesn't come undone in a crisis but also deals with it thoughtfully and resolutely. If you are calm, cool, and collected, you'll be mentally prepared to deal with problems as they arise (and they will!). You'll inspire confidence—as well as promotions for yourself. Conversely, a nervous demeanor conveys your jangled anxieties to those around you, making them as ill at ease as you are.

9. **Look the Part**
   Being well put together—with the right outfit for the right occasion—is key to professional advancement. An equally important adjunct to this is being physically fit and having good grooming and personal hygiene habits: meaning clean, well-styled hair, a decent manicure, and subtle makeup that doesn't scream "Come hither." The way you look is another personal reflection on your boss—either plus or minus.

10. **Address the Thorny Issues**
    Say you've discovered a mistake in an important report that at this moment is on the press—or worse—has already gone to a client. There are thousands of glitches that can arise in a working situation. How you handle crises can be critical. The person who quickly assesses the situation, comes up with a workable plan for damage control, then goes directly to the boss with problem and potential solution in hand is the one who gets top marks. The ostrich who buries her head in the sand, hoping the problem will somehow just disappear, is likely to disappear herself. Never go to your boss and ask "How should I handle this?" without having your own suggestions ready.

11. **Anticipate**
    Never expect everything to go smoothly, according to Plan A. *Always* anticipate the areas in which things could go wrong; according to Murphy's Law, they probably will. Be sure to have Plan B at the ready.
    For example, if your boss is going on a business trip,

think ahead to what he or co-workers might have forgotten to bring with them. Take it upon yourself to include additional backup materials that could come in handy. This kind of creative anticipation inspires an escalating paycheck.

12. Be Decisive

Once you're in any sort of decision-making role, be prepared to do just that—make decisions. The waffler who is buffeted this way and that by her own indecisiveness and overreliance on the opinions of others will be frozen in her career path. Carefully weigh the options—including the time frame you have to work with—and make your decisions within that span. Successful executives are both incisive and decisive.

13. Keep Getting Smarter

The "dumbing down" of America is a new phrase pundits are slinging around. It refers to the belief that the Generation Xers don't read books or newspapers anymore. Instead, they get all their "information" from movies and TV.

Is this you? We doubt it, but for the few who'll admit they rarely pick up a newspaper or a book—get smart! There's no room at the top for people who don't keep themselves clued in to what's going on in the world.

14. Lighten Up

As a poet once wrote, "Laugh and the world laughs with you, cry and you'll cry alone." Nobody likes a sourpuss. Invariably, people try to avoid the company of anyone whose demeanor spells doom. It's just too depressing. Instead, they'll choose somebody who's upbeat and pleasant to be around. Everyone likes to be with a positive person, someone who sees the light at the end of the tunnel. Sad sacks sap other people's energy, bringing them down in the process. While making yourself indispensable, show the world your sunniest side, even on your down days.

Learn How to Speak on Your Feet

Knowing how to address a group can be a woman's secret weapon. Although most people dread speaking in public, it can work wonders for your career *if* you learn to do it right. Bosses place a high value on employees' communications skills. Someone who can present ideas effectively, whether it's at the conference table, making a new business presentation, or addressing a large group, is a big step ahead of the crowd.

There are certain tricks of the trade that all good speakers practice. They know that communicating effectively, whether it's to six people or sixty, can advance their career faster than a speeding bullet. Here are some tips to follow if you want to be a star player:

Around the Conference Table

Some women handle their participation at business meetings so poorly they could just as well have phoned it in. Even when they have something important to contribute, they politely wait to be called on and, even then, don't project their message forcefully. Here's how to do it right:

- Pick a seat at the middle of the table, if at all possible, not at the end where it's easy to be ignored.

- Don't wait for an opening—make it!

- Try to speak at the beginning of the meeting, so you'll be noticed immediately.

- Get to your point straightaway, with just the necessary facts and no extraneous details. Women often are criticized for not getting to the core quickly enough.

- Avoid sprinkling your message with vague or apologetic words like "I hope," "I feel," or "This may not be right, but . . ." It's too wishy-washy and sounds unconvincing.

- If your boss is at the meeting, never focus completely on him or her; make eye contact with *everyone* present so nobody feels left out.

- Don't wait for the "right" moment to present your ideas—it may never come! Jump in and talk!

- Don't rush when you speak—nobody's timing you, and they'll keep listening as long as you have something meaningful to say.

- Don't limit your remarks to your own bailiwick; if you have valid ideas on other areas of the discussion, even if it's outside your job, speak up.

At the Podium

Before you give a speech, prepare yourself thoroughly. Besides giving yourself sufficient time to research and write it, you need to rehearse as thoroughly as if you were starring in a Broadway play. Some people find that tape-recording their speech several times is an effective way to perfect their presentation. Try it out on a close friend, before a mirror, or even deliver it to your doggie. You can never practice a speech too often. Winston Churchill rehearsed his speeches so many times that he practically wound up memorizing them. That's why they were so dramatic. He knew his lines so well that he delivered them as eloquently as any Shakespearean actor could have.

Giving a good speech is really a grand performance opportunity that you should never blow. Here's how to seize the moment and run with it:

- Make sure your appearance is picture-perfect—no wrinkles in your clothing, no runs in your panty hose, and no bra straps showing. Don't wear jangling bracelets or swaying earrings. They're too distracting. And adding a touch of color, perhaps a red blouse under your suit, helps to make you stand out.

- Have someone introduce you before you speak so that your audience clearly understands *who* you are and *why* you're qualified. You need to be ''set up'' before you utter one word. Writing your own introduction is best. That way you can put in all sorts of outrageously wonderful things about yourself that your ''introducer'' might not say, otherwise. Besides, it guarantees that the essential facts—job, title, etc.—will be accurate. This is a common practice smart speakers use. It just takes a bit of tact. Say something like ''Here's an intro you may want to use. My office put it together to save you time. Feel free to change any of it.'' Nine times out of ten they'll be so grateful that they'll use it verbatim.

- Keep your speech as brief as possible—long enough to cover the subject matter but short enough to be interesting. After all, you don't want people nodding off. Twenty-five minutes max; fifteen minutes is better.

- Find a way to bond instantly with your audience. Research shows that people make up their minds whether or not to listen to you within one minute after you begin speaking. You can establish rapport by talking about something you think you have in common with your audience, whether it's the city, the organization/cause, the latest episode on *Seinfeld*, etc. Anything goes, as long as you can tie it to your speech.

- Also use eye contact to connect with your audience. In that all-important opening minute, don't imitate an ostrich by burying your head in your notes. It's always a good idea to memorize at least the first page so you can start off with a bang.

- Check the lighting in advance of your speech. If the lights are too dim, your speech won't have the same impact. Because the mind processes information through both sight and sound, your audience can lose interest because it's difficult to follow what you are saying.

- Use body language effectively.

    Always lean slightly forward; don't pull back. This demonstrates that you're reaching out to your audience.

    Use your hands, but only with natural gestures.

    Keep your body loose, not stiff and ramrod straight.

    Don't fidget with your fingers, glasses, or hair. It makes you seem nervous and ill at ease.

- Show enthusiasm when you speak. Learn to ''walk'' your voice up and down so that it sounds alive. If you speak in a monotone, you'll lose your audience really fast.

- Make it easy for people to follow your train of thought. Use the three T's:
  ACT I: Tell them what you're going to tell them.
  ACT II: Tell them.
  ACT III: Then tell them what you've just told them.

Why Bother Being Indispensable?

Just why are you breaking your back to make yourself so indispensable? Besides the pride you take in your job, let's face it—you're working to make money, and the more the merrier.

Some women—and you may be among them—have a problem asking for money. They think it's crass and overly aggressive. Besides, you'd like to believe that the company is paying you what you're worth. Not always true! Some companies pay as little as they can get away with.

Asking for a Raise

So, how do you go about getting more? In large corporations, pay levels are usually predetermined for every job category. Assuming, of course, that your performance review is up to par, or better, you can usually expect an annual increase. The downside is you take what you get, even if it's less than you feel you deserve. There's not a lot of room for salary negotiation; it's cut and dried. In small and medium-sized companies, there's usually a little more flexibility. It's often up to you to push for the most money you can get.

Regardless of the size of your company, here's how to do it:

Tips for Trading Up

1. Know what your job is worth in the current market, so that you don't ask for an unrealistic amount.

2. Prove your point. When you meet with your boss, highlight how you've saved the company money, improved its profits, or enhanced its image in the industry. Be as specific as you can. Generalities get you nowhere! Bring along any complimentary letters from customers or colleagues. Subtly mention the overtime you've put in. (Go easy here! You're probably not the only one who puts in extra hours.)

3. Mention any special courses or training programs you've taken to upgrade your performance.

4. Never bring up personal needs, like wanting to buy a new car or that your rent has gone up. Nobody cares about your problems.

5. Focus on your future goals. Exactly what do you plan to accomplish in the coming year(s), and how are you going to do it? Again, don't generalize. Quantify with numbers whenever you can.

6. Time your meeting carefully. If the company is going through a down cycle, hold off. Ditto, if your boss is in a bad mood.

7. Be prepared for a possible turndown. If your boss bases it on your performance, talk it out, and find ways to improve.

8. Don't threaten to leave if you're turned down—unless you're prepared to do just that.

9. Try not to go away empty-handed. If budgetary restrictions preclude a raise, ask for something other than money—a car allowance, a better title (with a raise to come when business is better), or an assistant who's already on staff, etc.

10. Put your rationale for a raise in writing. Be succinct and businesslike. When you meet with your boss, hand her a copy and keep one for yourself to use as a "talk sheet."

KEY POINTERS FOR KEEPING YOUR JOB

- Get up with the birds.
- Be as flexible as an acrobat.
- Sing in the rain.
- Speed it up.
- Button your lip.
- Walk in lockstep with your boss.
- Put your boss in the best possible light.
- Keep your cool.
- Look the part.
- Address the thorny issues.
- Anticipate.
- Be decisive.
- Keep getting smarter.
- Lighten up.
- Learn how to speak on your feet.

five

Losing It: How to Get Fired

There are two little words that pierce your heart like no others: "YOU'RE FIRED." These hurt almost as much as your lover saying "Good-bye." You can usually find reasons for *that*. Getting sacked is different. You feel it's the very essence of *you* that's being rejected—your ability, intelligence, and behavior.

The first question a firee almost always asks herself is "Where did *I* go wrong?" According to Tom O'Brien, owner of a recruiting firm that bears his name, "Few people lose their jobs due to a lack of skills . . . Folks fired for nonfinancial reasons, usually lack the ability to get along and communicate well."

Invariably, most people find there are things they would have done differently. When pressed, they conclude that they didn't play by the company's rules in one way or another. You would be wise to scrutinize which ones you broke and make sure you don't repeat your mistakes in your next job.

To help you avoid the painful process of losing your job, the following are a few things *not* to do!

1. **Go counter to the company's culture. Ignore their established systems. Try to show them that your way of doing things is better than theirs.** Buck the corporate culture, and you'll be out in no time flat. It's one of the

few things in life that's literally set in cement. Trying to do things your way is like trying to make living in Manila the same as living in Milwaukee. Slightly impossible! A company's culture develops slowly over time. It's not always 100 percent perfect, but they feel it works for them. If you charge in and try to change their way of doing things, they'll probably show you the door.

2. **Be absent a lot. Call in sick or make your "dental appointments" on Fridays or Mondays.** Excuses like this become transparent over time. Phony long weekends are going to get you in the long run! If you want to earn your keep, you have to put in your time.

3. **Answer every question the boss asks you, whether you have the information or not.** People who give the impression that they have the answers to everything better be damn sure of their facts. Talking off the top of your head can destroy your credibility in the blink of an eye. And, if people act on your misinformation, the ramifications could be enormous, not only to you, but to your company. This is a great technique to use when you want to talk your way out of your job.

4. **Cheat on your expense account. It doesn't really matter how little or how much.** Bosses have been known to check up on client lunches and other supposedly work-related charges. If you value your job, don't put in for expenses unless they're absolutely legitimate. When traveling on business, be as careful of spending the company's money as you would your own. Don't run up room-service charges. Ditto with keeping a lid on the valet bill. If it's company policy not to travel first class, don't.

5. **Falsify your credentials.** Some creative individuals list degrees from colleges they never attended and say they held positions they weren't even offered. Many a person has been canned for embroidering her résumé. It may take a while, but invariably you'll be found out.

6. **Tell little white lies.** To cover a mistake, try lying. Make up an answer or pass the buck. If you go this route and slip just once, your boss will be on guard. Moreover, she'll lose trust in you that she may never recover.

   Invariably, anyone who thinks she's shrewd enough to pull the wool over her boss's eyes on trivial matters will invariably try to get away with big, fat whoppers. Eventually, you'll trip yourself up and get sacked.

7. **Just Say "No."** You're asked to do something you consider "beneath you"—like answering someone else's phone or photocopying. Or you're handed an "inconvenient" assignment, like having to go to an out-of-town meeting at a moment's notice. Maybe you're told to do something that's not part of your normal routine. Refuse to do it and just say, "It's not part of my job." In today's competitive environment, you're expected to go the extra mile—no matter what. Say "No" often enough and they'll soon say "No Thanks" to you and your job.

8. **Supplement Your Salary.** Take home "little" things—pens, pencils, paper—then graduate to the good stuff—a desk lamp, blank videotapes, a VCR, and perhaps a lonely little laptop computer. What the heck—the company won't miss them! They make tons of money, anyway! And why not cut down on your home phone bill? Make *all* your personal long-distance calls from the office.

   In today's sophisticated telecommunications world, many companies track employees' telephone activity: the number of outgoing and incoming calls, and, for sure, long-distance use.

   Stealing by employees—because that's what it is—has become so rampant that some companies have had to resort to security guards checking out workers when they leave. Don't ever take to not-so-petty larceny. Word has a way of getting around, and they'll be lying in wait to collar you when you finger something bigger. Is it worth it to lose your job and wind up with a black mark on your record over something you could have bought with your own money?

9. **Procrastinate.** Always put off till tomorrow what you don't feel like doing today. After all, it'll keep—it isn't that vital—and you're not really in the mood.

    Procrastination could be called the Eighth Deadly Sin. It has cut short countless careers that could have flowered but died in the bud. Adopt this acronyn: DIN, which stands for Do It Now! Whether it's as simple as returning your phone calls or as complicated as coming up with a new ad campaign—*don't put it off!* If your unreturned phone calls wind up costing the company money, you'll soon be able to procrastinate all you want—on the unemployment line.

10. **Make your desk or office into a home away from home.** What better place to read the latest John Grisham novel, do your makeup, or use your instant hot rollers? Did you ever see a man slather lather on his face and then shave at his desk?

    Any of these, per se, will not get you fired. However, it gives such an unprofessional appearance that it will color people's opinions of you. Combine this with a lackadaisical performance, and they just might say you're not really focused on the job. If you must redo your makeup at work and can't get to the rest room, just be as unobtrusive as possible.

11. **Become the office gossip.** Be the big-mouth know-it-all— the one who's got the scoop on everybody. The Office Gossip loves to share her info, especially juicy items like the boss's supposed affair with his secretary, or the marketing director's purported cocaine habit. If enough of these steamy tidbits and their source boomerang back to your superiors, you'll find yourself out on the street.

12. **When the pressure meter goes up, lose your cool.** If you fall apart at every crisis—burst into tears (a supreme no-no), or erupt into ballistic temper tantrums—you're in

trouble. If you're unable to function or deal intelligently with the problem at hand, you're creating the impression that you're unstable, unreliable—and *very* expendable.

13. **Do it the easy way.** When you send letters or reports, don't bother checking for the proper spelling of people's names and their correct titles. Don't do thorough research, or back up your reports with the necessary data. Just do it the easy way—off the top of your head. This kind of laziness can definitely help earn you a well-deserved pink slip.

14. **Be a chronic whiner.** Complain, whine, and complain some more: "This assignment is so boring," or, "I hate working with Robert Jones" (a longtime client). And be sure to groan—"WHY do we have to work late again?" Do your best to stir up the same discontent among your co-workers. You'll soon be complaint-free and out of a job.

15. **Shorten your work week.** Come in late—after all, you need your beauty sleep. Take long leisurely lunch "hours"—you have a life, too! Be sure to leave promptly at five, even if there's work to do. Soon you really *will* shorten your work week—to zero.

six

Getting Back on Track

Let's say you goofed up, you've learned from it, and you want to get on with your life. There are definite dos and don'ts when you've lost your job and have to find a new one. For out-of-work individuals, we recommend these key strategies:

1. **Get in motion.** Don't take too much recovery time. Contact everyone you can think of.

2. **Stay in the field you know.** After the Ford Motor Company fired him, Lee Iaccoca had numerous job offers. He wisely opted to go with Chrysler because the automotive industry was his field of expertise. He felt his best chance was to stay there, not to try a totally new career area. The Chrysler offer wasn't the most lucrative, but he felt he could make it pay off. And did he ever! When your confidence has been shaken to begin with, adding the pressures of learning a new industry makes your chances for success all that much slimmer.

3. **Never complain, never overexplain.** When you're asked why you left your job, be brief, and keep negative opinions about the company and your boss to yourself. Here are a few innocuous reasons you can give:
   - "I felt it was a dead-end job."
   - "The company and I weren't a good fit."

- "The job became too routine. I needed more of a challenge."

4. **Act confident in public.** Look and talk as if your search is going well but you want to survey the field further before you make a final decision.

5. **Keep up your appearance.** Don't dress down or let your hair go. Just because you're out of a job is no excuse to go around in jeans and sneakers. Always look as if you're heading off to the office. Look successful even if you're worried about next month's rent.

6. **Concentrate on where you want to *go*, not where you *were*.** Don't dwell on the past and never look back. Don't beat yourself up about what happened. Switch it to the back of your mind. Replace it with positive visions of the future.

7. **Don't get overly upset when former business associates "forget" to phone back.** Just swallow your pride and call them again. Sometimes it's that second or even third phone call that gets you an unexpected job tip. Be persistent, but polite.

8. **Expect to be confused.** Getting fired is like falling off a cliff without a parachute. If you can convince yourself that it's okay that your future direction is temporarily up in the air, you'll find your new job much more quickly.

9. **Get out of the house.** Have at least one appointment a day, even if it's just for lunch with a friend who can't possibly help you.

10. **Restructure your life as quickly as possible.** Put yourself on a nine-to-five schedule. Sleeping late and not setting daily dates and goals are major mistakes. *Don't let one day go by without doing at least three things to advance your job search.*

seven

The Romance and Business Merger

Is love in the air at your company? Office romances, once strictly taboo, seem to be flourishing nowadays—and why not? Work is the natural place to meet a potential mate. *Fortune* magazine explains it this way: "People who work together have, almost by definition, similar backgrounds, talents, and aspirations." With over 46 percent of women in the workforce, the office may be the most natural and very best place for you to meet a man. It certainly makes more sense than picking up a stranger at a bar. Besides, with smaller staffs than ever, people spend longer hours together, in close proximity. It's not surprising that at least 33 percent of all romances begin at work. As Stephen Manes, coauthor of *Gates, A Book About Microsoft and Its Founder,* explained: "In that kind of intense work environment, you not only practically live at the office, but you get to use your brains on each other, which is really the most erotic thing there is."

Fortune also surveyed some two hundred CEOs in 1994, to get their views on office romance. The majority of them believed in "letting love between employees take its course, even if office amours may occasionally give rise to trouble." That's a real sea change. Just a few short years ago, you were supposed to deny the fact that you were even mildly interested in a co-worker, much less found him sexually attractive. *Fortune* says such attitudes are not only old hat but puritanical. People involved in an office affair are more productive and happier when they know their company doesn't frown on interoffice romance.

Having said all this, should you let your libido loose and bed down a co-worker? It's a multiple-choice answer.

On the positive side, there are zillions of stories of business colleagues who merged romantically—at least for a time—if not forever. To begin with, you have a lot in common. It's easy to strike up a conversation with any attractive man you spot. You know, like, "Hey, what do you think about Joe's promotion?" No need to forage for things to talk about.

The workplace brews many a love potion. Every company has tales of couples who met at the photocopy machine, locked eyes at a sales meeting, or rubbed elbows at the company softball game. Couples manage to find each other, one way or another.

Your office can be the ultimate happy hunting ground. So, while you naturally keep your mind on your work, there's no harm in casing the joint, looking for Mr. Possible. Your workplace can be better than the busiest bar when it comes to meeting men.

To prove it, here are a few true stories of office encounters that turned into full-blown love and marriage.

Office Amours—For the Better: Love Crashes In

Romance can happen in the strangest of ways. You never know when or where the thunderbolt might strike. Take Liza, for example. At twenty-six, she worked as a receptionist for a large auto manufacturer in New Jersey. She greeted all visitors when they arrived at the company's offices. Her desk in the ground-floor lobby looked out on acres of rolling hills and lush landscaping that surrounded the main building.

One day she looked up and to her horror saw a huge tractor come crashing through the glass doors—headed straight for her! At the wheel was Doug J., owner of the contracting company in charge of landscaping the grounds. He'd been driving around, supervising his crew, when for some unknown reason the tractor went out of control. Almost numb with fear, Doug finally was able to bring the vehicle to a screeching halt—eight inches from Liza's desk!

In those few seconds, he was sure he was going to die—and so was she. Miraculously, neither one was hurt. Instead, after catching their breath, Doug and Liza took one look at each other, and that was it! The attraction was fatal, but the accident was not. They've been happily married for ten years, have two children, and still laugh about how they met.

Dodi and Jed had a kind of collision, too—minus a runaway tractor. It was more a meeting of the minds. In her mid-twenties, Dodi was an account executive at a large advertising agency. One now-memorable day, she was introduced to Jed, the company's new creative director, who happened to be young, attractive, and equipped with all the seldom-seen manners of the old South. A Mississippian, he never let New York change his genteel southern ways. He always stood up when a woman came into his office, stepped aside to let women enter the elevator, and was the first to find a spare chair in the office cafeteria when Dodi or any other woman joined the table. This kind of thoughtfulness, plus the fact that he was tall, lean, and had big blue eyes, was hard to resist.

Even though the agency had no policy against employee dating, Dodi was a very private person and reluctant to start anything with a colleague. She kept her increasingly-frequent conferences with Jed on a strictly-business basis, but she sensed the chemistry was there on his part, too.

One day, after concluding a client meeting, they looked at each other and both blurted out, at the same time, ''Would you like to have a drink tonight?''

They laughed, left the office, and began a sweet, very discreet relationship that went on quietly for a year. And—yes—they got married and are living happily ever after.

Sexual attraction in the office, however, doesn't have to lead to the bedroom—or the altar. According to some experts, it can simply result in increased productivity. David Eyler, coauthor of *More than Friends, Less than Lovers: Managing Sexual Attraction in the Workplace*, rhapsodizes that "sexual energy can drive people into a better working relationship. It doesn't have to be destructive . . . It's high time we started taking advantage of all that energy in some constructive way."

It's not always wine and roses, though. Many business and romance mergers have been known to backfire. Read on.

Office Amours—For the Worse!

Invariably, there's a handsome guy in the office who's an equally adorable flirt. What happens when that sexual energy hurls you into his ever-ready arms? Instantly, the very air you breathe seems charged with electricity. In the first flush of passion, office amours can be irresistibly exciting. Just make sure you know with whom you're dealing so you don't get burned in the process.

If you have a sneaking suspicion that he's hitting on every attractive woman in the office, watch out! While the affair with you would undoubtedly enhance *his* stud status, *you* might wind up with egg on your face. And, if he's the kind who kisses and tells—well, who wants to be the butt of office jokes? If you get involved with such a skunk and it ends badly, just act as if it never happened. If anyone brings it up, change the subject. Refuse to give it credibility. You don't have to explain or justify your actions. Men don't! Eventually it'll all be forgotten, as soon as another piece of juicy gossip makes the rounds.

Today, many companies turn a blind eye to intimate relationships between single co-workers, with heavy emphasis on single. For example, some firms make only one stipulation: neither of the parties can be in a direct supervisory position over the other. This, of course, is to prevent either the appearance—or the reality—of favoritism.

Now, let's say your romance is with your direct supervisor, who's not only sexy and successful, but single, too. How do you handle it? Very carefully. On his side, he has to be very wary of any show of partiality. On your part, even if you've "got" him, don't flaunt it. That green-eyed monster—jealousy—could do you in. Your co-workers, who are probably on to your affair, will be resentful, especially if you're blithely bending the rules: coming in late, leaving early, and not doing your job.

And, if the boss/lover not only condones your behavior but also covers up for it, you've set the stage for a first-class office rebellion. The end result could be the unemployment line for both of you. However, if only one of you has got to go, guess who it will be?

Aside from that, dating the guy who decides on (or influences) your salary can be a tricky business. Why? Suppose you split up with him under unpleasant circumstances, and he decides he doesn't want you around anymore? So, he transfers you or maybe he starts criticizing your work. He could also take it out on you via your paycheck. Why risk it?

So, if you're single and get the urge to have a fling with someone on a higher or lower level, beware of favoritism. Don't take it or give it. It could easily do you in.

What if you're attracted to a boss who's very much married? That's a whole other story. You'd better be mighty careful, because you're really asking for it. It's true, some women have had affairs with their married bosses and eventually wed them. It's equally true that many others have wound up brokenhearted and had to quit their jobs because it was too painful to stay. Rarely is Don Juan willing to leave his wife, kiddies, and comfortable nest to undergo a costly divorce—unless his marriage is really on the rocks. Yes, he may be genuinely attracted to you, treat you like an angel, and the sex may be sublime. But, almost invariably, it won't end at the altar—if that's your ultimate goal. The odds are not in your favor.

Take our friend Kelleen, who fell head over heels for her handsome investment banker boss. He just *happened* to be married. For six months, they met in romantic, out-of-the-way restaurants and hotels. He gave her expensive gifts and promised her a "big promotion." He led her to believe he was unhappy at home, with the proverbial "wife who didn't understand him and hadn't grown along with him." He swore to Kelleen it was just a matter of time before he left his wife. Yeah, right. That's one of the oldest lines in the book. Kelleen finally realized that this mythical breakup was never going to happen. The atmosphere in the department became so tense that she couldn't handle the pressure and finally left. Happily, she moved on to greener pastures, winding up with not only a better job but with a fiancé who was younger, handsomer, nicer, and single.

Be Discreet

One word of warning applies to all office attractions—*discretion*—whether it's a casual dating situation or a live-in relationship that could evolve into marriage. You may feel you've found your "forever" soul mate, and the urge to brush bodies in the hall or steal a kiss in the supply closet can be overwhelming. Don't do it!

Your co-workers (and superiors) can pick up on those steamy vibes much more easily than you think. This kind of hanky-panky can give the impression that your mind is on matters other than work, not to mention the grist you're supplying for the office gossip mill.

Speaking of the company grapevine: resist the urge to tell even your closest chums about your pulsating passion. Rarely do bosom buddies keep quiet when there's a juicy tidbit like this to pass along. Pretty soon you and your loved one will be the hot buzz of the moment.

Keeping your office romance under wraps is just a good idea, period. What if your bright, shiny love affair should tarnish and go kaput? You'll have enough trouble dealing with your own tears, trauma, and eventual recovery. You don't really want the entire office involved in the dissolution of your dream, do you? On the other hand, if you have found Mr. Right and the two of you keep it quiet, what could be a greater high than floating into the office and announcing that you two will soon be one?

Now, having said all of the above, here are some tips to help you with romance in the office:

- Sexual attraction doesn't *have* to wind up in bed.

- Sexual energy can make everyone more productive.

- Steer clear of guys who like to brag about their conquests.

- Never flaunt your affair among co-workers.

- Married bosses rarely get unhitched.

- You never know when true love could come crashing in.

- If the attraction is mutual, enjoy yourself, but be discreet.

Sexual Harassment

When does it go from office flirtation and/or romance to sexual harassment? In Kelleen's office romance with her married boss, the sex was completely consensual. In other words, neither party was forced into the relationship. But what do you do if your boss or a senior executive comes on to you and you want no part of it? This kind of situation can be very touchy. How do you handle it? Try thinking like a diplomat. It's best to avoid World War III if you can. Of course, this assumes his approach has been basically nonthreatening. Let him know politely, but firmly, that you're not interested. You could always tell him you're seeing someone, even if you're not. This is an easy out. No one loses face. Just look him straight in the eye and say, "Sorry, I'm involved with someone." Don't amplify or feel compelled to make further excuses. If you do, you could be inadvertently leading him on. Make sure you say this in a businesslike tone of voice, without smiling, so he'll know you're serious. And, with any luck, he'll accept your turndown like a gentleman.

Another scenario could be that you're faced with a not-so-nice guy whose behavior becomes blatantly offensive. He asks you straight out to sleep with him and implies that your job is at stake. Now you have a serious problem.

If he persists, and you just keep trying to brush him off lightly, maybe even good-humoredly, you're not resolving the situation—you're just making it worse. Let him know *right off the bat* that you will not tolerate such conduct, and that if he doesn't cease and desist, you'll take action—like reporting it to the Human Resources Director (HRD).

The woods are filled with women who let such obnoxious behavior slide by. Big mistake. If you eventually decide to file formal harassment charges, it's your attitude and reaction while the harassment was occurring that determine the legitimacy of the complaint. Acting as if it doesn't bother you lessens the chance for your complaint to be taken seriously. All the guy has to say is, "Hey, she never seemed to mind. She just smiled and let it go."

If you have told him off, and the situation remains unresolved, make good on your threat and go immediately to your HRD. Explain your problem and listen to his/her advice. Most enlightened companies, especially large, publicly held corporations, take sexual harassment seriously and have a specific written policy on it. It tells employees exactly what to do and whom to contact. It's important that employees who feel they're being harassed follow these internal complaint procedures to the letter. Those who fail to do so may have waived their right to successfully sue. Human Resources departments can be extremely helpful and sensitive to your problem. Most cases are resolved in-house, and handled fairly for all parties involved.

However, it doesn't always happen that way, particularly in smaller, privately held companies or nonprofit organizations, both of which are sometimes run like little kingdoms. If you work in this type of organization and your HRD is not helpful, then your next step could be to consult the U.S. Equal Employment Opportunity Commission (the EEOC) or a state Fair Employment Practice Agency (virtually every state and many large cities have them) before seeking a lawyer. These agencies are there to enforce civil rights laws, including those regarding sexual harassment, and their services are free. Most lawyers are not! Even if you choose to go to an attorney, remember that your accusation should be clear-cut and provable. If you don't have solid evidence, you'll just be wasting your money.

Just because you're female, and sexual harassment is a ''hot'' issue, doesn't mean you can accuse someone of it and automatically be believed. Besides, it could have a domino effect. Once you point the finger at someone, be prepared for the possibility that he'll accuse you of wrong-doing as well. Your harasser could twist your accusation around and say the sex was consensual, or that you came on to him. Or he could trivialize your side of the story and say you're falsely accusing him of harassment to gain something else. Remember, companies, judges, and juries listen to both sides—his as well as yours. After all, that's what happens in a democracy.

This is not to say that you should keep quiet if you've been subjected to harassment. But before you attempt any action, think of the possible consequences. You could be labeled a "trouble-maker" and become "unemployable" to other companies. Such cases can drag on for years, and you may not win. In the meantime, you could be without a steady income. The multimillion-dollar awards we hear about are few and far between. There are thousands of cases that are thrown out of court or settled for peanuts.

Here's a true account, typical of some of the small companies where the CEO rules like a king and sees himself as accountable to no one. It's the down-and-dirty golden rule: He who has the gold (i.e., pays your salary) makes the rules.

Jennifer, a highly respected professional in the health-care field, was employed by a well-known hospital. For over three years she worked closely with the powerful chief of staff, Dr. X (known in-house as Dr. Strangelove), who fancied himself as irresistibly attractive to women, including his wife. He began to kid around with Jennifer, and then started telling her smutty jokes, a departure from their normal working relationship. He followed that up by "play-fully" grabbing her rear end whenever the opportunity presented itself, and even when others were around. She tried to ignore it until the day he put his hand up her skirt. That did it. She knew she couldn't take it anymore.

She reported the incidents to the hospital's Human Resources Director, who discussed them with Dr. X. He denied everything. As we've already warned you, when the person you're accusing of mis-conduct is high ranking, and in this case, head honcho, things can get very sticky. End result: Jennifer got no satisfaction from the HRD. She finally went to a lawyer, who advised her that she had a genuine case if she wanted to pursue it. Her lawyer contacted Dr. X, who immediately chose to "settle" the complaint rather than go to court. Under the terms of the agreement, Jennifer was "allowed" to resign, with a small financial settlement.

Dr. X, in the meantime, proceeded to smear her reputation with everyone in the close-knit health-care industry, portraying her as a money-hungry bimbo who would do anything to get a raise. If Jennifer had thought of it, she would have put Dr. X on notice as soon as she learned of the "smear campaign" to stop him before the damage became too great. She also could have consulted an attorney to see if she had a viable claim against him for slander. However, she was too depressed to take any further action and went for a long period without a job, saddled with a heavy load of emotional trauma. Ironically, Dr. X still rules the roost at the hospital, even though his treatment of Jennifer and other women employees is common gossip among his colleagues.

It doesn't always end so dismally, however. Here's the equally true story of Annie. Twenty-seven and happily married to John, she was working in the advertising field and liked her job a lot. Annie was a little naive, and it took her a while to realize that her boss was hitting on her in a big way. At first, she thought he was just kidding around, asking her every Monday how often she'd gotten "laid" over the weekend. And, every time she wore anything red, he told her it was a sure sign she "needed a little."

Annie ignored him as best she could, but finally worked up her courage and explained that such remarks made her uncomfortable. He apologized sweetly, and all was well—for a week. Then one day he grabbed her in the conference room and tried to kiss her. She pushed him away and ran out the door.

Annie didn't tell her husband about the incident because she was afraid he'd go to the office and punch the guy out. Or, even worse, he'd blame *her*—"How come this guy is still coming on to you if you've told him to stop?" So she hung on for several miserable months until her boss got tired of looking at her anxious little face whenever she was in his presence. He fired her for "poor performance." Annie was so shocked and humiliated that she finally told her husband the whole story.

John encouraged Annie to march straight to a lawyer, who told her she had a viable complaint because the sexual harassment had risen to the level of creating what is known as a "hostile work environment." She was advised to report her boss to the company's HRD. They investigated thoroughly, and Annie was awarded a settlement big enough for a down payment on a house. Even better, she got a new job almost immediately. To top it off, within six months she heard that her bastardly boss had been fired, due to the company's "restructuring."

It doesn't always turn out that well, however. Sometimes even large corporations don't handle sexual harassment cases to everyone's satisfaction. For example, if your alleged harasser is a top executive—higher-ranking than the HRD—things could take a different turn, for many different reasons. Here are some:

1. The Human Resources Director fails to take adequate action on your complaint because the executive involved is his/her senior. Also, if the executive has years of credibility, whose word are they most likely to take—the harasser or the harassed employee?

2. Mr. Important Executive goes ballistic at being accused of such an outrageous deed and strikes back, charging you with inferior job performance, or attempted blackmail in order to get a promotion, or whatever. Now not only do you have to defend yourself, you also have to prove to the company that your sexual harassment charge is true.

3. The company acknowledges that maybe Mr. Big screwed up to some degree, but it's not clear as to exactly what happened. In many cases, you're much more expendable than he is. He may get a slight slap on the wrist, while you could be shown the door, with whatever severance the company decides to hand you. Believe it or not, one woman who brought action against her boss was asked by his attorney what kind of perfume she used, implying that she deliberately wore a provocative scent to seduce him!

You should be aware that there are many gray areas as to what constitutes sexual harassment. Isolated or relatively trivial incidents, such as occasional teasing, harmless sexual remarks, or being asked out a couple of times are not considered to be sexual harassment. In legal terms, there are two kinds of sexual harassment. The first and most callous deals with "pocketbook injury," and is called *quid pro quo*, meaning "this for that." That's when you're offered raises, promotions, favorable assignments, good performance reviews, etc., in exchange for sexual favors. If you don't go along with this "put out or get out" demand, you could be passed over for a promotion, given a poor evaluation, or even lose your job.

The other kind of sexual harassment is called creating a "hostile work environment." This happens when you're placed in a work environment that makes it difficult to do your job. Sexual touching, ridicule, or a pattern of gender-based abuse ("Come here, 'babe' and give me some of that"") are all examples of hostile environments. The abuse can be physical, verbal, and even nonverbal. The first two offenses are obvious. The third—nonverbal abuse—includes displaying pornographic objects, stalking, leering and lip licking, or ostracizing a person because of gender.

Hopefully, you'll never be the victim of any form of sexual harassment. Not only is it demeaning, it also causes tremendous confusion and anxiety. Fortunately, it's out in the open these days. Women no longer have to suffer in silence. Now that you've read what it is, what it isn't, and how to deal with it, here are a few more pointers:

- If you feel you're being sexually harassed, it's very important to follow your company's internal complaint procedure without deviation.

- Contact the person your company has designated to handle these kinds of complaints.

- Your accusation should be clear-cut and provable.

- Remember: not all companies handle harassment as satisfactorily as others.

- If you can't afford a lawyer, go to the EEOC.

- Taking legal action is serious business. Be prepared for the consequences.

eight

Business Myths and Realities

There are far too many myths, half-truths, and downright distortions about business. Let's set the record straight! At least part of it.

Myth #1: A woman has to act like a man in order to succeed.

Reality: If your idea of acting like a man means being brusque, using four-letter words, and shouting a lot, you're dead wrong. The world of business is polite and low-key for the most part. Bad tempers and obscene language are inappropriate for everyone. Such behavior is even more unacceptable in a woman. Sound sexist? Sorry, that's the way it is.

Myth #2: The company will always treat you fairly.

Reality: Wipe the words "It isn't fair" out of your mind. You're just being naive. What seems "unfair" to you may appear perfectly equitable to someone else. Companies are composed of human beings—not robots—and humans aren't always fair. People play politics. They look out for Number One first, then try to take care of their buddies. If you happen to get in the way, watch out, because "fairness"—as far as you're concerned—could go right down the drain. If this happens to you, chalk it up to experience. Next time, tune up your radar so you can protect yourself better.

Myth #3: It's nice—but not really necessary—to be computer literate.

Reality: Today's worker, from entry-level to upper management, has no choice but to be computer savvy. In our computer-driven world there's no excuse for computer illiteracy. Get with it or get lost.

Myth #4: Talent is always recognized and rewarded.

Reality: Eventually, but it takes time and seasoning. Beginners can't expect from Day One to be praised, coddled, and loaded up with fat salaries and jumbo raises. You have to prove yourself first. You can speed up the process by the way you perform in your job. Do it right, do it quickly, and do it with a smile.

Myth #5: It's not *what* you know, it's *who* you know.

Reality: *Who* you know can get your phone calls answered and crack open the door for an interview. But it's *what* you know—your smarts, capabilities, and dedication—that will keep you employed and on the fast track. In other words, who you know has a short shelf life if you can't back it up with performance.

Myth #6: Women are not good at math and should avoid careers in finance.

Reality: One of the biggest breakthroughs in the eighties and onward was the massive march of women on Wall Street. Today, women are not only chief financial officers of major companies but also owners of, and partners in, hundreds of successful brokerage houses. Childhood conditioning to the contrary, many women handle numbers just fine, thank you.

Myth #7:   The best jobs go to the best-looking women.

Reality: Maybe yes, maybe no. Whereas good looks can help when you're beginning your career, they could be a hindrance when you reach the higher echelons of power, depending on how you handle it. Some exceptions may be found in those fields traditionally open to women: retailing, cosmetics, fashion, publishing, public relations, and some facets of advertising.

However, in our experience, we've found that attractiveness can work against a woman in more highly structured organizations. Psychologists say it's because people don't equate brains with beauty and find it hard to believe that a woman could be blessed with both. This may be unfair, but that's the way it is. We hope this is changing. You can prove them wrong. You don't have to apologize or try to hide your good looks; just make sure your professionalism shines through first so that your appearance is almost secondary.

Myth #8:   Women can't handle top-level jobs, high-stress situations, or criticism because they're too emotional.

Reality: As with many myths, there's a grain of truth in this. Young women beginning a career, particularly those with no role models to fall back on, sometimes do get emotional. Their reactions can range from misty eyes to full-blown tears to overpersonalizing whenever they're criticized by a superior. No one has bothered to teach them to keep a stiff upper lip. On the other hand, little boys—from the cradle on—are chided not to be "crybabies."

The myth, nonetheless, lives on, in spite of the fact that very few women in top positions lose their cool. They know that it's unprofessional, inappropriate, and not particularly useful. Most senior women know better than to reveal this type of vulnerability and "flip out" over their jobs. Plus, why would they give off vibes that imply they can't hack it when the going gets tough? There are plenty of seasoned women in high-stress positions, confronted daily by deadlines, bottom lines, and life-and-death decisions, who handle them as well as men do—or even better, for that matter.

Besides, coping isn't gender related; it's unique to the individual. Men are no more immune to stress than women. Countless men fall apart under pressure, but they usually exhibit it differently. We've all heard about very senior male executives who, when under the gun, drink excessively or are prone to angry outbursts.

Tip: If you really have to cry, do it privately—*never* in the office or in front of anyone you work with.

Myth #9: Women can't see the big picture because they get too bogged down in details.

Reality: Not true! Besides, these two abilities are not mutually exclusive. You can be good at details and still have a clear view of the so-called Big Picture. Because women traditionally have begun their careers in the lower echelons, usually as secretaries, they're used to taking care of the bits and pieces. Hence their reputation for being detail oriented versus having the capacity to conceptualize. Men have always been seen as strategists and planners, not the ones to worry about dotting every *i* and crossing every *t*. It's exactly the same with women at the top. They, too, know how to prioritize and not sweat the small stuff.

Myth #10: Affirmative Action makes it virtually impossible to discriminate against women in business.

Reality: Get real! They said that twenty years ago, too. While business seems pretty open at entry to mid-level, the air gets thinner the higher you go. Men tend to mentor and promote people who remind them of themselves. That could leave you a bit out in the cold.

Like it or not, at the very top levels, the corporate world is still a men's club. The trick is to try to neutralize this natural male bias. For example, men beginning their careers instinctively know better than to whimper when criticized, or to come back from lunch loaded down with gobs of shopping bags. Somehow they manage to give the impression that their mind is always on the job, even if all they're doing is rehashing Sunday's football game.

Myth #11: Hard work alone will take you to the top.

Reality: In your dreams! While we can't overstate the importance of working hard, there are other key elements—like luck, timing, and chemistry—that can work for or against you. Being fortunate enough to be at the right place at the right time has made the difference in countless careers. And, there's always chemistry—that mysterious movement of molecules between you and others—that can either propel you to the peak or paste you to the same old plateau.

Myth #12: "Overnight success" exists—and it could happen to you.

Reality: Scratch the surface of practically any so-called "overnight success" and you'll discover years of sharpening skills, plus plenty of good old-fashioned hard work. People who emerge into the spotlight of fame and fortune generally have paid their dues—and then some. If you want instant success, try the lottery!

nine

Tales from the Top

Do you ever wonder why some women make $100,000-plus per year while others live from paycheck to paycheck? Why do some stay stuck on the same step while others leap up the ladder? What's the secret of their success?

We wanted to get the real scoop for you. So, we interviewed some of the country's top business and professional women and asked them to tell all. Eureka! We struck pay dirt!! There really are legitimate formulas for success that you can follow.

We found strikingly similar traits, regardless of background or career choice, in every woman who made it. If you met any one of them, you'd probably like them instantly. Without exception, they're bright, personable, and well put together. Some people might find it hard to believe that these friendly, down-to-earth women are some of the most successful executives in America. That old wives' tale about high-powered women being hard as nails just doesn't fit.

All of them believe in doing whatever it takes to get the job done. When they started out, it didn't matter if it involved working weekends or nights, and it still doesn't. It didn't make a difference if the work was grubby or glamorous, menial or mental. They were willing to break their backs to get the job done.

Every one of them had this "will-do" attitude from the beginning. One executive we interviewed told us that when she started out she never regarded any assignment as a put-down. "I felt so fortunate to get my foot in the door that I was not only happy to make coffee, I would have fixed soup if they'd asked."

This alone, however, didn't propel them to the top. There are hordes of hardworking, intelligent, and personable young women who never seem to move forward. In trying to isolate the single quality these high achievers felt was responsible for their success, we asked them to go back to the beginning. Was it their education that started them in the right direction? Did they, perhaps, meet a mentor at a critical point in their career? Were they fortunate enough to have a parent, teacher, or boss who believed in their abilities and encouraged them?

The answers were both "yes" and "no." While these women thought there were many factors that played a role in their success, all—without exception—said that they had always had an inner belief that they were destined for big things. Some described in minute detail the dreams and mental images they had when they were very young. This ability to project and visualize themselves at the top, years before it actually happened, was a common thread in most of their lives.

Perseverance also played a big part in their careers. They simply refused to take "no" for an answer. One high-powered executive told us that when she started out she had her heart set on a particular company. Although she was repeatedly told there were no openings, she kept trying anyway. On her twenty-seventh attempt, the firm's head honcho reluctantly agreed to an interview, just to get rid of her. The result is history: she not only got the job but also used it as a springboard for the enviable career she's enjoyed over the years. Many of our interviewees said this kind of dogged persistence was key to their climb.

And here's how they did it, in their own words:

Judith Price

Founder, *Avenue* magazine, a monthly publication for New York's movers and shakers.

Defining quote:

"I always tell people I have a hearing problem.
I can't hear the word 'no.' "

Judy's refusal to be discouraged from the beginning was just part of the reason for her success. She adds: "I never had a mentor. I've always been a self-starter. If you're just an average young woman with no connections or clout, you're wasting your time waiting for a mentor to rush to your side. It hardly ever happens that way. If you think about it, why should people put themselves out for a young woman who hasn't proven herself yet? Sure, if your father is the head of a huge company, a lot of people will want to help you, just to curry his favor. If that isn't the case, then you have to do it yourself.

"I would also advise a woman who's beginning her career to focus on 'winning'—not on being 'right.' If I'm trying to sell an idea to someone who isn't buying, I always manage to see his or her side. When someone tells me they're still not interested, I tell them I have a hearing problem. I can't hear the world 'no.' So, then I try another route."

Judy is recognized in the industry for knowing how to run with an idea. She cautions, "Another mistake a lot of young women make is to think that if they come up with a great idea, they'll be an instant success. Everyone has good ideas; you not only have to have them, you have to know how to make them work. And even that isn't always enough. You have to find a way to make your concept unique. Otherwise, someone else with the same idea can come in and undercut you."

When asked how important she thought her education was, Judy explained, "I happened to go to an Ivy League college, and they practically invented networking. It's great to be able to call former school chums and ask who they know at such-and-such a company. But there are other ways to network if you didn't go to a big-name university. You can get involved with a charity that has a roster of high-powered volunteers. But don't do it just for the contacts. Find a cause that's important to you, so you'll feel great about helping someone."

Judy landed her first job at Chase Manhattan Bank and went from there to *Time* magazine as a researcher, then a reporter. It was while she was at *Time* that she came up with the idea for *Avenue* magazine. She dreamed of an upscale version of *People*, directed particularly to affluent New Yorkers. Judy said, "I figured people like to look at pictures more than they like to read. By creating a pictorial magazine for influential New Yorkers, I filled a niche that didn't exist. It was a unique approach and it worked."

Judy's idea for *Avenue* not only took off; it continues to thrive in the often dicey field of publishing, where magazines bite the dust daily.

Anne Sutherland Fuchs

Senior Vice President of Hearst Magazines, Group Publishing Director

Defining quote:

"My mentor was simple survival."

Anne is another woman who made it big in the publishing field. The former publisher of *Vogue*, Anne left for an even bigger job at Hearst. In this post, she's responsible for some of the most popular publications in the country: *Harper's Bazaar*, *Town & Country*, *House Beautiful* and *Marie Claire*.

Anne's business career got started for a very practical reason—she was dead broke. "In the beginning, my 'mentor' was simple survival. I *had* to make it, just to survive. Nobody needed to tell me that only hard work would pull me out of that hole. So I worked like a demon at every job I had. I went from dawn to whatever time it took to get the job done. My daily routine *still* is to get to the office at the crack of dawn."

Another part of Anne's work style is to set short-term, well-defined goals. "Once I achieve them, I go on to the next. I never make five- or ten-year plans. Short-term goals motivate *me*, and they do the same for the people I manage."

Anne also believes that successful people possess a heavy dose of what she calls "Star Quality." "It has nothing to do with how you look or speak," she says. "It's that indefinable something that means you work all weekend on your presentation and breeze in with it on Monday, as if it had been a snap. It was anything but. It was plain hard work. That's 'Star Quality.' "

Susan Falk
Former President/CEO of the Limited Express, a chain of women's speciality stores

Defining quote:

"If you don't have a goal, how can you reach it?"

Susan is another self-described workaholic. When we asked her what advice she would give a young, ambitious woman, she answered, "I'd tell her to do two things. First, she should ask herself, 'Where do I want to go from here and what will it take to get there?' For whatever reasons, some women can't see themselves moving to a bigger job. They create their own barriers. If you don't have a goal, how can you reach it?

"Second, I would tell her it's important, especially in the beginning, to look for female role models who have the kind of success she wants for herself. It's not enough to admire these women from a distance. You have to zoom in on their work habits—how they speak, how they dress, how they handle confrontation, how they deal with their colleagues . . . even how they write a memo. This is particularly important for women, because they're usually out there all alone. There's no 'Old Girls' Network' to show them the ropes. And mimicking the mannerisms of men won't work. Don't even think about it.''

Susan Lucci
Star of TV's *All My Children*

Defining quote:

"If you do what you really love, you'll be a success."

A second Susan who succeeded, in a totally unrelated field, is the undisputed Queen of Daytime TV—soap opera star Susan Lucci of *All My Children* fame. Susan credits her success to two factors: single-mindedness and her family's all-out support.

Although she was an extremely shy child, Susan always wanted to be an actress. "It was my first love," she says. "And I've always believed that if you do what you really love, you'll be a success. No one can stop you if you go with your God-given talents.

"I was so fortunate to be raised by parents who showed their support by attending everything I was involved in. Whether it was a school play or a cheerleading session, they were there for me. That gave me a lot of self-confidence."

Susan says she never doubted for one minute that she would succeed. "When people told me I had an impossible goal, I just thought: 'It might be hard for others, but it won't be for me.' " Susan also is a firm believer in education. "During my senior year in college, I was one of five finalists for Miss New York State in the Miss Universe contest,'' she recalls. ''The last event of the pageant happened to fall on the same day as my college finals. I had to make a choice. I decided to forgo the contest, even though it probably would have helped my career, especially if I'd won. My education was more important, a decision I haven't regretted for one minute.''

Susan's starring role as Erica Kane in *All My Children* has led to numerous made-for-TV movies, all of which have been extremely successful. But she's equally well-known for having been nominated a record sixteen times for an Emmy—and not having won once! Her reaction? ''I just frame all my nominations and go on doing my very best.'' We hope that by the time you read this, Susan will have that Emmy on her shelf!

Susan's ability to keep from getting discouraged and to continue giving her all is what sets her apart from many women who would let a similar rejection throw them.

Kay Koplovitz
Founder and Chairman, USA Network

Defining quote:

''If you think you've spotted a future trend,
go for it.''

Kay Koplovitz's vision and determination created another enormous success story. Founder and chairman of USA Network, one of the country's leading TV cable channels, she told us, ''The idea for USA Network began in my mind when I was a graduate student in 1968 at Michigan State. I wrote my master's thesis on satellite technology. It was crystal clear to me, even then, that this was the wave of the future. I had this vision that cable could be brought into everyone's home through satellite. Nobody believed that a woman could bring this off. It took me ten years to convince anyone it could work. Eventually, I found the financing to get it off the ground. It finally went on the air in 1977.''

Today, USA Network is watched by millions across the country and Kay Koplovitz is one of the highest-paid women in America. ''If you think you have the ability to spot a future trend, always listen to that little voice inside you and go for it. That's the way giant companies like Federal Express, Microsoft, and Apple Computer got started, too. Someone had a dream about filling a void that most people didn't even realize existed.''

Cathy Cash-Spellman
Best-selling author and cosmetics executive

Defining quote:

"Take the job home with you."

Another super-successful woman, who made it big despite career and personal obstacles, is Cathy Cash-Spellman. Even though she started out in the days when women—regardless of qualifications—were automatically asked, ''How fast do you type?'' Cathy managed to make it big—and still continues to conquer new territory. It wasn't always smooth sailing, though.

Divorced at twenty-three, and with two small children to support, she realized she needed a career, not just a job. Fresh out of college, Cathy took a typing course and went to work as a secretary at the J. Walter Thompson Advertising Agency. She soon became a copywriter—but in those Dark Ages for women, she had to type her male co-workers' copy first, before she could start writing her own!

She left the agency, became a creative director at Revlon, and eventually landed a plum position at Bloomingdale's, New York's trendy department store. As Vice President of Communications, she was the store's youngest VP ever, and the first—and only—woman on its board of directors. Later, as president of her own advertising agency, she was part of the team that developed two of the world's best-known perfumes—Opium and Armani.

But Cathy's first love—as well as a major part of all her jobs—was writing. Once she had a steady income, she wanted to take that talent to the next level and try her hand at turning out a novel. Every day she rose at 5:00 A.M. and pounded away at the typewriter before getting her children off to school and setting out for the office. It paid off. To date, she's written four best-sellers, including *Paint the Wind* and *Bless the Child*. Even Hollywood has taken notice—a major movie studio has optioned her latest book, *The Playground of the Gods*.

When asked if, along the way, she'd met any mentors who made her career climb easier, Cathy cautioned: "Finding a mentor can be helpful, but don't expect to be taken under someone's wing for life. It's not like being permanently adopted. A mentor can just be a person who believes in you and gives you the right encouragement, at the right time, even if you're young and inexperienced."

Cathy has two tips for women in business: "Contrary to popular wisdom, I'm a big believer in taking the job home with you. Eat, sleep, and drink it. That's the best way to beat the competition. After all, they're smart and ambitious, too. Why not keep a step ahead of them? Men do it, why shouldn't we?"

Her second piece of advice is to not pop up with an answer as soon as someone asks a question. Think it through first. Always know what you're talking about.

Sandra Derickson
President of G. E. Capital Auto Financial Services
Defining quote:
"Never turn down a new assignment just because it's a lateral move."

Sandra Derickson believes it's entirely possible for a woman to make it, even in the so-called "man's world"—if you have the right stuff. "I started at the bottom with an entry-level job at a bank. Over the years, I held every conceivable position they had to offer. My advice is never turn down a new assignment just because it's a lateral move."

When we suggested that a lot of people resist anything that's not a clear-cut promotion, she smiled and said, "I've always thought that was a big mistake. If a step sideways increases your know-how, do it! Don't always insist on moving straight up. You might get there and find yourself out on a limb because you're in over your head. If you take advantage of any opportunity to broaden your knowledge base, you'll be that much better off."

Sandra said her three watchwords have always been: passion, sacrifice, and balance.

"You need passion, first and foremost, because if you don't enjoy what you do, you're not going to be able to make it work. If you love your job, it's a lot easier to work incredibly long hours, travel constantly, and spend time away from your family. I had to do all of that or I'd have been stuck in the same rut forever. Sacrifice, unfortunately, goes hand in glove with success. Be prepared to make some sacrifices. Finally, make sure you add balance to your life. All work and no play make you a very dull person—not only to others, but to yourself as well. My challenge has always been not to bore myself to death."

Sandra Derickson has some tips for women on the move: "Be decisive. Don't second-guess yourself. Make decisions without waffling, and without looking back. 'Would have' and 'should have,' after the fact, not only are a waste of time, they undermine your self-confidence.

"And last—don't forget how you got where you are. Lots of people probably helped you along the way. Be sensitive to, and supportive of, the needs of others, just as they were to you. Stepping over bodies you've kicked on the way up—or after you've gotten there—can come back to haunt you.''

Muriel Siebert
President/Chairman Muriel Siebert and Co., Inc., stock brokerage firm

Defining quote:

"Have a sense of humor, even if you screw up."

Muriel "Mickie" Siebert, the first female to hold a seat on the all-powerful New York Stock Exchange, is another outstanding woman who broke through the barriers in the late sixties. Back in those dinosaurean days for women, Mickie dared to defy the un-written—but understood—"men only" membership policy. In 1967, she became the first woman to hold a seat on the Exchange, a move considered so unorthodox that one newspaper ran the story under the headline: "Now the Girls Want to Play, Too."

And Ms. Siebert *did* play, scoring one touchdown after another. In 1977, she was offered the prestigious post of Superintendent of Banking for the State of New York, the first woman ever to even be considered for that position. She held it for five years—during which time not one single New York bank failed—before deciding to return to her own firm full-time.

Mickie's trajectory to the top was somewhat unique. A college dropout, she labeled a formal education as "useless" in helping her reach her goals. "To me, many college courses just stuff your memory. They don't teach you how to think. On the other hand, accounting appealed to me from the start. Give me a page of numbers and they sing out. So I took a lot of accounting courses because they were easy for me.

"After two and one half years of college, I headed straight for New York. I had to lie to get my first job. When one brokerage house I applied to asked me if I had a college degree, I said "no." They didn't hire me. When the next firm asked me the same question, I said, 'Of course,' and was hired on the spot for $65 a week. You can't get away with that today, though. Everything is checked and double-checked."

When we asked Mickie how she'd had the gumption in the sixties to think she could get a seat on the New York Stock Exchange, she answered: "A business associate encouraged me to apply and told me he would sponsor me. I knew I was qualified, so I did."

We asked Mickie if she got her seat right away. "Hardly. Every possible obstacle was thrown at me—like having to get letters of credit, which men weren't required to do. My would-be sponsor literally ran out the door when I told him I was going ahead with my application." The rest is history. Today, Muriel Siebert is the president of her own brokerage firm and a respected, colorful member of New York's financial community. She's come a long way from that $65-a-week job she started with. Her advice to fledgling businesswomen is, "Have a sense of humor. You have to be able to look in the mirror and say, 'Mickie, you sure screwed up today!'"

Josie Natori
Chief Executive Officer, The Natori Company, fashion design firm

Defining quote:

"If you jump into the traffic of life, something's
bound to happen."

Josie Natori, one of the country's leading fashion designers, is another woman whose humor keeps her going.

"My mother used to tell me angels can fly because they take themselves lightly. I always try to keep my sense of humor, no matter what. Just because things aren't going my way, I don't fall into a funk or bark at people. That doesn't mean I laugh everything off, but I do try to keep things in perspective. If something goes wrong, it's not the end of the world. If it's fixable, I fix it. If it's not—I move on."

Josie is a prime example of a woman who never felt she had to act like a man in order to succeed. Her femininity and gentleness work in perfect harmony with her determination and strength. Nicknamed "Sweets" for her kind and thoughtful nature, Josie left a lucrative career on Wall Street to make a foray into the fast-paced world of fashion. It was a big, brave gamble, but it paid off handsomely.

Born in the Philippines, Josie Natori headed to New York at seventeen to study economics at Manhattanville College. After graduation in 1968, she joined Bache Securities and later the huge brokerage house, Merrill Lynch, where, while still in her twenties, she was named a vice president.

In 1977, at age thirty, Josie took a deep breath and decided to switch careers. "Although I loved the excitement of Wall Street, I really wanted to do something more creative that would help the Philippines. I also felt it was time to start my own business." With nothing definite in mind, Josie decided to try her hand at the import/export business—first with straw baskets, then with furniture, and finally with clothing, all manufactured in the Philippines. By chance, she showed a buyer at Bloomingdale's a traditional Philippine hand-embroidered shirt. The buyer thought it would make a terrific nightshirt for women if she lengthened it. It flew off the shelves. Within three months, the store's stock sold out.

Overnight, Josie was launched into the loungewear business. Orders poured in from such upscale stores as Saks Fifth Avenue and

Neiman-Marcus, all clamoring for the colorful, new Natori sleep shirt. Josie's timing was nothing short of brilliant. Her bright and pretty nightshirts were an idea whose time had come, replacing the pristine, staid lingerie of the late seventies. Women were ready for a change. Josie's designs were so attractive that some women even wore them out to dinner!

When we asked her if she'd had a business plan before she started her company, she laughed. "How could I? I had no previous fashion experience. I was just open to trying anything that might work. Sometimes I think it's better not to have too many preconceived ideas. Just jump into the traffic of life, and something's bound to happen."

"Wait a minute, Josie," we asked her. "Aren't you setting yourself up for failure if you just do anything that strikes your fancy?"

"I never even thought about failing," she answered. "I come from a family of career women, so I saw for myself that a woman could be successful in business. My grandmother was a classic entrepreneur heading multiple enterprises, from an ice plant to drug stores, to a plantation—all in the Philippines. My mother also was a terrific businesswoman who helped my father run his construction company."

When asked what advice she would give a young woman who wants a career but isn't sure where to start, Josie replied, "I'd tell her to just get in motion—then things will happen. You don't have to be 100 percent certain. As a young person, how are you supposed to know everything?"

We reminded "Sweets" that it's easy for young women to become discouraged and asked her how she had managed to avoid this. She answered, "You've got to be an optimist. My father taught me that something good will eventually come out of even the bad things that can happen. You have to have faith that the sunshine will follow the rain. It always does."

Patricia L. Francy

Treasurer, Controller—Columbia University

Defining quote:

"If you have a little humility when you're young,
people are more willing to help you."

Add still another woman whose optimism carried her to the top.
Patricia Francy is the Treasurer of Columbia University—the first
woman in that post in its entire two hundred-year history!

However, "Patty" Francy, who now heads a department of
150-plus people, practically got her job by default—she didn't even
bother to show up for the first interview!

While she was working as an administrative assistant at Columbia, Patty's boss suggested she try for a spot as a budget officer in
the university's central administration. "I didn't go for the interview, because I wasn't interested in being a numbers cruncher,"
Patty says. "But my boss finally convinced me I'd be good at it.
Sometimes, someone else can see a capacity in you that you don't
know you have. When he assured me that my co-workers would
help me learn the ropes, I changed my mind. So, I made it a point
to show up for the second interview!"

Good thing Patty did, because she not only got the job but was
quickly promoted from budget officer, to budget manager, to director
of finance, acting controller, controller, and finally treasurer.

Patty Francy feels her nonaggressive attitude was partly responsible for her getting the job. Her soon-to-be boss thought this un-
assuming manner was a big plus.

"I'm not saying women shouldn't be assertive," Patty goes on
to say, "but only after you have the skills under your belt. In the
beginning, you're basically an assistant. Act like one! Older, more
experienced people don't appreciate know-it-all kids. Have a little
humility when you're young. People are much more willing to help

you. Cocky kids put people off. When you're young, you don't know what you don't know.''

When asked how she thought young women should show their self-confidence, Patty replied: ''Through their actions—by being competent, for example, not by talking about themselves. Actions count more than words. Just show everyone you're hungry to learn and that you'll handle your assignments quickly and correctly.

''Astute individuals—and most bosses are astute—interpret an employee's 'humility' as a show of respect for those who are wiser and more experienced. People will discover soon enough what you're all about, but not if you toot your own horn.''

When we asked Patty if acting humble meant being meek and mousey, she laughed. ''An outgoing personality can be a real resource, if you know *when* to use it. Every company has its own rhythm. There are times to chitchat, and times to show your leadership skills. Take note of the male executives around you. They've always known how to 'compartmentalize.' Talk and act one way at work, another way after hours. Just as you dress one way for the office, and differently for a party.''

Patty believes the most important thing a young career woman can do is not to look for the perfect job, but to go where her interests lie. ''Pick your field and take the job. See it from the inside out—from within you—not the outside in. That's the only way you'll know if it's right for you.''

As far as salary is concerned, Patty thinks that many women are their own worst enemies when it comes to getting raises. ''Women can be sweet-talked into stalemating themselves,'' she says. ''For example, someone who has excellent administrative skills can get snookered into staying in a lower-paying job because her boss tells her she's 'indispensable,' offering her compliments instead of cash. These women take praise as 'psychic income.' They think it's enough; it's not. That's one reason why some women wind up making 70 percent of what men do.''

Patty goes on to say, ''I was always fortunate enough to know my own self-worth. Growing up in Oregon in a safe, secure family environment, with very supportive parents, gave me a real sense of self. My family told me I could be anything I wanted to and that I'd be successful at it. This made me very optimistic about life. I didn't know that a career would make me happy, but I was delighted to find that it did. Working with intelligent, motivated people and being compensated fairly for it is very satisfying.''

Based on her experience, Patty tossed out some practical advice for a woman beginning her career:

1. Always bring something new to the table. Read, investigate, ask, think. Then speak up. This may mean taking a risk, but running your idea up the flagpole is one of the surest ways to be recognized.

2. When you're a beginner and asked to attend a meeting, listen to silences, to what's *not* being said. Senior executives often make decisions about major issues prior to convening. Or they may withhold confidential information that can't be shared with the whole group. Be sensitive to this. Don't ask questions that could interfere with higher-ups' prerogatives to keep certain matters off the table.

3. Be present mentally as well as physically. Bosses do notice when employees are burning the candle at both ends. You can't be mentally alert if you're spending too many late nights out, indulging in excessive partying. I know, I did the same thing in my twenties. When you're being paid to do a job and turn in sloppy work, you're actually putting your boss at risk. His or her self-preservation dictates that this won't be tolerated for very long.

Nancy Lane
Director of Corporate Relations, Johnson & Johnson

Defining quote:

"Always deliver far more than anyone expects you to."

Nancy Lane is not only the first woman, but the first African-American, to be named a divisional vice-president of Johnson & Johnson, the world's largest manufacturer of health-care products. She used her top-notch education and the opportunities it provided for networking. (You'll note over and over in this book that meeting the right people along the route is one of the best methods for wending one's way up the slippery slopes to career success.)

After graduating from Boston University and the Harvard Business School, Nancy never let her old school ties loosen. She kept involved and in touch with her former schoolmates through alumni organizations and plain old picking up the telephone. She became the first African-American woman to be named president of New York's prestigious Harvard Business School Club, one of the country's premiere alumni organizations for networking. She also joined women's associations that brought her in contact with leading female executives.

"These organizations can be helpful in many ways," states Nancy, "particularly for a woman. They are great door-openers and the best way imaginable to meet the kinds of people you really want to know—in both your business and social life. It's only natural. To begin with, you've got interests in common—and you just take it from there."

Nancy rose through the ranks at Johnson & Johnson over a twenty-year period. She agrees with Sandra Derickson of GE that women should always be open to branching out into different avenues—even if those changes don't involve raises or clear-cut promotions. Nancy reiterates that while "titles and job up-grades are important, they have to be accompanied by the chance to be stretched and challenged."

If business and college-related organizations have played a major role in Nancy Lane's career ascendancy, what about a mentor?

"I never had one," she responds. "Instead, I have what I think of as 'my team,' people I turn to when I need them. Because they have a different expertise than mine, they've helped me over the years and still do."

When asked how being an African-American woman has influenced her career, the usually bubbly Nancy turns serious. "It has impacted—that's for sure," she responds. "Although there are a lot of minuses, there are some pluses too. You're forced to be more driven. Knowing you have that hurdle in front of you makes you grit your teeth, and say—'I'll show 'em!' "

And, what would Nancy's advice be to young women—particularly young black women—on the cusp of their careers? "I'd tell them it's as simple as always delivering far more than anyone expects you to. That's where it's at."

Terrie Williams

Founder/President, Terrie Williams Agency, a New York PR firm

Defining quote:

"Never use excuses like racism, sexism, or any other 'ism' as reasons to give up."

Another African-American woman—this one a dynamically successful entrepreneur—Terrie Williams built her own business from scratch, after starting out in a totally unrelated field. She had two things going for her—fierce ambition and perseverance—both of which she attributes to her parents. "My mother was the only one of nine children to graduate from high school," she relates. "She and her siblings were raised on a dirt-poor sharecropper's farm in the south. My father also started with nothing and built a successful trucking business. I had strong examples at home that told me to go with my own ambitions.''

Terrie earned a cum laude degree from Brandeis University and a Masters in Social Work from Columbia. ''I wanted to help people, so I was interested in either social work or psychology. I ultimately chose social work because I couldn't hack the statistics courses required for a psychology degree.''

Her first job as a social worker was at New York Hospital. Her work brought her in daily contact with terminally ill patients and their families, as well as women who'd had multiple abortions. She soon felt frustrated and, ultimately, depressed. ''It was tough,'' she relates, ''working in situation after situation where I really couldn't do anything substantive to help.''

At this juncture, Terrie made a gutsy choice, acknowledging that although social work was an altruistic field that might be gratifying to others, it was not right for her. ''I asked myself what did I really want? I pulled out a pad and wrote in big letters—Creativity, Glamour, and Big Bucks—legally, of course! Most important, I wanted something that was mine.''

Terrie homed in on public relations as a field she felt could fulfill her multiple goals. But first she had to learn all she could about the business, which she did. She started by taking two intensive PR courses, followed by a brief stint as program administrator for the tiny, fledgling Black Filmmaker Foundation (BFF).

She left BFF to become director of Public Relations at *Essence* magazine, at thirty the youngest VP in the publication's history. Public relations was obviously the right choice this time, and Terrie's career trajectory was hot. But her newfound success didn't diminish her dream of starting her own company. So how did she make it happen?

''At a party for a mutual friend, I met megastar Eddie Murphy,'' she related. ''I'd heard that he was looking for a PR agency, so I got up the nerve to tell him that I was interested in being that agency.

A week later I sent him a proposal detailing what my (then-unborn) company could do for him. A month later, I made the follow-up phone call, and what do you know? Eddie came on the phone himself and told me: "Terrie, your ideas are great and I would love to have you represent me!"

Not every start-up firm begins with as important a client as Eddie Murphy, but The Terrie Williams Agency didn't stop there. Soon Terrie landed some of the hottest names in the entertainment business, including Janet Jackson; rap entrepreneur Russell Simmons of DEF JAM records; Johnnie Cochran (of O. J. Simpson's "Dream Team"); singer Anita Baker; best-selling author Stephen King; and companies like HBO, Con Edison, and New Line Cinema. Today, Manhattan's Terrie Williams Agency bills more than $2 million per year, and is rising fast with a bullet, as they say in the record biz!

Terrie believes that being a black entrepreneur in a white-dominated industry has made her "stronger and more disciplined. You've got to be a hundred times better than your white counterparts to succeed. That's just a fact of life."

Like so many of the women who "made it," Terrie believes in positive reinforcement from the inside out. "My advice to young women is—never stop learning. I read everything I can get my hands on. I stuff my brain with information, whether it's business related or not. You never know when some seemingly unimportant fact can prove useful—both careerwise and socially."

And finally, she says—"Surround yourself with people who believe in you and encourage you. And—never use excuses like racism, sexism, or any other 'ism' as reasons to give up."

Summary

Although every successful woman we talked to found her own unique way to the top, you've probably noticed there are some similarities running through their stories. So that you can adapt them to your own work habits, we've put them in capsule form. Take at least one or two a day as needed!

Attitude

- Have a can-do/will-do attitude.

- Be doggedly persistent.

- Be self-reliant, with or without a mentor.

- Don't get discouraged if others disagree with your ideas.

- Do what you love and love what you do.

- Never fear to be the first to try something new.

- Keep a sense of humor and use it on yourself, too.

- Show self-confidence through actions, not words.

- Don't be a know-it-all when you're a beginner.

- Be assertive, not aggressive.

- Don't let sexism, racism, or other "isms" throw you.

Work Style

- Work from dawn to dusk.

- Make the toughest job look easy.

- Take the job home—eat, sleep, and drink it.

- Don't abuse people on your way up; it can boomerang.

- Don't sacrifice femininity to be "one of the boys."

- Bring your mind, as well as your body, to the office.

- Always provide more than you're expected to deliver.

Job Strategy

- Come up with new ideas to get recognized.

- Realize an idea is great only if you can make it work.

- Find new ways to network.

- Keep networking even after you've made it.

- Set short-term goals.

- Plan your next step while you're in your present job.

- Find role models whose success you want for yourself.

- Study and imitate their habits.

- If you spot a future trend, go with it.

- Use lateral promotions to increase your know-how.

- Prepare to sacrifice time away from family and friends.

- Make sure you're compensated, not just complimented.

- Listen to silences; they can speak volumes.

- Never stop learning.

ten

The Ten Commandments of Business Success

Hey—it's a jungle out there! The world of business is rougher than ever before. Killer competition, downsizing, office politics—all combine to make survival a tough task. Only those sufficiently savvy to realize that unwritten, but rigid, rules of the game exist will survive and conquer. Don't bother looking for them in your employee manual. They aren't there! But, for you, we've taken the wisdom of some of the world's most successful people and distilled it into our Ten Business Commandments. If you're serious about success, follow them and start your climb to the top. Reread them! Paste them on the fridge! Engrave them on your tongue! Do anything, just so you'll obey them to the letter.

1. **Thou Shalt Learn Thy Corporate Culture.**

    Pure and simple, when people refer to a company's culture, they mean its customs and style. Every corporation has its own. Each company's customs are different, just as language and traditions vary from country to country. It's up to you to learn all the mores and manners that make your company tick.

    The corporate culture should never be taken lightly. It includes everything from dress codes, to the way you talk to each other, to whether the office mood is casual or button-down serious. It affects every minute of your business life. Is it the "company way" to arrive early and stay late; to take short lunch breaks or long, leisurely ones; to pop into someone's office unannounced, or to set up an appointment beforehand? Is it okay to call top management by their first names or is it always Mr./Ms. Big Cheese?

Many a job has been lost because an employee chose to ignore the company's traditions. Some of these customs may seem insignificant to you, but the company considers them sacrosanct and not to be fooled with. Follow suit or file out!

2. **Thou Shalt Follow Through on Whatever You Say You'll Do.**

Get to be known as Ms. Reliable. Be the kind of person who, when given a job, gets it done not only correctly but certainly on time and better yet, early. Nothing can kill your business reputation more quickly than having people feel they can't count on you to complete your mission. Go out of your way to follow through on everything, whether it's an assignment or something you've volunteered to do.

3. **Thou Shalt Be a Team Player.**

Life in business is all about teamwork. Everyone has to work together to achieve company objectives. It's like that old football analogy—everyone on the team has a specific job to do—at a specific time—or else they can't score. Teamwork means that even the star player can't just go off and do his own thing. Once agreed to, the coach's orders must be followed or the game plan falls apart. Can you imagine what would happen in a company if ten people went off in as many different directions to solve the same problem? Nothing would get done. You must become team oriented in order to succeed.

Team playing doesn't mean your individuality can't shine through; it just has to be channeled to fit within the framework.

4. **Thou Shalt Not Burn Thy Bridges Unless Thou Can Walk on Water.**

You never need an enemy. Don't assume because someone is on a lower level than you, it's okay to push her/him around. It's not. The enemy you make today can be your boss tomorrow. At the very least, it could be someone whose help you'll want someday. Business conflicts are inevitable. It's how you handle them that counts. Having a difference of opinion is one thing; going for the jugular is another. Don't try for a total win. It's not necessary to jump up and down in a victory dance. Sure, a hands-down triumph is a high. But if you've left a lot of broken bodies in your wake, you may have won the battle but you'll lose the war.

If you have a point to make, do it calmly, impersonally, and without name-calling. You'll be just as effective, if not more so. Employers are leery of "loose cannons," people who explode when mistakes are made.

5. **Thou Shalt "Talk Smart."**

Don't talk yourself out of success. How you speak can create the image that you're on top of the situation or, conversely, that you don't know what's going on. Women, in particular, persist in talking like women in places where success depends on talking like a man. Their mistakes include everything from indulging in "overspeak" when they should be getting to the point, to apologizing when offering an opinion ("This probably isn't important, but . . ."). Women also shouldn't "small-talk" about family problems. It creates the perception that you can't handle your life, much less your job.

A few pointers—don't "walk" your voice up when you ask a question. It trivializes your query. Second, avoid speed-talking. Your message will be lost, especially if you're quoting figures. Numbers should be spoken s-l-o-w-l-y.

Third, avoid "Rambling Mouth Disease." When you have something to say, stick to the essential facts and get to the bottom line without extraneous detail. Fourth, learn to tolerate silence. Women have been brainwashed to think that it's their responsibility to keep the conversation going. Unless you have something important to add, keep quiet. There's an old joke that it's better to be silent and thought a fool than to speak out and remove all doubt. Seriously, listening attentively can make you look considerably more intelligent than rambling on at will.

Last, when you do speak out, look people in the eye, keep your head up, and speak your piece. Looking down at the floor and being hesitant when you talk makes you appear unsure of yourself.

6. Thou Shalt Look Smart.

Believe us, clothes make a first impression that can launch or sink you. *You don't get a second chance to make a first impression.* The nuances of business dress codes are usually unspoken. You have to figure it out for yourself. Take a good look at the way top management dresses. That's your guide. There's usually a distinct difference between the way senior and junior executives dress. If you're a wannabe senior, copy their style. Forget about expressing your individuality via your office wardrobe, and never show too much flesh at company parties. Money doesn't have everything to do with dressing well. You can achieve a great look without going broke.

7. Thou Shalt Persevere! Persevere! Persevere!

The old saying that "persistence alone is omnipotent" is dead-on right. Scores of educated, genius-I.Q. executives bomb out because they don't persevere. If you really want to make it to the top, you can never use snags or setbacks as excuses for not getting the job done.

If one way doesn't work, try another. If a client turns you down on a sales call, come up with a fresh approach and try again. If your first idea doesn't fly with the boss, think up another one.

Almost invariably, when top-flight executives are asked for the secret of their success, perseverance ranks at the top. Ray Kroc, who founded McDonald's Restaurants, wasn't successful until age fifty-five. He lived by this motto:

> " . . . Nothing in the world can take the place of persistence. Talent will not; nothing is more common than unsuccessful men with talent. Genius will not; unrewarded genius is almost a proverb. Education will not; the world is full of educated derelicts. Persistence and determination alone are omnipotent."

8. **Thou Shalt Keep Thy Learning Curve Up.**

In business, it's expected that you're good at what you do. If you're not, you obviously can't hold on to your job. But if you want to climb up the company ladder, you have to spread out like ivy.

First, learn what other departments in your company do and how they fit into the overall scheme of things. If you're in the communications department, for example, learn how finance works. What's your company's price-earnings ratio? Is the net income up or down? Don't know? Find out. People in the accounting department should educate themselves about their company's marketing function. What new products are on the horizon? What improvements are planned for the current line?

Second, never assume that you "know it all." There are always new takes on your own field of expertise as well as on business in general. Complacency can be your worst enemy.

You become truly valuable to your company when your expertise is not isolated and confined to just your own bailiwick. You also become eminently more promotable. And, should you want to change jobs, other companies will be much more interested in you if you have skills beyond your area of expertise.

9. **Thou Shalt Keep Thy Personal Life Personal.**

Never forget—in business any personal information you give co-workers could be used against you. There are plenty of office barracudas who wouldn't hesitate to use any little morsel of information to drag you down. Don't confide your fears, lack of confidence, and health problems to anyone but your most trusted, tight-lipped friends. And don't necessarily think you can confide in your boss because you believe he or she is above such petty behavior. Not all bosses are!

A case in point: During our friend Terry's interview for a publishing job, she naively decided to give her prospective boss an overly detailed rundown of her weaknesses as well as her strengths. She wanted to be perceived as being oh-so-open and truthful. In fact, her self-deprecation was actually an example of being honest to a fault. Since Terry's overall credentials happened to be top-notch, she got the job. Her work was excellent, and she was given more and more responsibility. The one flaw in this pretty picture was that her raises didn't match her job performance. Whenever she asked her boss about it, Mr. Rotten would inevitably bring up her self-described "weaknesses"—conveniently using them as an excuse for not giving her more money. She learned her lesson. When she moved on to her next job, she kept her self-doubts to herself.

10. **Thou Shalt Remember Money Is the Bottom Line.**

Every company is in business to make money, not lose it. This may sound obvious, but the biggest mistake made by beginners is not understanding this simple premise. When the company earns more money, usually you will too. In other words, there's more for everyone to share—like raises and bonuses.

If the secretary who handles customer calls in a rude or slipshod manner stops to think it could cost the company business (and affect her paycheck in the process), she'd probably talk to customers a lot more professionally.

Every single step you take on the job should help the company stay in the black. You'll really become valuable to your company—and possibly even be promoted—if you can come up with ideas that'll help them save money and make more of it. Don't be bashful. Jot down your ideas and pass them on to senior management. When you become known as someone who's always thinking about how to increase the bottom line, you're sure to make a beeline to the top!

Part Two

The Right Man

eleven

The Pleasures and Pitfalls of the Single Life

Finding the right man is a principal part of what this book is all about. But, let's be frank. While a great guy is an important addition to your life, you can still have a terrific time before he comes along. Believe it. We did, and you can too! It's all in how you handle it, which is entirely up to you.

Once you realize that you're not half a pair of scissors without a man, your life can be as complete and fulfilling as you want it to be. How can you make this happen? By being active, involved, and curious about the world around you. Don't wait for life to happen *to* you—make it happen *for* you. You'll not only be stimulated, but much too busy to be lonely. You'll also be a far more interesting and desirable person to be with. And most important, your self-confidence will have a chance to grow in the process.

Women who are on an obvious out-and-out manhunt have an air of desperation about them that repels, rather than attracts, people—especially men. These women generally have such shaky self-esteem that they feel they must have a man, any man, to make their lives meaningful.

Too many women fall into the trap of thinking that their identity depends on being part of a couple. The truth is there are very few things a woman can't do without a man, in this day and age. When you earn your own living, you have the kind of economic and emotional independence that enables you to live your life almost exactly the way you want to.

Not so long ago, women felt that they must have a man in tow in order to enjoy life. Today every woman knows she has the freedom to travel anyplace, anytime, buy her own furs and jewelry, or go out on Saturday night with her girlfriends and have a helluva good time.

As for marriage, women are waiting longer and longer to take the Big Step. In fact, so many women today are postponing marriage that the term ''old maid'' has virtually been axed from contemporary lingo. Even pressure from family and friends to ''find a man and get married'' has lessened a lot—the heat is off.

The Cycles of Love

Our friend Sara, a top cosmetics company executive, didn't march down the aisle until she was thirty-seven. Over the years, Sara dated a variety of men but wasn't willing to settle until she found one whose goals and values meshed with hers. A girlfriend happened to tell her about Jim, who was newly divorced, very successful, and very single. Liking what she heard, Sara schemed up a way to meet him. She decided to leave a phony but intriguing message at his office that would force him to call her back. She knew she had to be extra clever, since Jim was a high-ranking executive who probably wouldn't return a phone call from someone he didn't know. The message Sara left was to ask Jim why he hadn't RSVP'd to her note inviting him to a dinner party she was giving for a mutual friend. (It was an invitation, by the way, she never sent, for a party she never gave.)

Curious about her message, and also very polite, Jim returned her call to explain that he'd never gotten the invitation. Quick-witted Sara said she must have sent it to the wrong address, but could she make up for "leaving him out" by buying him a drink? She convinced him to meet her for cocktails, and they immediately clicked. One year later they were married. By the time she was forty-two, Sara had three children, an extremely devoted husband, and the kind of life she'd always wanted. Although she had to kiss a lot of frogs before she met her prince, she's royally happy now.

Jim was not the first man in Sara's life, of course. She'd been involved with the usual number of bozos that life throws every woman's way—including the "soon-to-be-divorced" married man, a charming rogue with a fear of commitment, and the typical assortment of love-'em-and-leave-'em types. But Sara had loads of self-esteem and, in spite of a few bumps in the road, she never let the bad times damage her sense of worth. This kind of inner confidence made it possible for her to hold on until she found the man she knew was right for her.

Almost every woman we know has gone through cycles similar to Sara's—falling in love, dumping or getting dumped, binding up the psychic wounds, and starting all over again. In this sometimes gut-wrenching process, all of us eventually come to realize the kind of man we're looking for, and the ones we want to avoid. Number one on your hit list should be guys who attack your self-esteem.

Self-Esteem Abusers

For a cautionary tale about what Mr. Wrong can do to a woman's confidence, take our friend Amanda. Twenty-one and just out of college, Amanda landed a job at a New York advertising agency. On the surface, she appeared strong-willed and outgoing, but beneath the facade she wasn't really all that sure of herself. Actually, on a scale of one to ten, her self-esteem registered about a four. A newcomer to New York City, where she didn't know many people, Amanda was scared of the possibility of flubbing up on her first job.

Along came Bob. At age thirty-two, he seemed to have it all together. A successful sales executive, he was good-looking, mature, and seemingly s-o-o-o sensitive.

Amanda was thrilled to have this sophisticated older man interested in her. Bob made her feel wanted and secure. He made a big fuss over her, introduced her to his friends, and took her to trendy restaurants. Amanda was on cloud nine. At last, she had a soul mate! Whenever she was with him, he encouraged her to tell him her problems and always seemed to want to help her solve them. She felt a surge of self-confidence. He became her main focus. After all, she thought, he's crazy about me! She made him and their relationship her first priority, not realizing it was at the expense of her own needs.

Clever Bob. He was equally happy to have this attractive woman in his life who seemed to hang on his every word. He advised her how to handle her job, helped her find an apartment, and told her it wasn't necessary to turn to anyone else—not even her parents—for advice. After all, he assured her, she had *his* total support. Mr. Ideal, right? Wrong!

Bob was a Class-A control freak who relished having the power to manipulate Amanda. As long as she was "needy" and he could direct her life, things were okay. When Amanda began acting a little more self-reliant, making her own decisions and not constantly turning to him for counsel, the trouble started. He decided to sneak a look at her diary to see what was up. Surprise, surprise! He discovered his little bird was becoming more and more resentful of his superior air. She was beginning to feel smothered and wanted more independence to live her life her way.

Bob's immediate reaction was to try to clip her wings. It was easy enough for him to chip away at her self-confidence. After all, she had provided him with the weapon to do it—her vulnerability.

He began to put her down, needling her about her small-town background, reminding her how unsophisticated she was, and sarcastically squelching her hopes for a promotion at work.

He went even further and attempted to destroy her reliance on her family's emotional support. Although he tried to isolate her from them—a classic control maneuver—it didn't work; the bonds were too strong. One night, Amanda asked Bob to join her father and stepmother for dinner. Reluctantly, he agreed. When the conversation turned into an all-out family powwow to help Amanda get that promotion she wanted so badly, Bob felt his influence over her was threatened. It dawned on him that his little "hatchling" was capable of flying out of his clutches at any moment. He sulked all through dinner, disagreed with her parents' suggestions, and abruptly told Amanda he was leaving. Of course, he expected her to follow. She didn't and never saw him again.

That night, something inside Amanda clicked. She was finally able to see that Bob was playing mind games. It had taken her a while to catch on, because clever, manipulative men like Bob sugar-coat and disguise their criticisms. They rake you over the coals without your even realizing it. Amanda's story is a classic tale of spending too much time with Mr. Wrong. If you find yourself in a similar situation, where your feeling of self-worth is constantly trampled on, drop the slimeball like a hot potato! No one is worth sacrificing your self-esteem for.

Self-Preservation Tactics

You say you can't end it? That the sexual attraction is too strong? That he takes you to lots of interesting parties? That he's exciting and you meet fascinating people through him? For whatever reasons, you may have convinced yourself you really, really *love* him. It's not love, it's need. A big difference! When you're so needy that your self-esteem is practically nonexistent, it's easy to make yourself believe that even Ivan the Terrible isn't all that bad.

There are lots of smart but needy women like Amanda who get suckered into staying in relationships that seem to work but, in fact, are emotionally abusive. We don't want this ever to happen to you. Here's our fail-proof formula for protecting your sense of self:

1. **Beware of relationships that are certain to be dead-enders.** Pure and simple, that means don't stay in what we call pretend romances. You know in your heart of hearts if you want your relationship to be long-term. Maybe you're sticking around because you've been sleeping together and that lulls you into thinking you're committed. Or, ask yourself if you're just hanging in there because you're lonely and frustrated and there's no one else on the horizon.

2. **Hang on to your standards.** Whenever your ego is particularly fragile, it's all too easy to lower your standards. Don't let your lack of self-esteem allow you to settle for just any man. Who wants to be holding hands with Walter Wimp? Take off the blinders and face reality! Even if it means a few lonely nights, trust us—it'll be worth it. Anyway, how can you meet Mr. Wonderful if El Wimpo is in the way?

3. **Identify what you want out of life and stand up for it.** Do you share similar interests and ambitions with him? Are your backgrounds compatible? If he's into country music and you live and die for opera, that's easy to work out. If you're a Southern Baptist and he's Greek Orthodox, even that can be handled. On the other hand, if your intrinsic values are miles apart, face reality. It probably won't fly.

   Opposites may attract—at first—but they usually don't stay the course. Take Anita and Tim, for example. Born and bred in New York City, Anita had her heart set on a career in investment banking; Tim's lifelong ambition was to be a rancher in Oregon. Another twosome: Georgia was the ultimate party animal; Matt's idea of fun was to stay home and watch TV. And then there's Alicia and Todd. She was a clotheshorse and spent every spare dime on looking good; Todd, a die-hard penny-pincher, held fast to every dollar.

In all of these cases, it wasn't a matter of right or wrong. Their values were just too incompatible.

4. **Never forget self-esteem is built first by succeeding at Life's Little Things.** The Big Ones will soon fall into place. To make sure this happens, always try to protect yourself from no-win situations, regardless of who or what they involve. Safeguarding your self-esteem is a twenty-four-hour battle. It has to be fought in all areas of your life. Like what? Like avoiding men who constantly put you down, or steering clear of supposedly close girlfriends, who are obviously out for themselves—at your expense. There are loads of clever, insecure people who know that one way to build up their ego is by squashing yours.

5. **Fake it until you make it.** This has nothing to do with sex. Rather, it's a powerful psychological technique for you to master. What it means is that, in social situations (just as in the office), you must act "as if" you have so much self-confidence that you could *be* and *do* anything. So what if it's only an act? It works. It'll get you a lot further in life than a scaredy-cat attitude will.

6. **Open your heart oh-so-carefully!** It isn't too smart to go around blabbing to every Tom, Dick, and Harry about what a nothing you are. It doesn't make the man more loving. Look at what happened to Amanda. Instead of feeling compassion for you, some guys will use your vulnerability to their own advantage. They just can't help themselves. It's such easy pickings. And they might wind up dumping you because you aren't "good enough" for them. After all, you told them so yourself!

Sad to say, there even are guys who deliberately seek out "wounded birds," women who make it obvious that they don't think much of themselves. These men can then manipulate the relationship to their own advantage and be in complete control.

P.S. The message here is that you should reveal your insecurities and doubts *only* to a very few tried-and-true friends. These are the people who have proven over time that they're worthy of your trust. If you feel you need professional help in this area, we've written a whole chapter on how to find the right person to deal with your psyche. Read chapter 24, ''Psyching Yourself Up: Crisis Time'' to find some of the answers.

7. **Never depend completely on a man for your sense of self.** If you rely on being part of a duo to determine your self-worth, you'll fall apart if he decides to take a walk. No matter how much you're wrapped up in someone, have other people in your life whom you enjoy—good girlfriends, male friends, relatives, close colleagues at work, etc. That way, when times are lean in the romance department, you'll still have some people telling you how terrific you are. And never let a man isolate you from these very important people (as Bob tried to do to Amanda). It's a sure sign of a manipulator at work.

Now that we've discussed how the wrong man can squash your self-esteem, how do you go about finding a guy who's right for you? You know, someone who'll make your self-esteem soar, not sink.

Where Are They?

Look around you. Men are everywhere. Just like sampling ice cream, your goal is to find your favorite flavor (fat-free, of course) and to make sure he has all the qualities that are important for a good relationship. And remember not to panic if you don't find perfection immediately. Take your time and sample what's out there.

In the meantime, where are the guys? They go where other men go. Besides the bar for the usual beer after work, they're playing tennis, golf, going to football games, browsing at bookstores and roller-blading in the park. Karen met her future husband taking karate lessons. She says the odds were great—five men to every woman. Linda met her current boyfriend at Denim & Diamonds, a New York country and western club, taking line-dancing lessons. And Marci is still heavily involved with the heart specialist she met while volunteering at a local hospital.

Sheila picked up her beau when she dropped her boots off at Jim's Shoe Repair, a New York City institution located in the heart of one of Manhattan's busiest business districts. Jim's attracts lots of young male execs who are constantly popping in for a shine.

Consider broadening your social sphere by taking adult education classes after work. Not only will you sharpen your mind, you might actually meet an eligible man who shares your interests. If you really want to zero in, take a course in anything that reeks of maleness—like sailing, driving race cars, etc. Beth, a smart, goal-oriented advertising executive, got both an MBA and a husband by taking classes at night, a much better time to bag a man who's also gainfully employed.

And don't forget your church or synagogue, political campaigns, automobile and boat shows, the golf course/driving range, laundromats (in your building and outside), and supermarkets (weekdays after 6:00 P.M. and Saturday mornings). Debra, an avid supermarket shopper, was once picked up by a guy whose opening line was "Can you tell me if this cantaloupe is ripe?" The melon may not have been ready to eat, but their romance ripened in no time flat. Although the relationship didn't last forever, Debra said they were two of the sweetest years she'd ever spent.

Don't forget your local health club. It's as good a place as any to meet someone. The guy who's waiting for your treadmill just might be waiting for your phone number, too. And our friend Jack tells us that upscale department stores are terrific places to meet women. In fact, he and his buddies have a standing joke about going to Bloomingdale's to "work" the cosmetics counters. So if they're out there looking *you* over, take advantage of the opportunity and give *them* the once-over, too.

On-Line Love

Melinda, an assistant editor who had just arrived in New York from the Midwest, was feeling desperately lonely one weekend. Her roommate was away, and there were no plans on the horizon.

So she booted up her computer and surfed the Internet until she arrived at the "romance" section of America Online. "I was really looking for a pen pal," she explains, "someone I could correspond with and become friends with over the Internet." However, Melinda found more than she had bargained for. That day she encountered Dan, a boat builder, who had posted what she thought was a "beautiful, endearing" clip about himself. Melinda answered it and they struck up a daily correspondence. Over a period of ten months, Melinda and Dan developed an intense friendship, revealing everything about themselves and their lives. By the end of the tenth month, they finally decided to meet—in Dan's hometown of Baltimore.

"I must admit I felt some trepidation," admits Melinda, "because we had shared so much about ourselves before actually meeting. But we hit it off right away. And, the fact that I really got to know him as a person first—without looks and sexual vibes getting in the way—turned out to be a big advantage." Melinda and Dan's romance has been hot and heavy ever since. They see each other every weekend, in her city or his. And they still correspond daily on the Internet. "A number of my friends are also meeting men this way," says Melinda. "It's a great means of getting to know someone over a period of time. You can keep putting off actually meeting the guy unless you feel sure he's someone you'd really want to be with.''

Curious about what happened next? One year later Dan proposed, and it looks as though Melinda just may say yes.

Puppy Love

Anna-Lea and Stacey, two sun-bronzed California girls, were driving through Los Angeles in their red convertible when they spotted a rare sight for that city—a pedestrian! The stroller, a handsome guy named Randy, was walking his dog, Herman—a frisky Dalmatian pup. Coincidentally, the two women had Stacey's dog in the car, and it, too, was a Dalmatian—named Sunny.

They screeched to a halt in front of Randy and introduced themselves. The three of them arranged a play date for the dogs. Well, the Dalmatians didn't mate, but Randy and Anna-Lea sure did. They became inseparable, and one year later they married. Every guest at their wedding got a T-shirt with Herman's smiling face on it.

The moral of this story is—get a dog! No matter what city you live in, walking your four-legged friend can be much more productive than signing up for a dating service or even answering personal ads.

Find a Can't-Wait-to-Get-to-Work Job

As we pointed out in the chapter ''The Romance and Business Merger,'' one of the very best places to meet men is at your job. You already have lots in common with your co-workers. After all, you're working together for the same goals. Plus—you've had the chance to get to know one another fairly well over time. Don't ever feel guilty about choosing a job because you like the kind of men who work there almost as much as you enjoy the job itself. Chances are if you don't cotton to the caliber of men you're with from nine to five, you won't like the job either.

Torre's first job in New York at age twenty-three was working as a writer with a group of bureaucratic engineers. They were mainly middle-aged, married, and living in the 'burbs. Nice people, sure, but to her they were too conservative and B-O-R-I-N-G. More importantly, they not only didn't appreciate her creativity, they squelched it. Every brochure she wrote was so severely edited, it ended up as dull as dishwater.

Eventually Torre moved to an advertising agency that was full of young, creative people, where new ideas were not only valued but necessary. She blossomed like a rose. In fact, she became a vice president of the agency at age twenty-six. And her social life took off like a rocket. Finally, she was with men who were on her wavelength.

The moral of the story is: Don't hang around a place where you're undervalued and your co-workers are so unappealing you can't wait to leave and go home each night. Be honest—if they all seem uptight, over-the-hill, and out of it, is this the best place for you? If there aren't at least a couple of people you can schmooze with over cocktails or coffee, you're in the wrong environment.

The Right Attitude

Now that we've told you where the men are, let's make sure you have the right attitude. What's that? Be as flexible as a rubber band! Never, ever, refuse a blind date. It doesn't matter if you're having a rotten day at the office—or if you feel so fat that you think you'll never be able to zip up your dress. Opportunities rarely, if ever, repeat themselves. Today's blind date may become tomorrow's soul mate.

Our friend Toni, thirty-two, attractive, single, and working in New York, had just broken up with Donald, a guy who constantly reminded her that she was five years older than he was. After the breakup, she was so depressed she OD'd on Oreos and ice cream and gained ten pounds in a month. Obviously, her self-esteem was not bubbling over. When a girlfriend phoned to ask if she wanted to be set up on a blind date, Toni reluctantly put aside her negative feelings and figured she had to stop hibernating. Brad (the blind date) turned out to be available, witty, six years her senior, and making an infrequent visit to New York.

Since Brad was a Detroit-based automotive executive and Toni was glued to her marketing job in New York, they began a long-distance romance. It started slowly, and, whenever their calendars coincided, they'd meet in various cities around the country. If Brad had to make a business trip to Miami, for instance, she'd try to join him for the weekend. (By the way, he always paid for her ticket.) Pretty soon their relationship blossomed into a serious one, and they began to take turns weekending in each other's home city. After a couple of years, they realized the relationship was for real and decided to make it legal.

Toni and Brad's chance meeting proves blind dates can be well worth it. They're a gamble you should always take. Yes, we're the first to admit that some blind date experiences are washouts, but they only require a few hours of your life, and you can always end them early. If you're reluctant to invest a whole evening, we recommend meeting for lunch or drinks.

You can usually trust a girlfriend to fix you up with a guy who has possibilities. Women take the assignment seriously and are generally more sensitive to the kind of man who would really appeal to you. When guys fix you up, they mean well but often don't really think it through. Regardless of who arranges the date, remember: *You meet people through people.* If you're home watching TV and feeding your face, you're not going to meet anyone.

Who Pays?

Most men we polled said that they expect to pick up the tab, especially on the first few dates. This, of course, assumes that it's *he* who's asking *you*. That's the rule of thumb: he or she who asks, pays.

But let's say he's taken you out several times, and you really like him—but he's not exactly flush with cash. Thoughtfulness is the key here. If he pays for dinner, you can offer to buy the movie tickets. If he cooks one night, you might take him out the next. Here are a few other ways you can reciprocate that aren't as awkward as grabbing the check or continually offering to split it:

1. Invite him to your place for Sunday brunch and rent a movie afterwards.

2. Ask him to join you on a picnic, complete with checkered tablecloth, wine, and fancy sandwiches.

3. Pick up tickets to a concert or sports event that you know he'd enjoy.

4. If you're dying to go to a chic, somewhat expensive restaurant or club, suggest it and casually add, "Let's split the tab."

5. If things are really going well, how about taking him to dinner to celebrate his birthday, a job promotion, your third month together, or whatever you can think of?

6. If he *won't* let you pay for anything, buy him a gift you know he'd like but probably wouldn't splurge on. It could be a special book, a couple of CDs, a gift certificate for a massage, or a baseball cap with his favorite team's logo on it.

    You get the idea!

Dates: Blind, Disaster, and Otherwise

Every woman we know has had some kind of disaster date at some point in her life. It's all part of the search. There's really no way to completely avoid the occasional dud. It happens to all of us. Friends and relatives with the best of intentions are sometimes way off base, setting you up with the kind of guy you wouldn't choose for yourself in a hundred years.

Take this example: Felicia, a TV newscaster who was sought after by every man in New York, was fixed up with Fred by mutual friends. Tall and handsome, Fred had always dated very glamorous women, mostly models and movie stars. He was delighted at the prospect of meeting Felicia and called her immediately.

She agreed to meet him at his apartment for cocktails—expecting that dinner in a neighborhood restaurant would follow. During drinks, the doorbell rang and there stood a delivery boy from the local Chinese restaurant. It seems that Fred's idea of showing Felicia a good time was eating sesame noodles straight from the carton while going through photo albums starring himself and every well-known woman he'd ever dated. Felicia was taken aback, to say the least, and took off without even waiting to open her fortune cookie. Fortunately, Felicia's ego was very much intact, and so was her sense of humor.

However, disaster dates are not always as harmless as this one. Our friend Carrie, a Minneapolis stockbroker, told us about a blind date she had a few years ago that still brings back bad memories. Carrie was set up with Bill, a business associate of a mutual friend, for a ski weekend at a popular resort. It was described to Carrie as tons of fun, with about twelve others invited.

Carrie eagerly accepted the invitation after checking with several of her friends, who also were going. Barely an hour after she met Bill, a big, bulky, former college wrestler, he offered to give her a tour of the ski house, which ended in a game room in the basement. There he proceeded to grab and grope her until Carrie, five foot two in her stocking feet, managed to shove him away and run back upstairs. She spent the rest of the evening as far away from Bill as she could get—counting the seconds until the weekend was over.

"On Monday morning I called the guy who introduced us and gave him a piece of my mind," she recalls. "I couldn't help wondering—did Bill feel I was so available that I would get physical with him minutes after we met? I felt hurt and humiliated. My friend's response was that he didn't really know Bill all that well and that he had seemed like a 'good guy.'"

It was a long time before Carrie would accept another blind date, and when she did, she made sure to check him out as carefully as she could. In retrospect, Carrie realizes that she was foolish to have accepted an invitation for a whole weekend with a guy she'd never met before. She also advises it's wise to set rules for time and place: no weekends with anyone on a blind date; lunch or drinks are usually the best way to go. It's easier then for either party to end it after an hour or so, if there's no chemistry.

We couldn't agree more. If it's a lunch date, the obvious excuse is that you have to get back to work, or have a 2:30 appointment. For drinks, the natural out is that you're meeting friends for dinner. Carrie's fiasco also underscores our theory that when it comes to blind dates, men, while usually well-meaning, often aren't sensitive to the nuances of what might make a couple click—nor do they always pick up on the personality traits of their buddies that could create total dating dissonance.

Another Date from Hell

Although we said earlier that women are usually better matchmakers, this isn't always true, either. Sharon, an up-and-coming young ad copywriter, confides: "Louise, a woman I didn't know all that well, called and told me that her friend Charles, a lawyer who'd recently split with his girlfriend, had seen me at a party and wanted to meet me. Although Louise was more of a business acquaintance than a buddy, she was bright and successful, and I figured she had good taste in men. I'd just broken up with my boyfriend and was kind of at loose ends, so I thought—why not?"

Charles called Sharon shortly thereafter and arranged to meet her in the lobby of Carnegie Hall to attend a concert, and then go to dinner. "We spotted each other, said hello, and he went to get our tickets from the box office," recounts Sharon. "On his way back, an elderly woman accidentally bumped into him, and he went ballistic. 'Get out of my way! Where do you think you're going?' he bellowed. That's how things started off," she recalled. "I can't stand rudeness—and he was inexcusably rude in the first five minutes. Then—when we got to our seats, he started grumbling when he saw that the evening's program was going to be some obscure work by Strauss. 'I hate listening to music I don't know,' he complained."

After these two negative incidents, Sharon was relieved that she didn't have to say anything during the concert. Later, at dinner, Charles spent most of the time talking about the many faults of his ex-girlfriend, plus giving Sharon a dull, detailed description of every big business deal he was involved in.

"He didn't seem even remotely interested in me or anything about me," said Sharon, "and I couldn't wait for the evening to be over. But the crowning blow came when we finally finished eating and he asked where I lived. When I told him my apartment was about twenty blocks from Carnegie Hall—he lost it again. 'I NEVER go more than six blocks from midtown,' he huffily declared, as though I had committed a cardinal sin by being geographically undesirable! 'But I guess I could make an exception and take you home.' 'Please don't bother,' I said, 'I'll get my own cab.' ' "

Sharon quickly hailed one and sped away from the crabby Charles—forever.

Believe it or not, he had the nerve to call Sharon for a second date. Luckily, she was able to say she was busy. He tried another time. Again, Sharon said she had plans. Not one to get the message, he asked her to name a night that was good for her. Sharon had to resist the impulse to say "How's never?" Instead, she took the diplomatic way out and said, "I'm sorry, but I'm seeing someone." (Obviously, she wasn't). When a guy doesn't want to take "no" for an answer, just use the old "I'm-involved-with-someone" excuse. If that doesn't work, resort to brutal honesty. "I'm sorry, I don't think it would work out between us" is a truthful yet firm statement that should get him off your back.

A Different Scenario

But, what if he had been Charles Charming instead of such a jerk? Let's say you've just gone out with a great guy, had a terrific time, and then nothing happens. No flowers, no follow-up phone calls, not even a fax. *Nada*, *niente*, nothing! So how do you get a guy you really like to ask you out a second time? If the first date was a roaring success and the chemistry was there, relax. He'll probably call you again, assuming he's not married or otherwise involved. But what if he doesn't? Today's dating etiquette has supposedly evolved to the stage where it's perfectly all right for you to call him. It's an okay thing to do—now and then—if you feel comfortable. Although guys say they love it when women ask them out, remember: most men want a challenge, not an easy win. A fact of life is that the majority of men prefer to do the chasing. Let them!

Avoiding a Frog

Whew! Finding the right man is hard work. Kissing all those frogs can give you a case of the creeps. Here are some guidelines for recognizing the unwanted toads who hop in and out of every woman's life. Our friend Bea Lund advises the following:

NEVER DATE A MAN WHO:

- has hips bigger than yours
- gets undressed in the bathroom
- says he hates eating in restaurants
- has a Barcalounger in front of his TV
- keeps a motorcycle in the living room
- won't give you his home phone number
- looks at other women while talking to you
- wants to call his wife or girlfriend on *your* phone
- doesn't know how to turn on his own oven
- thinks every woman needs a baby to be ''fulfilled''
- has little shoes hanging from his rearview mirror
- doesn't like to look at you when you're naked
- wants to try on your clothes

Procuring a Prince

Now that you've read Bea's version of who *not* to date, here's our no-joke guide to locating someone who's at least a possibility, if not the real thing. Be forewarned, however, that all women have their fantasies of meeting the perfect man who has everything—movie-star looks, lots of money, a beautiful bod, brains, money, a sense of humor, money, an important job, money, and—of course—he's great in bed.

If he exists, it's probably in your dreams. No guy is 100 percent perfect, but there are women who do expect everything in a man. Setting impossibly high standards only paves the way to failure and disappointment. All relationships involve compromise. It's up to you to determine what you can live with or without. So, let's get real. There are some qualities you have every right to expect in the man of your choice, and here they are:

- He treats you, your family and friends with respect.

- He's at least as smart as you are.

- He thinks your job is just as important as his.

- He's honest.

- He tries to lift your spirits when you're low.

- He notices the new haircut or dress.

- He doesn't force you to do anything that goes against your grain.

- He's not too shy to show affection outside the bedroom.

If your current squeeze has none of these qualities, you don't have much of a guy. Sometimes it does more for your self-esteem to stay home and read a good book than to be with a man you really don't like, could never admire, or who really isn't there for you. When we say "compromise," we aren't advocating dating a guy who has few or none of the qualities that are meaningful in life. Rather, recognize that there are some things in a man that just are not acceptable. Here's a quick summary of these nasty negative traits:

Characteristics of a Creep:

- He spaces out when you try to talk to him.

- He expects you to wait on him, never the reverse.

- He rarely, if ever, compliments you.

- He's annoyed by your tears and your problems.

- He doesn't want to hear about your dreams.

- He's never attentive in public; he just lets you fend for yourself.

- He's always looking at, and comparing you to, other women.

- He's totally selfish emotionally, sexually, and financially.

- He puts down your family and friends.

- He's addicted to drugs and/or alcohol.

- He lacks basic manners. Beware—this usually goes deeper.

- He has only one true love, *himself.*

To put all this in a nutshell—never date a guy who, at the very least, you wouldn't want to have as a friend.

Wrap-Up

Being single can be one of the best times of your life, if you work at it. Okay, we acknowledge that finding the right man is not an easy process. But it won't be a painful one if you heed our advice.

If you fill your life with meaningful work and exciting people, you won't feel that there's a great big void because the right man hasn't come along. Obviously, you don't need to wait for him to get a life. Besides, with a little more experience and seasoning, you'll have a much better idea of the kind of guy you want and deserve than you did when you were still wet behind the ears.

QUICK CAPSULE: FINDING THE RIGHT MAN

- You aren't half a pair of scissors without him.
- Don't wait for life to happen *to* you, make it happen *for* you.
- Be active, involved, and curious about the world around you.
- Never be too obvious about your search for a man.
- You can do virtually anything you like without a man.
- Accept blind dates.
- Go where the guys are.
- Always look your best—even for a quick trip to the supermarket.
- Work where the kind of men you want to meet are.
- A little more life experience will reveal the kind of man you really want.

twelve

Good Sex, Bad Sex, Safe Sex, and No Thanks

Ah, good sex! You're in love, life is exciting, and it's great to feel sexy. You feel more beautiful, more desirable—it's June in January, and all's right with the world.

When he knows how to light your fire, it burns brighter than the noonday sun. Great sex sizzles like nothing else in the world. Once you've had it, you don't want to give it up—ever. It's more than just thrashing around—it's a true meeting of the mind and heart, as well as the obvious.

This kind of chemistry works like Krazy Glue, bonding you together through thick and thin. But be aware that if the sexual magnetism isn't mutual, the relationship won't go anywhere. It doesn't matter if he dances as divinely as Baryshnikov, his mind equals Einstein's, and his looks make you melt. When the chemistry is kaput, there's not a whole lot you can do about it.

Naturally, we know that sex isn't the be-all and end-all. But it is important. Sex serves as a personality barometer, giving you a direct line to what he thinks, not only about you but about life in general. Invariably, his sexual habits will tell you all sorts of things like: Is he generous or selfish? Does he respect women, or are you just a convenient relief station?

Sex can help to define a relationship and provide a closeness that's unlike any other. When it's good, it swoops you up to a real high. But before you attempt that ascent, let's address the age-old question:

Quando? Quando? Quando?

When? When? When is it okay to have a sexual relationship with a guy? There are dozens of different opinions, depending on your religious beliefs, family upbringing, and what's acceptable in your own circle. However, if you do decide to become intimate, and your goal is a long-term relationship or even marriage, wait until the relationship has jelled. And, don't ever let yourself get pressured into a sexual relationship that you're not sure about.

Trust us, this advice may sound old-fashioned, but we know it works. So, sorry—but no, you shouldn't sleep with him on the first, second, or even third date, no matter how much you're attracted to him, if you want to keep him around. Why? Several reasons. Men like and need THE CHASE! It reinforces their masculinity. Your job is to play the game well and outfox him. If you say yes too quickly, you make it too easy and take all the fun out of it for him. Anyway, no man with any character demands that a woman succumb to his advances immediately. If you're in there for the long haul, you'd only be defeating your purpose.

Look at it this way: If the average Joe dated a megawatt movie star, do you think he'd immediately expect to get her between the sheets? Of course not! He'd wonder how special she could be if she hops into bed so quickly. Well, it's no different for you. The mental machinations of the male animal work the same whether you're a famous sex goddess or not. It just isn't challenging for a man to pursue a woman who falls right into his arms.

Remember Toni and Brad's romance from the previous chapter? Toni is firmly convinced that she and Brad are married today because she challenged him by not sleeping with him right off the bat.

She also didn't sit home waiting for his phone calls, and when he asked her out, she wasn't always available.

The fact that Toni and Brad got to really know each other as individuals first helped their relationship grow more than anything else they could have done. When a woman jumps into bed with a man too soon, it's easy for her thinking processes to become clouded. Sex is the ultimate bonding experience and can blind you to the faults and underlying personality of your bedmate. When sex enters the picture, the whole relationship suddenly moves to a different level. Once you've passed go, it's almost impossible to shift into reverse. At that point, it becomes much more difficult to get to know a guy in an easygoing way, with all the comfortable give-and-take that helps a woman and man become friends as well as potential mates. A few months later—if the passion has peaked and waned—you might wonder what you ever saw in the guy in the first place.

You say you don't really want to know or marry him, you just want to go to bed with him? You could even argue that you don't care if he calls you afterwards or not. Guess what? *We don't believe you!* Every woman alive, with the possible exception of the occasional nympho, is hurt if a man doesn't want to see her again after she's slept with him. Why risk damaging your self-esteem? Back off, slow down, and take it easy.

Like everything else in life, there are exceptions. If you're the rare woman whose intuition is so dead-on accurate that you can almost instantly size up a man, and know you'd be right together, then okay. Go for it, as long as you think you won't get hurt. Yes, there are some long-term relationships that have followed instant sex. But don't kid yourself—these are the exceptions, not the rule.

Okay, so you've waited the requisite amount of time, at least six or seven dates (yes, we're for real!), you've gotten to know him as a person, and now you've gone to bed with him. What's next? Don't even think about asking him to move in with you after a few delicious weekends together. That's the quickest way to scare him off. And don't tell him you've got an extra toothbrush on hand for him, either. Don't let passion push you into trying to engage him in any lovey-dovey commitments. In the beginning, never discuss your future together. Forget your fantasies and treat the time spent in bed as a—hopefully—loving experience, not an automatic avenue to a deeper commitment.

However, once you're in a sexual relationship, it's fair both to assume, and to ask the guy involved to confirm, that he's not sleeping with anyone else. He's got the very same right to expect equal treatment from you. Having more than one bedmate at the same time not only complicates matters—it's also dangerous in this era of AIDS and other sexually transmitted diseases.

It's a woman's nature to want to nest. If you're sleeping with a guy you really care about, it's only natural to think in terms of where the relationship will go from there. But, you'll really do yourself in if you come on too strong, too soon. Don't make him feel as if he owes you something because you gave him the "gift" of your body. After all, it was your decision to sleep with him. In the beginning, it's especially important that you play it cool. When he gets ready to leave the next morning, send him off gracefully. And if he goes out the door without saying he'll call you, or setting another date, play it smart and don't push.

Good Sex

Okay—your physical relationship has taken off, and you think it's great. But everyone's definition of good sex is different. Specifically, it depends on what gives *you* pleasure. For example, Natalie tells us it's exciting for her when her boyfriend is adventurous, always trying new things, plus remembering those special little touches that turn her on. On the other hand, Kelly's first priority is that he be gentle, that he realize sex is like a good book.

It has a beginning, a middle, and an end. For most women, if the foreplay is a flop, who cares about the rest?

Timing is important, too. Audrey prefers making love in the morning, because that's when her energy kicks in. Cathy, on the other hand, is a night person and hates romance in the early A.M. with the sun streaming in. She's just not in the mood until the evening.

If you want sex that pleases you, you have to make your needs known. How? *Tell him.* But very carefully and not in the beginning of your relationship. You're in male ego territory and if you get too dictatorial, too soon, he'll freeze. Wait a while before you get specific about your needs; no man wants a traffic cop in bed. The art of sexual communication is similar to holding a good conversation. The approach and the rules are the same. When you have a touchy subject to discuss, you work up to it. And you don't attack or preach. You make your point diplomatically, then listen to the other side.

It's the same for satisfying sexual encounters. You don't give instructions—but you do have input at the right point in time. We thoroughly agree that women should be equal partners, in and out of bed, but don't expect it to happen overnight. Some men still resent women telling them what to do. They want to play it their way—*period.* But most men won't be put off by their mate's suggestion to make sex a cooperative venture. Like anything else in life, however, your timing has to be right.

Then there's that question women have been asking for the past twenty years—should you be the aggressor sometimes? Should you seduce him—lead the way to bed, initiate the lovemaking?

In a way, it's the same as wondering if you can ask him out on a date. If you feel comfortable doing it, and you don't think he'll feel threatened—try it. He might love it. Again, make sure you pick the right moment.

No Thanks

Here's another touchy topic. What if you two are crazy about each other, but sometimes he's in the mood and you're not? It could be you're tired or you've had a bad day at the office and just want to turn your mind off. There's no reason why he should be offended if you explain. You're not a machine, to be turned on with the flick of a switch. Nor is he, for that matter. Don't be afraid to tell him "uh-uh, another time."

Bad Sex/Bad Partners

Once you've sampled the good stuff, bad sex is pretty easy to identify.

A quick caveat: You don't have to do *anything* in bed that makes you uncomfortable. You have a perfect right to tell him he can't lick your toes, tie you up, or put on your panties. If you feel uneasy about anything, just say "No!" It doesn't matter if the guy says you're a prude, or that if you really loved him, you'd make an exception. Dear Reader, always remember: if you don't like "it," whatever "it" is, that's the only reason you need.

The following is a roundup of partners we can all do without:

Eleven Terrible Turnoffs for Women

1. **Wham, Bam, Thank You, Ma'am**
   A few minutes of romance and off to sleep he goes. If this happens, especially on a regular basis, it's bound to make you feel empty, unsatisfied, and used. Why bother? You might as well have had a manicure instead.

2. **The Taker-Not-a-Giver Bedmate**
    We've all met him. He wants you to do something for him
    he would never dream of doing for you. A guy's habits
    in bed are usually the same when he's out and about. If
    he's selfish in the sack, chances are he'll be no different
    with his clothes on. Give him his walking papers, pronto!

3. **The Eager, but Artless, Gent**
    Yes, it's nice that he wants you, but his technique is so
    awkward you almost feel sorry for him. Beyond the basics,
    he doesn't have a clue as to how to go about pleasing a
    woman. The sex becomes so boring you start thinking
    about anything else—like the report that's due on your
    boss's desk the next morning.

    What to do about it? Give him a few hints. As we've
    said, sometimes mediocre bedmates can be taught to be
    better lovers. Especially if they're willing to learn. If this
    fails, it's your choice as to whether you want to remain
    in the relationship or not.

4. **The Me-Tarzan, You-Jane Bedfellow**
    Gentle he ain't, to put it mildly. He wants it, and he wants
    it now! He doesn't bother to ask, he demands. Even if
    you're fast asleep, he thinks nothing of shaking you awake
    to satisfy his needs. Send this savage swinging back to the
    jungle. He isn't your type or anyone else's. He's far too
    much in love with himself to acknowledge your desires in
    bed.

    Never forget, anything that depersonalizes you in bed
    (or anywhere else) is flat-out abuse! Psychological mis-
    treatment hurts just as much as physical cruelty. The
    bruises may not show, but they're just as real.

    Sex should never be forced on you, just as you should
    never attempt to bed an unwilling partner. You always
    have the right to say "no," and, of course, so does he.
    Anyone—male or female—should be able to change his
    or her mind when it comes to one's own body.

5. **The Wobbly Warrior**
    This kind of guy drinks himself into the Twilight Zone

because he thinks booze will get rid of his inhibitions. It probably will, but alcohol is also a depressant. So, if he's deep into the sauce, skip it. His performance will be lackluster (if he *can* perform), and worse yet, he'll barely remember it. You'd be better off reading a good book and improving your mind.

6. **Love-'em-and-Leave-'em Leo**
This guy sweet-talks you into bed, then says he'll call you—and you never hear from him again! You feel used and blame yourself for being taken advantage of. Learn from this. No matter how much he seems smitten with you on that first or second date, it's best to cool it. Wait until you've had a chance to sense where he's coming from, understand his values. The guy interested only in bedding you usually sends off signals. He's the type who talks about other girlfriends, delights in making you feel insecure, and almost always has a roving eye, even while he's with you. If you pick up those vibes—drop him fast, before you get hurt. Or, at least, stay out of the sack so you don't become just another notch on his belt.

7. **Paul Polluter**
When he's in residence, your apartment looks like a disaster area. He leaves his socks and underwear on the floor, his grungy shirt and pants draped over the chair, and your bathroom is a pigsty. You know the type—Mommy spent her life picking up after him, and he expects that special service to continue. So, you show him the hamper, drop hints about trying to keep the place clean. If that doesn't work, you have two choices: either put your foot down—hard—or be his live-in maid.

Careless hygiene habits can be even grosser. If he thinks a shower is strictly a party for a bride-to-be, obviously, he's not your ideal bedmate.

8. **Freddie Freud**
When you first meet him, you're intrigued. He doesn't smoke, drink, or eat red meat. He appears sensitive and caring and wants to save the world: the whales, the horny-

spotted owl, the rain forest, the ozone layer—you name it. Going out with him is interesting until you ask "How are you?"—and he wonders what you meant by that.

Freddie is a walking encyclopedia on psychology. He hesitates to make any decision without talking to his shrink first. He's big on group therapy, and you're often the topic of discussion. He asks the group to vote on whether you're suppressing his inner self and if he should keep on seeing you or not. He spouts psycho-babble to tell you he can't commit because of his fear of intimacy. You finally realize he's committed all right—to everything but you.

P.S.: Why is it always the guy who thinks he has the exclusive on "fear of commitment"? A woman has the same anxieties, but she's usually too busy calming *his* to acknowledge her own misgivings.

9. **The Squelcher**

This guy is into suppression of your very essence—all the things that make you uniquely you. He tells you not to laugh so loudly, to stop crying at a sad movie, and to calm down when something really gets to you. His favorite expression is: "What are you getting so excited about?" And this is the guy who yells so loudly while he's watching a football game on TV that the sofa shakes, the dishes rattle, and the dog cringes! You're too emotional, he's just enthusiastic! He not only rains on your parade, he tries to drown it. His twin tormentor is . . . read on!

10. **Judgmental Jeffrey**

He says your skirt's too short, your hips are too big, and you walk too slowly. He picks and picks and picks on everything about you—your friends, your politics, your career choice, the books you read. He's probably suffering from insecurity overload, but that doesn't help your sense of self. Odds are he won't change—so unless you're more than a little masochistic and can put up with his constant criticism, tell him to take his opinions somewhere else.

11. **The Abuser**

This is very dangerous territory. You're playing with fire if you give in to his demands for rough sex. When you balk, he tells you to lighten up. DON'T. Anything that hurts isn't fun. It's also off-limits. Abuse in bed invariably goes hand in hand with mistreatment out of the sack. You can hardly miss it. Give these cowboys a few feet, and they'll take a mile. This isn't just bad sex, this is a bad guy.

Safe Sex: A Matter of Life and Death

Whether the sex is good, bad, or indifferent, women have much more to fear than an unwanted pregnancy. With the onset of AIDS in the eighties, our world, sexually speaking, has taken a 180-degree turn. One-night stands have become an absolute no-no, unless every possible precaution is taken.

Safe sex is more than a preference, it's a definite *must*. Anyone who has ever visited an AIDS ward can tell you that this dreadful disease makes no distinctions. There are no stereotypes. Patients are not all gay, nor are they necessarily drug users. They are, in increasing and frightening numbers, heterosexual men and women who were victims of an unprotected sexual encounter.

Letitia Baldrige, the well-known chronicler of manners and mores, says it succinctly: "Always keep condoms on hand, in case he's unprepared. If he refuses, thank him for dinner, and say good night."

All it takes is a single sexual contact. Just one time, when the guy says he hates using condoms, and you're either too excited or too much in love to insist. Never think it can't happen to you. A sad case in point: Alison Gertz, the pretty, young heiress to a New York department store fortune, slept only one time with a friendly bartender she'd known for several months. A year later, she discovered she was HIV-positive. She spent her remaining time talking to groups of young people, warning them of the perils of unprotected sex. In five years, she was dead.

And we all remember Mary Fisher, who spoke so movingly at the 1992 Republican National Convention, and again in 1996. She became HIV-positive from sexual contact with her then-husband, whom she later divorced. She, too, devotes her time to speaking to countless groups, warning them about unprotected sex. No one knows how many lives Mary Fisher and Alison Gertz have saved through their openness and counseling. We pray this information will have a similar effect on you. Please read the following facts slowly and carefully.

AIDS is fast becoming the largest killer of women between the ages of twenty-five and forty-four. Most of them are partners of men who are bisexual and/or drug users. But a growing number of AIDS cases are reported among women whose mates are straight and do not do drugs.

Some basics. According to a hospital clinician, you can get AIDS through:

✔ infected blood or semen

✔ sharing needles

✔ unprotected sex

You *can't* get it through:

✔ toilet seats

✔ saliva

✔ casual contact with someone who is HIV-infected

The clinician also adds that ''the best protection is a latex condom with spermicide (nonoxonal-9). The least safe are spermicides alone (foams, jellies, etc.) because there's nothing to contain the sperm. (Condoms must be used *only* with water-soluble lubricants. You can harm the latex in the condom if you use petroleum jelly or other ointments.)''

According to this same expert, ''AIDS isn't the only sexually transmitted disease—there's also herpes simplex virus. This won't kill you, but it's lifelong, it can involve painful lesions, and it's extremely serious in pregnant women.''

Please, please, please protect yourself!

QUICK CAPSULE

Obviously, your love life is important, and there are endless things to be said on this subject. To help you remember what we think about the whys, whens and wherefores of sex, here's a short list:

1. Good sex and positive chemistry can bond you together.

2. A man's habits in bed are a clue to his character.

3. Don't jump into bed with a guy until you *know* him.

4. When it gives both of you pleasure, it's really good.

5. For a mutual turn-on, timing is all-important.

6. Don't be a traffic cop in bed.

7. Never feel guilty about saying no to something you don't like.

8. If you're not in the mood, just say so; you're not a machine.

9. Always keep condoms on hand.

10. Safe sex is a matter of life and death—Protect yourself.

thirteen

Thirteen Ways to Lose Your Man

Let's say you're in a fabulous relationship and you desperately want to keep it going. The last thing you want is for it to end. Nothing hurts more than losing your man, especially if you feel it was your fault.

The reason for a breakup could be as simple as a lack of communication. A man doesn't always think or react the way a woman feels he should. His communication style can be very different. What turns him off may be a real shocker to you because it seems so insignificant. Conversely, something that appears enormous to him could seem minor, or nonxistent, to you.

This being the case, here's Lesson 101, How to Lose Your Man. We hope you'll learn from it and move on to Lesson 102—Keeping Your Man Turned On Forever.

Believe it or not, almost all men have the same opinions about what turns them on—or off—where women are concerned. We sent out an anonymous survey to 100 men of all ages, from many different backgrounds and professions.

Some were hotshot executives, others moderately so, and some were just average Joes. But, regardless of their career accomplishments—or lack of same—they all had strong opinions.

So, listen up. This is the straight skinny, right from the horse's mouth.

Thirteen Terrible Turnoffs for Men

Fatal Attraction—The vote was unanimous. Every man we polled is not only turned off by the obsessive/possessive type of female, he avoids her like the plague. In her eyes, she owns him and watches him like a hawk. She makes him feel he has to account for every minute of his time away from her. He's even forbidden to talk to other women, including long-standing friends. We know one sweet-tempered guy who was dating this personality type. She went ballistic when she saw him talking to a female friend on the street. His first and final reaction was to get out of the relationship—forever!

Tip Time: No matter how much you care about him, always remember—he's not something you bought and paid for. Give him a long leash; if he really loves you, he'll shorten it himself.

Mimi Me-Me!—This gal tries to dominate every conversation with endless revelations about herself, her friends, her job, her shrink, her life, etc. She's totally focused on herself. Rarely, if ever, does she bother to ask him about his life, his family, his day, his preferences, etc. It's not a matter of merely catering to a man's ego. Any woman who constantly runs off at the mouth is a bloody bore. Men hate it when a woman gabs on and on about nothing or dumps her emotional baggage on him.

A good relationship is all about exchange, give and take. If this doesn't exist, it blocks the bond that might have been.

Dressed-to-Kill—Guys complained that women usually err on the side of overdressing for an occasion, rather than being too casual. Showing up for a weekend in the country wearing your black designer suit is obviously overdoing it. It's embarrassing for a man to escort a woman who doesn't know what to wear and when to wear it. Most men will never voluntarily tell you how to dress unless you ask. A sophisticated woman, who's sure of herself, never hesitates to find out what the dress code is.

The Makeup Maven—To her, more is better, especially when it comes to her face. She piles it on thick—heavy eye shadow, black eyeliner, blood-red lips and nails, and she reeks of perfume. Does it work? Absolutely not. Men think she's hiding something behind that mask and wonder what she looks like in the morning without it. Definitely not their idea of a permanent girlfriend.

Cosmetics work only when they add to a woman's natural beauty. And don't lose track of the fact that makeup is a day/night thing. Use less by day, naturally, but you can let a little loose at night. Natural is the key word here. Don't cringe because you think he'll mess up your flawlessly applied lip pencil. As for hair, go easy on the spray and slippery gels. Men like hair they can touch.

Helpless-to-a-Fault—Contrary to the old myth, a helpless woman is not appealing. No man wants a clinging vine. He expects her to handle life's ordinary chores, like balancing her checkbook, changing a lightbulb, or working her VCR. Most men prefer a woman who's able to solve everyday problems. Relying on a man to resolve routine tasks is eventually a turnoff.

The Bulldozer—Most men don't want to be steamrollered by women in dating situations. If a guy is taking you out, *he* wants to call the waiter over, give the order, and ask for the check. Ditto for hailing the taxi and giving the cabbie directions. Let him do it. Indulge his chivalrous instincts. You may be a steamroller in the office, but when a guy asks you out, particularly for the first time, drop the busy-executive routine.

Up until the sixties, a woman was not considered a ''lady'' if she spoke directly to the waiter. That's passé now; times have definitely changed. A tinge of that attitude, however, still lingers on. Most men will think you're too bossy if you try to call the shots in every social situation.

Tip Time: Learn to compartmentalize your life the way men do.

They can be all business in the office and very different at home or when they're with friends. And, they don't feel they're being phony when they do it. Men know there's a time and place for everything. It should be the same for women.

Telephonitis—One guy told us he gets really bummed out when a woman chatters endlessly on the phone while he's sitting there. A lot of men agree. It's a major irritation, a real guy thing.

Men and women view the telephone very differently. Most men see it as a quick way to communicate a message. On the other hand, women often feel the phone is an opportunity to socialize—using it as a substitute for a long, leisurely lunch. It's called, euphemistically, a "phone visit."

The woman who ignores her man to blab on the phone forever makes him feel he doesn't matter much. Even the married men we surveyed complained about their wives' telephone habits. So, we suggest monopolizing the phone when he's not around. If friends call you while he's there, make the conversation brief. On occasion, just let the answering machine pick up; that sends a real message that you care. It takes willpower to ignore that insistent ringing, but it'll also save you from cutting the caller off abruptly.

Out-of-It Olga—Intelligent men want to be able to converse with a woman. They find it a strain to be with someone who's so out-to-lunch that she doesn't read a newspaper, never watches the news, and is unaware of what's going on in the world. It's b-o-r-i-n-g, men tell us, and creates long, awkward silences.

Rambling Rose, her sister-under-the-skin, isn't much better. Her idea of a good conversation is a series of endless anecdotes that never make a point. She insists on telling long drawn-out stories about people he's never met, or wants to. Anyone who can't talk about anything outside of her own narrow world is the dullest companion there is.

The Tease—She gives such a come-on, he's already mentally in bed, having the best sex of his life, and he's barely said "hello"!

The looks, the innuendoes, the occasional touches to his face, his knee. He's ready, but she's not. In fact, she has no intention of following through. Most guys say they don't expect sex after one or two dates, and they resent a woman who's a tease. So, if you fall into this unfortunate category, forget the femme fatale bit. Also, don't discuss sex in-depth, unless you're a therapist or you really want some action.

Obviously, there's a big difference between flirting and hardcore teasing. Flirting is a subtle way to show you're interested. It never goes out of style.

The Tough Talker—She thinks it's clever to swear like a truck driver. Every other word has four letters in it, and some of her expressions would make a rapper blush. Guys refer to it as F-speak and it embarrasses them in public situations. Your language is saying you have no class. They may think twice about taking you any place that's important, where you might run into business associates. And forget about taking you home to meet Mother!

The Empty Refrigerator—The woman who has nothing in her fridge except a lone bottle of wine and a Diet Coke turns a man off—especially if it's over a weekend. As one male respondent explained, "Going out for breakfast after breakfast is the pits." Whether you're dieting, a vegetarian, or whatever, stock up on the bagels, bacon and eggs. A leisurely breakfast in bed, *à deux*, is not only fun, it makes the morning-after linger on.

Tip Time: A barren fridge gives him the impression you're not interested in the care and feeding of the object of your affections. Be prepared—men like to be offered food and drink, whether they want it or not. It makes them feel cared for.

The Bathroom Barbarian—Although it wasn't first on the list of no-nos, many men we polled complained about women whose bathrooms were more cluttered than the makeup counter at Bloomingdale's. It makes them nervous to have to move a dozen jars so they can shave. Ditto for wading through a jungle of dripping bras and panty hose to take a shower. On the other hand, a sexy nightgown—obviously on display—is a turn-on to a guy. The moral of the story is: Put away your everyday underwear and beauty bottles, and make some space for him.

Beth the Boozer—This is the woman who can't hold a man because she can't hold her liquor. In her attempt to get into the spirit of things, she gets too much spirits into her. She's never figured out her limits and just doesn't know when to stop.

Every man we talked to, without exception, said it's not only a turnoff, it's good-bye forever when a woman drinks too much. A man doesn't know what to do when a woman is totally wasted and out of control. He feels helpless and embarrassed. A guy usually can handle a drunken male buddy, but he's repelled by a woman who's trashed.

Tip Time:—If this problem applies to you, then you know it in your heart of hearts, although you may deny it, even to yourself. There's only one way out: get help. For millions of people, Alcoholics Anonymous has the answer. It works and it's free.

fourteen

Ten Terrific Turn-Ons

What Men Really Want from Women

Now that you've completed Lesson 101 and know what turns a man *off*, take heart! The same guys we polled shared with us the things women do that turn them *on*: Lesson 102!!

They're simple, uncomplicated, and within any woman's grasp. You may have heard some of this advice before, and even used it. But this time make a real effort, follow our suggestions, and you'll see instant results.

1. **Faithfulness**

   If you've embarked on a serious relationship and want to hold on to your man, your commitment had better include exclusivity on all fronts. The men we polled said faithfulness is one of the main qualities they look for in a long-term matchup. It goes without saying, if you've decided you love him, you wouldn't dream of sharing your heart—or your bed—with others.

   Tip Time: A man wants to feel that his woman is 100 percent true-blue, no matter what. So—think before you stray! It's better to openly opt out of a faltering relationship than to be caught in a clandestine clinch with an INsignificant Other. If you're feeling the urge to stray, it's better to reassess the whole thing.

2. **Hard Body**

It's no secret that men are attracted to women who keep in shape. But our polls show that men don't like the rail-thin waif look, either. Their preference is a woman with a grownup body, someone who's curvy and caressable. Most men we spoke to told us that an angular frame is a turnoff, not very feminine—no matter what the fashion magazines are showing.

Tip Time: Get in shape, fast! Join a health club, rent a fitness tape, or take up jogging. The key is consistency. We know several women who stay fit and still eat what they like by exercising regularly. Revving up the metabolism is the secret. Keeping fit is something you should do for yourself, whether or not there's a man in your life.

3. **Smiley Face**

Most of the men we surveyed ranked a woman's warmth and the smile that goes with it as one of the top three things that initially turns them on. Don't underestimate smile power; it goes a long way—if it's genuine.

Tip Time: If the reason you don't smile is because your teeth aren't great, get them fixed. For yellow teeth, try a toothpaste with brighteners in it. If that doesn't help, look into bleaching, a common dental procedure these days. If your teeth are buck, or crooked, don't fail to do something about them. Your best bet is a professional who specializes in cosmetic dentistry. Yes, it can be costly but it's well worth it. Don't think all this emphasis on teeth is petty. Your smile is as important as your face or figure.

4. **Har-Dee-Har-Har**

Men are attracted to women who not only have a sense of humor but also use it. It's not just a matter of laughing at his jokes. It's also being able to see the lighter side of life.

Sharing a good laugh with your lover creates instant intimacy. Many a couple has literally laughed their way into bed. Conversely, lots of men said they rejected a woman, not because of her face or figure, but because she was always so uptight.

Tip Time: Humor is sexy, doom-and-gloom is not. Humor is an ''upper'' that men find hard to resist.

5. Flexibility

A woman appears even more irresistible to a man when she's flexible, not set in her ways. Keep your mind open to new people, places, and things. Don't pout if plans suddenly change. Over and over again, our polls have shown us that men are attracted to women who are spontaneous and go with the flow.

Tip Time: If he's important, don't demand predictability 100 percent of the time. It makes him feel fenced in. So what if he changes your weekend plans at the last minute? If he's got a good reason, compromise. Ask yourself, Does it really make any difference? Usually it doesn't. If it happens all the time, that's another story.

6. The Sound of You

Do you screech when you talk, cackle when you laugh? The men surveyed in our poll told us that some of their top turnoffs are ''shrillness,'' ''a nasal twang,'' and ''an annoying laugh.'' Guys go for a low, well-modulated voice that projects warmth and friendliness.

Tip Time: If you suspect your voice is selling you short, tape a phone conversation with a friend and play it back. There are a number of things you can do to correct and enhance your voice. It's worth it—after all, eighty percent of your communication is verbal. Some strategies:

- Check out Speech Improvement in the Yellow Pages or join an organization like Toastmasters, which teaches people how to give a speech. It's national and it's very inexpensive.
- For one day, put a mirror on your desk and smile into it before you pick up the phone. You'll actually sound better—your smile comes right across the wires!
- If you get a lot of flak about your laugh, don't be discouraged. Maybe you can't control your chortle, but you can adjust the volume. Keep it on low.

– Wake up your voice! No one enjoys speaking to someone who sounds half dead. Put a little energy and enthusiasm into your talk. When your voice is alive and kicking, you'll be amazed at how positively people will respond to you.

7. **The Straight Shooter**

Guys say they feel most comfortable with someone who is not phony, not pretentious—what you see is what you get. The last thing men want is a woman who puts on airs (name-dropping, fake accent, etc.) or someone who doesn't play it straight. Men like to know where they stand with a woman. The straight shooter is real and honest in her dealings, not only with her man but everyone else as well. When she's with a date, she doesn't spend half the evening flirting with every man in the vicinity, and she always leaves with the guy she came with.

Tip Time: You've heard this a zillion times—but it's worth repeating: *Just be yourself.* Affectations of any kind are a turnoff. Why pretend to be something you're not? Men see through phonies. The most appealing guys we know are the ones who are the most turned off by pretentious women.

8. **The Scent of a Woman**

Did you know that every woman has a natural aroma that's distinctly her own? Men know this. One guy told us he was attracted to his future bride because he liked the way her skin smelled, pre-perfume: "A woman's very own scent always mattered to me. If I liked that, then whatever perfume she wore was a plus. When I first met my wife-to-be, her skin smelled like fresh lemons to me. That was a big part of the attraction."

Your nose knows. When you dislike a person, believe it or not, he or she can actually begin to smell bad to you. If you and your partner don't pass each other's sniff test, just keep searching until you find your smell mate.

Obviously, if you have the hygiene habits of a hobo,

you'll aggravate the situation. You know, like wearing the same dirty clothes over and over, declaring a ban on bathing, dispensing with deodorants, dental aids, etc. If this describes you, clean up your act. When Mother told you always to wear clean underwear, she really knew best.

Tip Time: When you use perfume, don't be heavy-handed. Just dab it on. You don't want to announce your arrival before you get there. And remember, perfume—like good wine—needs time to breathe. Put it on a few minutes before you head out the door and let it air. Choose your perfume carefully, though. Despite what some fragrance manufacturers would have you believe, an overpowering scent is a distinct turnoff. Those classic perfumes like Chanel No. 5 and Diorissimo are still selling because they're light! And the last thing you should ever do is to spray on fragrance in an enclosed space—-like an airplane or car. It's asphyxiating.

9. Money Manners

While almost all the men we surveyed said they expect to pick up the check on a date, no guy likes a gold digger. She makes him feel used. A man wants a woman who's considerate of his wallet. Take Cathy and Warren. When they started dating, he noticed immediately that she wasn't out to take him. She didn't insist on fancy restaurants or the most expensive bottle of wine. She always made him feel that she was happy to share his company no matter what they did.

Warren is a young lawyer who hasn't gotten to the big bucks yet. He's not cheap, just prudent at this stage in his career. Cathy understood this intuitively, even though they never discussed it.

Tip Time: He may be on the way up—he may even be there—but don't take him to the cleaners just because you feel you've got it coming. Okay—so maybe some of the best things in life aren't free, but you don't have to spend buckets of bucks every time you go out.

10. **Givers, Not Takers**

    In our poll, men listed consideration and kindness among the top three things they look for in a woman. Consideration goes far beyond money matters. It applies to every aspect of a relationship, from the way you treat his friends and family, to how you react to the world at large. A woman who's nasty to a cabdriver or a waiter sends a signal to a guy that one day she may turn on him, too. Act like Nurse Nightingale when he's sick. Bring him chicken soup. So, when he's had a lousy day, give him a break—don't insist on going out. Whenever you're with his family, go out of your way to be adorable. It's insulting to anyone—male or female—for a partner to put down the other's family and friends.

    There are two kinds of people in this world—Givers and Takers. Givers end up "getting" in the long run. Takers wind up alone. Just remember: Time wounds all heels!

If eight or more of the Top Ten Turn-ons sound like you— you're the kind of woman who holds on to her man. Remember— some of these qualities (scent, hard body, smile) are what attracted him to you initially. The ones that keep him happily glued to your side are basic character traits like honesty, faithfulness, flexibility, and humor. And these are the very qualities that will serve you best in all your relationships—personal and business.

fifteen

How to Keep Your Man Forever

What the Guys Told Us

Now that you know what turns him off and on, let's get to the next step—how to keep him forever.

The guys we polled in our anonymous survey in chapter 13 told us specifically what makes their little hearts beat faster, and what makes them run for the hills. Some of their answers are documented in previous chapters, but there are so many more goodies, we couldn't resist sharing them with you.

We asked these men to answer twenty questions about virtually every element of male/female relationships. They were requested to rate their answers on a scale of 1 to 10, with 10 being the most important. Read this section carefully. It's always interesting to know what the little darlings think about us, even if we don't buy into all of it. There are a few surprises, along with the predictable stuff. For better or for worse, here's what men told us really matters to them:

1) *When first meeting a woman, what attracts you?*

Matters Most	*Matters Least*
Face/figure/smile	Age
Warm personality	Ambition
Intelligence	Background/social status
Sense of humor	
Grooming	

Commentary: No surprises here except that we always think of men as being obsessed with big boobs. Not even one of our surveyees mentioned them. The only requirement noted for a great figure was a "trim butt."

2) *What's most important to you in a serious relationship?*

Matters Most	*Matters Least*
Faithfulness	Mutual interests
Flexibility	Spending habits
Consideration	Domestic skills
Sexual drive	
Desire to have children	

Commentary: Although these guys listed domestic skills last, we'd bet you dollars-to-donuts that once they're living with a woman, this kind of know-how suddenly assumes serious importance. There's hardly a man around—even in this so-called age of enlightenment—who thinks cooking and cleaning are just as much his job as yours. If you've found one, bronze him and put him on the mantel.

3) *A man's version of a "Blind Date from Hell":*

- "A woman with no personality, bad skin, and who's a chain-smoker."

- "Talks too much . . . can't dance . . . generally annoying."

- "A Mother Teresa type without the heart."

- "A no-personality, nontalking dinner date."

- "Talks a mile a minute about herself and things in her life that I'm not ready to become interested in."

- "She's possessive, she's overdressed, she wears

too much makeup, talks too much, and she cackles when she laughs.''

- ''Me, me, me, me, me . . . Well, enough about me. So what do you think about me?''

- ''Pick her up at her messy apartment, find out she doesn't know how to dress, and then she talks about herself all night.''

- ''Not having anything to say to each other—at all!''

- ''I spend a lot of money on her; she sits and talks about other guys.''

- ''Took her to a restaurant and, after several glasses of wine, asked her what she wanted for dinner. She was quite put off because she thought we had already eaten!''

4) *Why did you end your last relationship?*

- ''She lied *all* the time.''

- ''She kept telling me about other guys.''

- ''Her main focus was on having children.''

- ''She refused to accept me as I am.''

- ''She was too obsessive about her career.''

- ''She was too conservative—in all areas.''

- ''Just plain sexual incompatibility.''

5) *Do you expect to have sex on the first date?*

Answers range from little expectation to none. (''Unless she insists!'')

6) *When she brings up marriage:*

Men really don't like it, particularly in the early stages, with reactions from ''surprised'' to ''horrified'' to ''I may not return from the men's room!''

7) *Does it bother you when a woman uses four-letter words?*

Guys said it's a turnoff in public. Most felt it depended on the situation:

- "Once in a while, no big deal, but not around my mom!"

- "Makes me think she's a kid who's trying to act grown-up."

- "During sex it's great!"

- "It embarrasses me when we're with other people"

8) *How important is it to you that a woman "act like a lady" in public?*

Every guy felt it mattered to some degree, ranging from "very important" to "so-so."

- "She can act how she pleases, but just not like a tramp."

- "As long as she isn't smoking a cigar, I'll be okay."

9) *How important is it to you that a woman be aware of what's going on in the world?*

Overwhelmingly, guys voiced approval of a woman who's "with it." Comments ranged from: "It sure helps when you're having a conversation," to "I can't hack anyone—male or female—who's out of it," to "She looks stupid if she isn't able to talk a little bit about world affairs." Obviously, this is a two-way street. Any man or woman who isn't up on world events is just plain boring.

10) *The first time you go to a woman's home, what do you notice?*

This brought a mixed bag of answers:

- Colors and choice of art

- Warmth

- Femininity

- Her sense of organization and style

- Her bathroom—clean or messy

- "I look for someone who has a few funky items and is a bit carefree, yet not living in chaos."

Commentary: Now you'll believe us! Men notice these things. (See "The Female Lair" chapter.)

11) *At what stage of your relationship would you introduce a woman to your family?*

This can be a big clue to how he feels about you. A few guys knew exactly when they would bring you home to Mother—anywhere from two months to six months. Most said they had no time limit. Instead, it depended on whether or not he felt that you and he had long-term potential:

- "When I dig her enough to travel with her."

- "Far down the road—I've made that mistake before."

- "When I believe the relationship is getting serious and may have long-term implications."

And if he doesn't bring you home, take heart—it may have nothing to do with you:

- "Not for a long time—I don't want to scare her off."

- "Hopefully never. Trouble at home—enough said?"

12) *Would you date a woman you met at work?*

Most men said yes, they would date a colleague from work—and have done so. One man even confessed he had dated eight women at work, and all at the same time!

13) *Are you intimidated by a woman who has a bigger job/ income than you?*

If you're thinking of a fling, or even more, with a guy who's on a lower job level than yours—they don't care, if you don't. With rare exceptions, our poll revealed that men not only aren't intimidated by a woman who makes more money or has more power—they like it. One said he was "awed." Another admitted he didn't mind as long as she was generous! And another probably put it best: "Doesn't bother me as long as she doesn't push it in my face."

14) *Do you prefer to date women who have the same religious or ethnic background as you?*

Only a few of the guys said "yes" to this. All the others felt it didn't matter, but a few agreed that it's "easier" or "wiser" to be involved with women who have the same backgrounds as they do.

15) *Most irritating female habits:*

> *The All-Time Losers*
> Nagging
> Complaining
> Talks too much
> Too sensitive
> Takes forever to get dressed
> Messiness

16) *Picking up the check:*

No contest. He expects to. "Any true gentleman will always pick up the check. I consider myself a true gentleman."

17)   *Importance of how a woman dresses:*

Preferences	*Dislikes*
Sexy, but not cheap	Overdressing
Appropriate for the occasion	Heavy makeup
Natural, relaxed look	Too much perfume

18)   *Do you like women calling you to ask you out?*

No contest here—they love it!

Finale

So, what did our guy poll tell you that you didn't already know? Considering that this survey was totally anonymous, it makes the answers all the more interesting. These men weren't trying to impress anybody; this is how they really feel about women.

If one or more of your relationships has crashed and you don't know why, maybe this chapter gave you some answers. Use it as a guide to avoid future collisions.

sixteen

Breaking Up

As the song says, "Breaking Up Is Hard to Do." Hard? It's excruciating, especially if you're the "dumpee," the unfortunate one getting the heave-ho. Most of us would rather have a tooth pulled than go through an unwanted breakup, particularly if it was a deep-rooted love affair that's fallen apart. When this happens, your heart and head not only ache, but your self-esteem is pummeled to pieces.

Of course, sometimes you're the "dumper," the one who wants to sever the ties that bind. If you're stuck in a situation that's going nowhere because you don't want it to, putting off the breakup only prolongs the misery. And it can be just as painful to be the one who, for whatever reason, wants out. But if it's over, tell him—sooner rather than later.

Calling It Quits

How you say good-bye is all-important. It's never easy to deliver negative news, especially when you know it's going to hurt. Never do it in a cold, cruel manner. You don't want to burn bridges or make enemies. Find a way to extricate yourself that causes the minimum amount of pain for either one of you.

If it's a fairly casual relationship that you have to terminate, you have our permission to use this age-old solution: don't return his phone calls. If he gets you on the phone, don't be available to go out. Maybe he'll take the hint. Failing that, you have no other choice but to face the music and tell him gently that it's over.

There are some circumstances that—while obviously painful—almost help you to end it. These include a mate who habitually cheats on you and isn't about to change his wandering ways, or a man who abuses you—physically or emotionally. These kinds of men can slowly destroy your very essence if you keep hanging on in hopes that they'll change. Abusive men have the ability to convince a woman that she's worthless. She begins to feel that she's totally at fault and that she's the reason for the abuse. The signals to get out of these relationships should be blasting through loud and clear. There are women, however, who will endure this mental battering, thinking it will stop if they could only learn to please their tormentor. Therapists label this kind of behavior masochistic and advise intensive counseling.

We hope your situation isn't this bad. Let's assume, however, you've had it up to here and want to get out as soon as possible. The next question is: Where, When, and How to say "Good-bye."

Where, When, and How?

Even if he's done you wrong, the decent thing to do is to say farewell in private and in person—not over the phone, by mail, FedEx, or fax! (Yes—there are some people who've been ditched electronically, and many others who've been kissed off by mail.)

The obvious exception to a face-to-face sit-down is if you fear he could become violent or threatening. In that case, you may have to meet at a public place with a friend standing by in case of trouble.

Assuming that's not the issue, you should pick a private setting where you can calmly say your piece, listen to his response, and exit shortly thereafter. Once you've decided that breaking up is the only option, stormy recriminations and long-drawn-out scenes are definitely counterproductive.

When Love Fizzles Out

Okay, suppose that the guy in question was not a philandering rat or a sadistic manipulator. Maybe you had a mutually satisfying thing going for a while, but somewhere along the way you both started moving in different directions. Your needs and ambitions diverged and what once seemed vital and stimulating has become . . . boring. Or, maybe you've met a terrific man at work, and your lengthy business meetings have blossomed into romance. Whatever your reason for dissolving your relationship, whether it was rosy or raunchy, you have to make the break as cleanly and considerately as possible. Keep in mind that this is someone you once loved, and probably still like. You don't want to hurt him any more than you have to. Think of how you'd want to be treated if the circumstances were reversed. Obviously, you'd prefer to be told in private with a sense of compassion—and with some emphasis on the good times you shared, not just what went wrong. It's always painful to say good-bye to someone you've cared about, so do it with thoughtfulness and sensitivity.

Here's a possible example of a farewell that we hope won't leave too bad a taste in his mouth.

"I'm really sorry to say this, Joel, but I think we'd better call it quits. It was wonderful being with you, but I've met someone else

I really care about.'' This may or may not be true. If it isn't, some-times a little white lie can be the gentlest and easiest way to extricate yourself.

Live-In Disentanglement

Breaking up can be even harder to do if the two of you have been living together. Deciding who gets what—from the furnishings to the CD player, even the dog!—can be fraught with emotion. If you're not careful, this kind of tug-of-war can turn into a full-fledged battle that resembles a really nasty divorce.

There are a number of elements to consider carefully, along with the fragmented feelings of two "once-were" lovers. For example, does your breakup involve joint property? Also, is the apartment in your name or his? If it's your apartment, be gracious and give him a reasonable amount of time to move out (a few days to a week), and then see that he does just that. A guy with any pride will get out pronto. If it's his place that you've been sharing, you should do the same—ASAP. Even if you have to move in temporarily with family or friends, it's better than staying in your former love-nest with all its bad vibes.

The third possibility is that you have a joint lease or even pur-chased a condo or house together. This is where things can get really sticky. You may need legal advice as to who can or should buy the other out, or if putting the place up for sale is the only viable option. The same applies to jointly purchased possessions. First, try ami-cably dividing the property you've accumulated together. Failing that, a lawyer may be the last (and very expensive) resort.

Keep this in mind, though: If you're the one who wants out, be prepared to do a bit more compromising when it comes to the di-vision of property. Freedom from a dead-end relationship has a value that can't be measured in mere money.

Grieving Time

No matter what the circumstances, breaking off a serious relationship is a painful process that calls for recovery time. If and when it happens, you need first aid fast. Here's our prescription for healing:

First and foremost, feel free to cry your eyes out. Call close friends, your sister, your cousin—anyone you can trust, and tell them you feel really, really rotten and need a shoulder to cry on. Acknowledging your pain is part of the healing process. Suppressing grief only bottles up a lot of sadness that has to come out sooner or later. Just airing it helps you come to terms with what has happened and speeds you on the road to recovery. Besides, friends often have good advice; they've probably gone through it themselves. Having a sympathetic ear to listen to you soothes your soul. Most people need some time to mull, mourn, decompress, and hibernate before dating again.

Here's an exercise that might help. Take out a yellow pad and make a plus-and-minus list assessing the relationship. We helped our friend Donna do this when she was going through a breakup. We suggested that she write down her gains and losses—what the relationship with Richard did and didn't give her. When it came to her "gains," the first three things she wrote down were two great dogs and a nice apartment. She listed Richard as number four! Under losses, she wrote things like "He's moody," "Won't talk things over with me," and "We never go out." Actually, she started laughing when she looked at her list and realized that Richard, the supposed man of her dreams, came in last, after her adorable dogs and new apartment. This exercise put it all in the proper perspective for Donna, helping her to get on with her life.

Getting Back in Motion

And, speaking of moving on, after you've worked through the grieving process, the next step is to tell the world that you're available. No need to go into the nitty-gritty of the breakup, just mention that you're no longer going out with the guy. Say something like "I'm not seeing Milton anymore. If you know anyone interesting and think we'd hit it off, I'd love to meet him." Rehearse these words as many times as necessary so that you can get them out in one breath without breaking into tears.

As we've said, it's healthy to spill your guts to your closest friends, but you don't owe any explanations to the gossip-hungry, outside world. Besides, nothing's worse than a man or woman who talks incessantly about their ex. It's a sure sign they haven't recovered from their last relationship and really aren't ready to reenter the dating arena. "Never complain, never explain" should be your motto. Bite your lip and just say, "Yes, Milton's a great person, but it was time for us both to get on with our lives." Nothing more is necessary. Take the high road. Don't knock the guy, even if he's a jerk who did you wrong.

And try not to give the breakup too much drama. If you do, your friends just might ask your ex for *his* version. If it's critical of you, who needs that?

When you've just undergone a breakup, try to do lots of positive things for yourself, whether it's getting a flattering new haircut, losing five pounds, taking up yoga, meditation, prayer, or even spending some couch time with a shrink. And, it's especially critical that you have plans for the first weekend after you've broken up. Never, but never, spend it alone. Go out with your best friend, visit your family—do anything but sit home and suffer by your lonesome.

Once you start dating again, don't even think of telling your new male friends about the guy you just broke up with. If his name comes up, just say, "Yes, Kevin and I used to be together, but we're no longer seeing each other." Make it clear that Kevin is Pasadena, El Paso, over and out of your life!

Whatever you do, don't take the breakup out on yourself. He may have treated you badly, but that doesn't mean there's anything wrong with you—he just got away with it. And don't give him the satisfaction of turning to food or drink as substitutes for your lost love. Remember, the only affection they'll give you is a few unwanted inches on your hips.

It may help you to know that a decent guy suffers, too, when he breaks up with a woman, even if it was at his instigation. And, if he has real substance, he won't jump into the arms of some hot new babe just because he's lonely and she's available. He needs healing time, too.

The bottom line, though, is that breakups are usually dreadful, gut-wrenching affairs and something we wish we never had to go through. At this point in your life, you need a sophisticated pain-management program. Here's how two of our friends handled their healing.

Change of Scenery

If you can swing it, this is the perfect time for a change of scenery. A Club Med–type of experience, where you're thrown in with all sorts of new people who don't know anything about you and your problems, could be just what the doctor ordered. Our friend Tracey took off on a Club Med vacation to Morocco right after busting up with the guy she thought was the love of her life. Suddenly she was in an exotic locale where she didn't understand the language, the culture, or even the money.

Tracey was so busy trying to figure out how many dirhams there were in a dollar, she didn't have a minute to moan. Before she knew it, she'd snapped out of her funk and was having the time of her life. The fact that she met David, a darling lawyer from California— who went with her on multiple trips to the Souk (the exotic, local marketplace), and a camel ride, to boot—made it all the better.

New scenery was the best medication for Kimberly, a sports marketing executive, who was going through a particularly nasty breakup. In the midst of it, her company assigned her to cover a huge sports exhibition in Florida, where well-known male and female professional athletes were competing. Unlike most of the other deadly-serious marketing professionals covering the event, Kim was open, outgoing and had a sense of humor about her work. She suddenly became the most popular kid on the block. She had plans for everything—breakfast, lunch, drinks, dinner, and even moonlight swims.

In a couple of days, her mood went from bleak to blissful. She came away with renewed self-esteem, and the realization that she was well rid of her former fiancé. It was a revelation that would have taken her many months to achieve if she'd stayed at home with nothing but sad memories to haunt her days and nights. Instead, she rediscovered her old self and realized that she was attractive, desirable, and not the worthless person her ex had tried to make her believe she was.

Wrap-Up

Here's a list of Dos and Don'ts to help you pull yourself together after a relationship has ended:

Do

- Expect a breakup to hurt, whether you're the dumper or the dumpee.

- Realize that it happens to everyone at some time.

- Take time to grieve.

- Talk it out with a couple of close girlfriends or relatives.

- Get back in circulation as soon as you can.

- List your gains and losses on paper—you might be surprised by the results.

- If you can afford it, get away for a week or weekend—a change of scenery can help you put everything into perspective.

- Take advantage of any business situations that throw you in with new people.

Don't

- Discuss the breakup with everyone you meet.

- Spend the first post-breakup weekend alone.

- Waste time blaming yourself; love is a two-way street.

- Turn to excessive food or drink; it's a self-destructive and fattening way to get over the pain.

Part Three

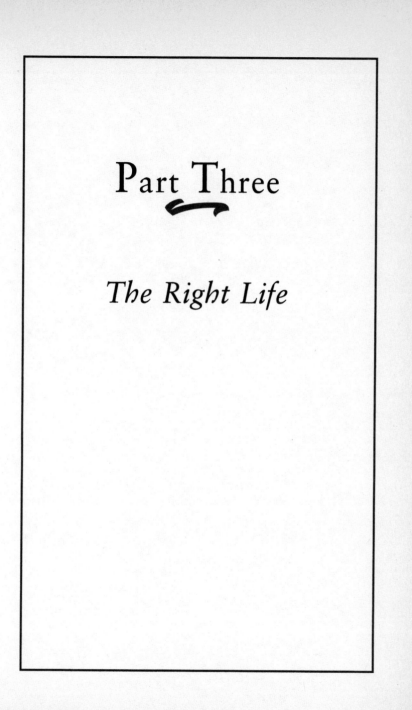

The Right Life

seventeen

Creating Your Style

The Bridge to the Right Life

How you look, dress and live are like pieces of a puzzle that fit together to create a style that's uniquely yours. Trust us when we say that style is much more than a five-letter word. It's a direct bridge to the Right Life, a better life. You may not have thought of it that way, but your sense of style is as much tied into your sense of self as your career and love life.

When you know you've done your best to look good, you have the added ammunition to help you handle whatever glitches life may bring. This sense of self should also extend to where and how you live. It's equally important to make your home so appealing that you're happy just to be there. When you feel positive about all aspects of your life, there is a spillover effect that directly reinforces your self-esteem and performance.

The Duchess of Windsor once said that "a woman can never be too rich or too thin." Well, we insist you can never be too young or too broke to develop a personal lifestyle that makes you feel good about yourself. Everyone feels financially pinched at times, but you can't let that become an excuse for living like a beach bum. There's no time like the present to develop a lifestyle that enhances your self-image. You've got to make it your business *now* to look and live well—otherwise you're missing out on some of the best parts of life.

Style? What Is It?

How do you define style, and, more importantly, how do you get it? Let's start with what it isn't. Style is *not* about beauty, wealth, or even fashion. Beautiful women come and go, but the stylish ones hang in there forever. Plus, lots of wealthy people don't have a clue as to what style is all about. Fashion victims are a dime a dozen. Women with style have their own special identity that projects authority and confidence. They have that magical thing called "presence," plus the staying power that gives them an added edge in life. Elsa Klensch, the noted TV fashion commentator, says in her book *Style*: "Stylish women can go anywhere and achieve anything. A stylish woman gets the best table in a restaurant, has the empty cab stop for her on a rainy day, and receives better service in department stores, as well as from her hairdresser."

Believe that? We do, because we've seen it in action. At twenty-two, Marianne noticed that salesclerks ignored her while they would fall all over themselves to wait on a well-dressed, stylish woman. It wasn't until she'd developed her own image that it began to happen for her, too. Let's briefly trace how Marianne reversed herself from "chunky and frumpy" to streamlined, stylish, and successful. Slightly overweight, Marianne was still wearing the oversized sweaters and faded peasant skirts she bought in her sophomore year in college. Needless to say, these clothes did nothing to flatter her figure. Her hair, which should have been one of her best features, was overpermed and had no particular shape.

However, she was smart and driven, and easily landed an entry-level job at a radio ad sales firm. After a few months, Marianne became bored by the daily routine and lack of challenge. She wanted to move up but didn't know how to go about it. One day, she took a good look around and saw for herself that the most successful businesswomen had a particular flair in the way they dressed, handled themselves, and lived. Most importantly, they had the Right Attitude.

A word on Attitude: how you feel about life shows on your face. Your facial expressions can detract from, or enhance the way you look. We know a very pretty young woman whose darting eyes and nervous grimaces actually diminish her good looks. Another acquaintance of ours, while not a great beauty, is perceived as being prettier than she is because her overall body language—her eyes, her smile, and the way she carries herself—radiates warmth and inner confidence. All of us shy away from people who give off negative vibes. We're much more attracted to a positive personality. This is all part of presence—a key component of style.

Women with a positive presence have that certain something called *Style Power*. Not all of them were born with it, but they were willing to spend the necessary time and energy to acquire it. Many young women are not—they simply don't focus on how to dress or live. Instead of developing the kind of personal style that sets them apart from the crowd, they choose to mark time until they have more money, a better job—the excuses are endless. Unaware that it takes time and effort, not merely money, they don't do anything to improve their overall lifestyle, making themselves the losers in the process.

Back to Marianne. She decided one way she could move up the corporate ladder was to take a clue from the successful women she admired. She went on a diet, got into a fitness regime, and began dressing up. She tossed out her collegiate wardrobe and invested in a few good basics—a couple of well-cut suits, a blazer, and classic pumps and handbags. Finally, she decided it was worth it to have her hair cut and styled by a top hairdresser. It all paid off. Her business associates began to take note of her new professional-looking persona, and soon Marianne was promoted to a better job. It wasn't just her clothes and haircut, of course. She had a lot of good things going for her—including smarts, skills, and ambition. However, her total exterior makeover gave her something she hadn't had before: presence.

Dear Reader, we know you don't want to let the Right Life slip through your fingers, as Marianne almost did. How you set up your life at this very moment has significant implications for the future. The way you dress, live, and handle yourself today can affect your future. Now is the time to begin to live well. Explore your personal style so that your life can evolve into what you really want—The Right Life for you!

eighteen

Looking Good: Dressing for the Office

In life, appearance counts more than we might like. In business, it's critical! That's why people invariably make such a big deal out of the way you dress. Although clothes are superficial, they matter a lot. Rightfully or not, in business you're judged as a total package. Of course, the way you're perceived begins with your ability to do your job, but it also includes the way you speak, dress, and act.

People make decisions about your professionalism based on how you look. During times of reorganization, downsizing, or change, your overall image can be the deciding factor in whether or not you keep your job. If there's a choice between two equally capable people—and one looks the part and the other doesn't—the former wins hands down.

Your clothes either reinforce the impression you hope to make as a capable professional or detract from it. In business, a book is judged by its cover—and so are you.

The Company Look

Remember: every company has its own dress code. The first rule is to realize it exists, and then observe how others are interpreting it. Notice what your co-workers are wearing. Your way of dressing must be in sync with the company's way if you expect to succeed. You may think that other executives look dowdy—no style, no flair. Quite honestly, your thoughts don't count as much as what the company thinks is appropriate.

Your second rule is to dress conservatively whenever you're in doubt about what to wear. This is especially important when you start a new job. The last thing you want is for your boss to be critical of your clothes.

Dress As If . . .

A good rule of thumb is to dress as if you were the boss. Notice what she's wearing. People will react to you differently; they'll take you more seriously. In other words, dress up to the job you aspire to, not like the junior staffers. If they wear pants or jeans, you don't. Instead, you dress like the highest-level, most successful female executive around.

Suit Yourself

There's nothing like a suit to create a businesslike impression. It's the best investment you can make. Suits range from spartan man-tailored classics to feminine and subtly sexy. Always wear a suit when you want to look your best and most in-charge self. Basic solids—white, beige, black, navy, or gray—are always practical.

To add color, accessorize with a scarf, or button up a bright-colored blouse in a soft fabric. There's nothing like the effect a woman creates when she removes her jacket to display a silky, feminine blouse. In wintertime, wool or silk sweaters also look great with suits; in summer, dressy T-shirts and camisole tops are cool alternatives.

A navy blue or black blazer is one of the most versatile pieces of clothing you can buy. Wear it in the office or put it over a T-shirt and jeans on the weekend. An inexpensive blazer can be personalized and made to look much more costly by adding bright brass buttons.

UNDERNEATH IT ALL

Even if you're a size 32A, *always* wear a bra (Victoria's Secret has some great ones). Ditto for panty hose. Bare legs belong on the beach, not in the boardroom.

Baubles, Bangles, and Beads

Rid your business wardrobe of tight sweaters, decolleté dresses, hip-hugging slacks, short leather skirts, stiletto heels, and patterned panty hose. And then eliminate the distractions—earrings and bracelets that swing and jangle, or elaborate layers of clothing that confuse and intrigue. Omit avant-garde styles with flashy colors: neon green, eye-opening orange, etc. Sometimes, you can add one funky element to your office outfit and get away with it, depending on where you work. One! Not two!!

The overall idea is not to wear clothing that sends out mating signals. Save your come-hither clothes for after-hours. Wear duds at the office that make everyone know you're there to work, not play.

Some companies are relaxing their dress codes, at least for Fridays. Realizing that many staffers go away for the weekend, they permit more casual clothes. No neckties necessary for men, and women can wear pants and a good-looking Gap T-shirt. This is the time you can sport your funky outfit—but don't go overboard. Keep it in good taste. No scuffy sneakers, no exposed belly buttons.

A Shoe-In

We'll be quick. You don't need to make a statement with your shoes. For the office, plain pumps with a closed toe and low-to-mid heel make the best impression. Sandals or klunky shoes can create a look that is unbusinesslike. Keep your footwear in good repair— no worn-down heels or scuff marks. Always be sure they're comfortable. When your feet hurt, it shows on your face.

Bag It!

Your handbags also should be simple and classic. Big enough to hold the necessities, but not so large that you look like you're headed for a sleep-over. Buy bags in basic colors that match your shoes. And again, recommended shades are black, navy, beige, or bone. Who wants to change handbags every day, anyway?

Hair and Makeup

We all have our bad-hair days, but you'll have fewer of them if your style is simple and easy to maintain. Find a flattering cut that you can fix yourself, in between visits to the salon for trims and touch-ups. This way you'll always be in shape for an unexpected meeting or assignment. Hair is still your crowning glory. Don't ever let it get greasy and dirty, or allow dark roots to peek out. And death to the unmade-bed look! Run a brush through it! Big ''mall hair,'' teased and sprayed to the limit, is also out. You're too pulled together for that. Besides, you *know* the natural look is in.

When it comes to makeup, less is much better in the office. A little lipstick, foundation, blush, and quiet eye makeup are all you need. Overly made-up faces send out a very unprofessional message.

From Brassy to Classy

This is a true story, whose heroine is now prospering at a leading special events company. Carly had a problem common to a lot of young women just starting to work in an office. She didn't take a close enough look at how other people dressed. Oblivious to her environment, she wore what she thought was the height of fashion. Completely unaware that her skintight sweaters, leather miniskirts, and clunky shoes sent the wrong signals, she looked totally unbusinesslike.

Lucky Carly—her boss, Brenda, saw beyond these office no-no's and sat her down. She tactfully told Carly that her way of dressing was holding her back. She got the message. She refashioned her wardrobe and today is a vice president at the same company. End of story!

Carly was indeed fortunate. Having a boss who cared enough to speak openly to her was a huge plus. Many others (could you be among them?) may be self-destructing simply because their style of dress is inappropriate for their corporate culture, and no one has taken the trouble to tell them.

Business Style

Successful career women took the time to educate themselves as to what style is all about. They learned to choose classic clothes—easy and uncomplicated that can be worn year after year. They've found it's best to dress so that they're seen as a professional first, and a woman second. In business, you need to learn how to strike a balance between your professional and female personas. It's better to be known as a person who has great ideas, not "that woman who wears the crazy earrings."

Some successful businesswomen plan what they're going to wear as carefully as they plot their schedule. One woman we know "programs" her wardrobe for the week by writing it in her Filofax. Under each date, she notes what she'll wear that day. This not only helps her organize her wardrobe and save time, it also reminds her to rotate her outfits so she isn't seen in the same thing too often. This system saves wear and tear on clothes, too. When TV commentator Barbara Walters was on the *Today* show, she always laid out her clothes the night before, because she had to get up at 4:00 A.M. It worked so well for her, we started doing it too. Try this timesaver; it works.

When we asked Christa, a young retailing executive, who has Style with a capital *S*, what her secret was, she answered without hesitation, "Most of the clothes I buy for the office are in basic colors: navy, beige, black, cream, white, and sometimes red, because all of them work together. I save pastels and brighter colors for the summer.

Christa feels it's also important to have one or two good accessories, like a nice silk scarf and a good leather handbag that's not too big. She adds, "My shoes are not necessarily the most expensive ones, but certainly nothing too trendy, usually a classic pump, or loafers for casual wear. I also think one or two well-designed leather belts are important because they can give you different looks at different times."

Christa continues: "I learned to buy clothing in sets, because the more coordinated you are, the less chance you have of making a mistake. For example, I try to buy two or three good-looking suits, rather than a lot of separates. When I want to dress casually, I wear pants suits instead of mixing a lot of different slacks and blouses. Also, a single color gives you a leaner, longer look."

She also says simple jewelry helps give her a pulled-together look. "It's not necessary to have real jewelry in order to look good," she advises. "My staples are an imitation pearl necklace and earrings, a pair of faux gold earrings, and a few simple pins for my jackets. I think a classic gold watch, though, is an accessory every woman should have because it's one of the first things people notice. It doesn't matter if it's real gold or costume jewelry."

Christa also believes a good haircut is a great investment. To economize, she has her hairstylist cut her hair and then she blow-dries it herself.

While Christa gets A-plus plus in style, what do *you* do if you don't have her ability and want to acquire it? One way is to find a role model in your company to emulate. Notice how the most successful women dress. Then, look in a mirror and compare how you measure up. You could also pick a well-known person whose sense of style is considered world-class. Audrey Hepburn, for example, was always thought of as the epitome of classic style. After her movie career wound down, she became the United Nations Ambassador for UNICEF (The United Nations International Children's Education Fund). She shed her glamorous designer duds for tailored suits and dresses and wore pants and boots when she went into the jungles and villages of Africa.

Jacqueline Kennedy Onassis, another style icon, parlayed her perfect taste into a lifestyle that not only included being married to the President of the United States, but also helped her achieve universal recognition as one of the world's most admired women. While working for Doubleday as a book editor, she wore simple suits or a pants suit when appropriate. She projected her professionalism first, and Jackie O. second. Today, Hollywood's Sharon Stone's sense of style seems right on target for most occasions. It's never too much, never too little.

If you analyze these three women's wardrobes, you'll find an emphasis on classic shapes, basic colors, and simple designs that are never too trendy, elaborate, or complicated. Their style was, and is, as important to their images as their God-given good looks.

Streamlining Strategies

We confess, we were fashion victims years ago—wore one piece of jewelry too many, fell for fads over classics, and were occasionally overwhelmed by baggy clothes that made us look like unmade beds. To avoid making the same mistakes, pull out that trusty yellow pad and scrutinize your wardrobe. In one column write "Classic Keeps" and in the other "Throwaways." Do this no matter what, even if you decide not to toss anything out. In time you'll probably agree with your list.

It's also helpful to have a friend whose style you admire go through your closet with you. Try on each piece of clothing and have her say "yes," "no," or "maybe." Isolate the clothing she labels "no" and "maybe," and put them in a section of the closet all by themselves. Either tie a red ribbon around these clothes to separate them from other items in your wardrobe or store them in a shopping bag. Watch and see if you can't live without them. If you find you don't wear them for more than a year, either donate them to charity or give them to a friend who wants them.

Streamlining your wardrobe does more than give you extra closet space. It's easier to get dressed in the morning if you don't have to plow through racks of junk to find what you want. It'll also tell you what items you need to buy: another blouse for the black suit, a new pair of beige shoes for summer, some brass buttons to replace the ones that fell off your blue blazer, etc.

Sorry, but it doesn't matter how much you paid for a piece of clothing. If you've made a fashion flub, it's better to eat the expense than to wear clothes that are wrong for you. Speaking of cost, a question that's often raised is: How much should I spend on my wardrobe? To quote fashion expert Elsa Klensch: "The answer is simple. As much as you can afford . . . work clothing should be viewed as an investment."

Finding Your Way

Finding a style that's appropriate for you in the office isn't a snap. You'll probably have to work at it all your business life. To determine what's right for you, get all the help you can. Read fashion magazines and books, shop the stores and keep your eye on what the power dressers of the world are wearing. You'll soon realize instinctively what's right for your body, your office and your way of life.

Dressing Up

- Appearance in business is critical to your success.

- Know your company's dress code and don't buck it.

- Dress as if you were the boss.

- Let your clothes say you're there to work, not play.

- Suits create the most businesslike impression.

- Keep shoes, handbags, and jewelry VERY simple.

- Spend the money for a good haircut.

- Tone down your daytime makeup.

- Dress like a professional first, and a woman second.

- Save time by laying out your clothes the night before.

- Buy basic colors; they're easier to mix and match.

- Jewelry can be fake and still make a style statement.

- Learn from world-class role models.

- Don't fall victim to every fashion trend.

- Streamline your wardrobe—toss the stuff you haven't worn for a year.

- Educate yourself to find your look.

- Don't resist change; let your style evolve over time.

- Buy classic clothes; they'll always look right.

- Go for the best you can afford—it's a wise investment.

Take It Off

If you're feeling chunky, clunky, and overweight, there's no time like the present to make some changes. The shape your body is in definitely affects your self-image, your career, and your love life, too. But, most important, you should want to shape up for yourself. To feel fit is to feel fantastic.

There's a whole new mindset today about fitness and exercise. It used to be like cod-liver oil: good for you but so yucky going down. Now, total fitness is as much part of our everyday lives as brushing our teeth. Today's woman chooses foods that are both tasty and good for her body. She reads the nutrition panel on everything she buys and tries to purchase food with the fewest preservatives and lowest fat content. The fact that many foods aren't as fattening as they used to be is almost a bonus.

Fitness has made a 180-degree turn. All we used to want from diet and exercise was to look better. Now, we know fitness has a lot more going for it. It not only makes us feel attractive and energetic, we know it's good for our minds as well as our bodies.

Interestingly enough, successful businesspeople usually buy into the fitness ethic, and, as a result, are totally in shape. Why? It not only gives them more stamina and energy for their jobs, it helps relieve the stress that life in the fast track brings. And, for sure, they know it's hard to be taken seriously in business when your appearance is not up to par. It suggests a lack of self-control.

While you're busy keeping fit for you, remember staying in shape also has a spillover effect on your job. A positive appearance is a plus in any career. It's amazing that people don't wake up to this simple fact sooner.

If your body is bulging in all the wrong places, you'll never look as good as you should—no matter how great your wardrobe. It's almost impossible to hide figure flaws. Bite the bullet and de-bulge yourself! The only way we know to make that happen is through diet and exercise. No one ever said that this combo was a piece of cake. The ''no pain, no gain'' slogan is truer than ever. We don't claim to be diet gurus, but do confess to reading, clipping, and exchanging every diet tip that seems to make sense. Been there, done that!

Tried-and-True Tricks of the Trade

All right, already! So, you've heard some of these things before! Never you mind, you must be interested in losing a few pounds if you're reading this chapter. To tone up, trim down, and look as slinky as you can, here are a few hints that the experts keep repeating:

1. Don't go schlepping to the supermarket on an empty stomach; shopping when you're hungry can ''force'' you to buy something wicked. Even a quick cup of coffee can zap your appetite for a little while.

2. Never go to a party or restaurant when you're famished. Hors d'oeuvres at the former and the bread basket at the latter can do you in for the day. If every canapé contains at least 100 calories and if you wolf down five, you've practically eaten half your dinner allowance.

    Instead, before you go out, crunch into an apple, or drink a glass of tomato juice. B-o-r-i-n-g, but effective. They'll squelch your appetite and save you from overindulging.

3. According to diet wizard, Dr. Stephen P. Gullo, a psychologist who specializes in weight control, ''Most people gain weight during the first ten minutes (of a restaurant meal) when they don't know what to do with their fingers.'' Don't you be one of them. Instead, let yours grip a glass of juice or cold water—or, better yet, his hand!

4. Avoid foods that say "Alfredo," "Milanese," and ditto for breaded, or "sautéed"—a sneaky word for fried. Try poached, grilled, or roasted instead.

5. When you want to imbibe, try to do it only while you're eating. A glass or two of wine before dinner weakens your resolve to stay on a diet. A wine spritzer is a good choice—fewer calories, plus you can nurse one for a long time.

6. Buy and eat low-fat or fat-free foods whenever you can.

7. If you think you're one up when you have cappuccino instead of dessert, think again. A cappuccino can have the same calorie count as a bowl of ice cream. Just order plain old American coffee. Yes, it's okay to add a little milk, not cream.

8. The later at night you eat, the less chance you have of losing weight. Your body doesn't burn as many calories when you're catching Zs as when you're awake and moving around. Establish a cutoff time for dinner, say 8:00 P.M. at the latest, and stick to your guns.

9. Never scarf down your food! If you shovel it in, your stomach doesn't have a chance to tell your head that it's full. Take it s-l-o-w and you'll take it off.

10. Try eating smaller portions than you'd normally consume. Who says you have to finish everything on your plate? That's a hangover from toddler time.

The Shape You're In

Okay, so you've finally started to lose a little weight, but your diet seems to be dragging on forever. Speed it up and firm up with exercise. Yes, we know, lots of us dread even thinking about it. We're too busy, don't have any energy to spare, can't afford to join a gym, don't want to be seen in a leotard, etc., etc. We've not only heard them all, we've used those excuses ourselves!

Alibis aside, we all know that exercise not only keeps you physically fit but also boosts your morale, combats stress, and can help to prevent diseases—like heart problems, osteoporosis, and circulatory disorders. Don't think these ailments only strike little old ladies in tennis shoes; they can begin as early as your twenties. So, why aren't you working out now? Everyone is capable of some form of exercise. Even if you just walk part of the way to work, or forgo the elevator for the stairs, you'll help your bod look better. There are other easy things to do—like a twenty-minute walk three times a week, maybe even with your man of the moment.

Sounds dull? Then dance your shoes off! Dancing is great exercise, and it doesn't even feel like work. And, of course, there are health clubs, which not only offer a wide variety of sweat-burner classes but also can be great places to meet a new man, who'll undoubtedly be in great shape to boot.

But one of the best ways you can score a triple play—exercise, help your career, and expand your social life—is to participate in the so-called "social sports," golf and tennis. Our friend, marketing executive Stedman Graham, suggests that businesswomen take to the golf course if they want to move up the career ladder. Men have been doing this forever. Mucho business is conducted while strolling the fairways and at the "Nineteenth Hole," golfers' term for the clubhouse bar. Golfing enables guys to "coddle" their clients in a relaxed environment. You can do the same. An important business contact who turns you down for lunch or drinks just might accept your invitation for a round of golf. Tennis is another option. You can have lunch before the match, or cocktails afterwards.

Oh—you say you don't play golf or tennis? Take lessons! They could be a great investment in your future.

Wrap-Up

Are you convinced now that looking good is one of the key components of a successful career? Blow this and you could get blown away yourself.

Only you can control the way you look. There's no magic pill, no fairy godmother to wave her wand and give you the perfect look. Our suggestions in this chapter are just to get you started—the rest is up to you. Rarely will anyone pull you aside and tell you that the way you dress is holding you back. If you want to look your best—so you can do your best—you've got to work at it. Read fashion magazines to get ideas on current trends that you can adapt, note what successful well-dressed women are wearing, and get yourself in the best possible shape you can.

nineteen

Tips from Your Courtesy Coach

Believe it, manners in the millennium will be just as important as they were when you were growing up. When Mother told you to "always mind your *p*'s and *q*'s," she knew what she was talking about. Manners make you stand out from the pack. Don't ever think they're old-fashioned or out-of-date. Trust us: good manners can make or break you—in your job, romance, and the rest of life.

Did you know, for example, that it's common practice in corporate America for an executive to invite a prospective employee to lunch to test her or his etiquette IQ? Understandably, they want to hire people who know how to conduct themselves appropriately whenever they're representing the company. A lot of those candidates flunk, but you won't, if you take the Courtesy Coach's tips to heart.

Dining Out

Sit down, place your napkin on your lap, keep your elbows off the table, and don't slouch. Never talk with your mouth full and don't make noise smacking your lips. Yuck! And for heaven's sake, don't make potty pronouncements when you're leaving for the rest room. Just excuse yourself.

Dining In

Same as above, plus: When you're a dinner guest at someone's home, never complain about food you can't, or don't want to, eat. If you have religious or medical restrictions, some people think it's okay to call ahead and alert the hostess. If you feel this is an imposition, just move the food around on your plate and pretend you're eating it.

Bring a small gift for your host. It's not mandatory, but certainly gets you brownie points. And don't fail to take time out the very next day to send a *handwritten* thank-you note. Nothing beats it!

While it's impolite to eat and run, it's equally discourteous to overstay your welcome. Say good-bye and thank your hostess for the lovely time. She probably needs a while to decompress and clean up. By the way, it's nice to offer to help—but don't insist if she says no.

The Business Meal: Dos and Don'ts

When you're going out for a business meal, remember the purpose is just that—business—and not an unbridled opportunity to indulge in culinary or liquid delights. Here are a few ideas to keep in mind if you want to make a positive professional impression:

- **Don't hold up the order because you can't decide what you want.** Be ready when it's your turn, otherwise you'll come across as indecisive and wishy-washy. It's also rude to make the rest of the table wait while you ask the waiter a thousand questions.

- **Skip messy dishes.** Pasta that slips off your fork or corn on the cob that gets stuck between your teeth have the potential to make you look silly. Avoid them, along with any dishes you have to work at too hard, like lobster or a Cornish hen. You'll be so busy dissecting your food that you won't be able to participate fully in the table discussion.

- **Don't steal someone else's bread, water, or wine**. Remember, your bread plate is to the left and your water and wine glasses are placed to the right. This way you won't accidentally grab someone else's roll or drink. The way we remember it is to say to ourselves that drinking water is always the right thing to do.

- **Don't wave your knife and fork around when you're speaking**. You'll come across as a redneck if you don't put them down! The really proper way is to place them vertically on your plate, the fork on the left as it was originally set, and ditto for the knife on the right with the blade facing in. If you don't get all of this exactly right, don't worry. You're home free as long as you're not waving knives and forks in the air.

- **Don't leave the spoon in the soup bowl or cup while you're talking.** Put it down, faceup, on the serving plate. This shows you really know what table manners are all about.

- **Don't order the most expensive entree on the menu, whether you're the host or the guest.** You'll appear greedy—as if you're taking undue advantage of a free meal.

- **Don't order wine or liquor if no one else does**. And, never, ever, overimbibe at a business luncheon or dinner. Today, there's little or no pressure to drink. However, if others decide to indulge and you follow suit, never have more than two. Besides, a drink at lunch can destroy your effectiveness for the rest of the day. Plus, if your boss smells liquor on your breath when you return to the office, it could actually cost you your job if it happens too often.

- **Don't fight over the check.** The person who did the inviting is the one who pays—regardless of gender. There are no exceptions to this rule.

- **Don't try to stiff the waiter**. Tipping etiquette requires that you leave the waiter a tip for his/her service. The rule of thumb is to leave at least 15 percent of the total amount, before the tax is added on. It's easy to figure it out in your head if you do it in two steps. First, take 10 percent of the pretax total, which is easy to calculate, then divide that amount in half. Add the two numbers and you get 15 percent. Let's say your bill is $40 (pretax). Take 10 percent of this, or $4, and then half of $4, or $2. Result? 15 percent, or $6. If the service is fantastic, you may want to leave 20 percent, although it's not necessary. Some people leave the larger amount because it's easier to figure out.

New-Age Manners for Business

Today, it's very common for women to host business lunches and/or dinners for male associates who may be twice their age. Let's say you've set up a lunch date with a male client who's old enough to be your father. How do you handle it? In the first place, your professionalism is not undermined because of your age or sex. If your company trusts you enough to entertain clients, you've obviously got what it takes to do the job. Just act as if you're equals, regardless of his age and/or importance. And you'll appear more in charge if you pick a restaurant where you're known and are a frequent diner.

If you want to avoid any potential awkwardness, arrive at the restaurant early and tell the captain that you're the host, and are to be given the check, no matter what. You can even give him your credit card beforehand to run it through. At the end of the meal, he'll bring you the slip for your signature. It's basic business courtesy to arrive early when you're the host (so you can welcome your guest), and on time when you're the guest. If you're going to be delayed, it's courteous to alert your guest or at least call the restaurant and ask them to pass on the message.

Let's say you and a few clients are celebrating the successful launch of a new product and the occasion calls for a bottle of wine. Don't be intimidated. The polite thing to do is to ask your guest if he/she prefers red or white. (The old rules about drinking white wine with fish or fowl and red with meat are no longer set in stone.) After you've settled on white or red, just ask the waiter or wine steward to bring you the wine list. While he's there, ask for his suggestions. Don't be afraid to tell the waiter you want a good value (your company might not appreciate a $150 bottle of wine popping up on your expense account).

If you're the guest, thank your host verbally at the end of the

---

P.S.: Even though a new day has supposedly dawned, some waiters are still in the Dark Ages when it comes to treating female customers as well as they do their male clients, especially when a woman is hosting the meal. If you're treated badly, don't let the waiter get away with it. Your Courtesy Coach gives you full approval to complain to management. Explain that you'd like to continue to patronize the establishment but won't be back unless the service improves. It's best to put this in writing on company stationery and send it to the owner in an envelope marked confidential (otherwise, he/she may never see it). In the meantime, find another restaurant where they appreciate your business and treat you courteously. Who needs Neanderthals serving you, anyway?

meal. If you want to make an even bigger impression, follow it up with a short *handwritten* note. A personal message that you've taken the time to write carries far more cachet than any hi-tech missive. Sure, communicating by fax or E-mail is easier, but electronic sentiments never have the same warmth or weight.

Career Courtesy

Had a door slammed in your face lately? Only inconsiderate slobs do this. Most polite people look over their shoulder to see if anyone is behind them. Only those who wouldn't know manners from mayonnaise don't.

A few other tips on those little niceties of office life that'll make you stand out:

Basics:

- Always hold the elevator door open for others

- Step aside for seniors (who knows, he/she might be your next CEO!)

- Never pull rank on co-workers. You might meet them on their way up while you're on the way down!

- When you're sending out for lunch for yourself, be thoughtful enough to ask your boss and other nearby co-workers if they want anything as well.

Phone Fundamentals:

- If given the opportunity, answer your own phone. It shows you don't think you're a big shot.

- Always return phone calls yourself, the same day if possible. If CEOs can do this, you can too.

- A secure professional doesn't play the game of having her secretary call someone and wait until the other party gets on the line before she picks up. It's demeaning to whomever you're calling.

- If you happen to pick up the phone of a co-worker who's out for personal reasons, never disclose this information. It's poor business manners. Forget about saying "She's at the doctor's," "Her mother is very sick," etc. It's nobody else's business but hers. Many people, and your co-workers may be among them, will consider it rude on your part if you violate their privacy by sharing personal information.

Within the Office:

- Never sit on a co-worker's desk or put your feet on it. It's a territorial thing.

- Be on time for meetings. If you're perennially late, you give others the impression that your time is more valuable than theirs. That'll irritate them before you open your mouth.

- Don't go into your boss's office if she isn't there—even if it's just to deliver a memo. It's invasive. If someone happens to see you, they may think you're snooping.

- Even if your company has an open-door policy, avoid barging into someone's office, particularly if they're on the phone. And don't lurk outside either. They may think you're trying to eavesdrop. Stand at the door briefly and wait until you catch their eye. You'll either be waved in or not.

- If you're in someone's office and they take a phone call, offer to step outside if you think the conversation may be private.

- Never, ever pick up and peruse papers on a co-worker's desk, and don't try to read them upside down, either!

- If you're in someone's office and they stand up or glance at their watch, take the hint and leave.

Romance Etiquette

Never assume that just because you're brilliant and adorable, guys are going to fall for you if your manners are from Hell. No, you don't have to be Miss Priss, but what man worth having wants a woman who's a mannerless klutz? None that we've talked to. So, if your table etiquette isn't up to snuff—read up on it. Also, know your limits liquor-wise. Skip that "one-for-the-road." People tend to be more critical of a woman who's trashed than they are of a man. She's expected to know better. If you tend to go a little wild and crazy in public—it's smart to tone it down when you're around his family and friends in the early stages. No one's saying you have to change your personality; just put it in low gear when you're in situations like this. Remember, the hottest flame can be doused by your Significant Other's inner circle. If they perceive you as an oaf, chances are slim that you'll make the cut.

Don't Be a Dining Dork!

When he takes you out to dinner, conduct yourself with style. Don't order the most expensive items on the menu—forget the foie gras—unless he suggests it and you know his wallet can handle it. Don't hassle the waiter with a laundry list of your personal peculiarities: "I'm lactose intolerant and could never eat that" or "Don't you dare put a drop of butter on the salmon," can be boorish at best. If you have dietary, medical, or nutritional no-no's, keep your directives simple and spare. Never make more than three requests of a waiter. Otherwise, you'll create a complicated scene right out of the movie *When Harry Met Sally*.

If you want to go the old-fashioned route, relay your menu selections to your date and let him order for both of you. You'll come across as mannerly and disarmingly feminine. This can be particularly effective when you're with someone new. You can always switch to ordering for yourself the next time around.

Dating Dos and Don'ts

Never be too nosy with someone you'd like to hold near and dear! Save the personal queries until the romance has had time to take root. Skip questions like "How much do you make?" or "Why did you break up with your ex-girlfriend?"

If he sends flowers, call or write immediately to let him know you received and love them. Don't laugh—sending a casual thank-you note or a funny card will make a man feel like a king. Most people don't take time for these little niceties, so you'll definitely stand out in his mind.

If he invites you to dinner at his place, ask if you can contribute something—dessert, special bread, etc. If he says you don't have to bother, bring a bottle of wine, anyway. When you arrive, offer to help in the kitchen or with setting the table. Don't just sit there like a lump! And, of course, the same rules apply if you're invited to his family's home.

If a guy ever misreads your good manners and accuses you of "putting on an act," ignore it and him! He's obviously not operating on your level. Toss him back. There are plenty of other fish in the sea who take etiquette to heart.

A man's manners are a strong indication of his character. Pure and simple, manners are not a contrived collection of rituals. They're just a way of showing basic consideration for others. And, that's what you'll want in a permanent mate. So, it *is* important that your guy behave like a gentleman, just as Mother said.

Etiquette in Everyday Life

It's the little courtesies—as well as the not so little— that'll give you away. They'll tell the world if you've mastered the basic niceties of life or if you're still among the Etiquette Impaired. Here are a few things you definitely should not flub up on:

- **Miscellaneous Manners:** When you go through a door, don't slam it in someone's face. Never crash through revolving doors—you can hurt someone who's ahead of you. And, of course, you'll always ask permission to smoke, wherever you are. When possible, use your beeper or cell phone in private, unless there's an emergency. It looks so show-offy to talk on your phone in a restaurant or walking down the street. And, finally, be on time. Punctuality is said to be "the courtesy of kings." Sure, lots of people are habitually late, but don't you be one of them.

- **Expressions of Courtesy:** Always say "please" when making even the simplest request. Think of how different it sounds when you demand "Give me the menu" as opposed to "Please pass the salt." And—whether your date has taken you to dinner, the movies, or a stop at Starbuck's—always say "thank you." It's such a simple courtesy, but so effective. "Please" and "thank you" are two expressions that can never be overused. When someone sends you a gift, don't fail to acknowledge it with a brief thank-you note. As a reader of Ann Landers recently wrote: "Until you have sent a thank-you note, you cannot: wear it, show it, read it, watch it, eat it, spend it, play with it, or use it.''

- **RSVPing:** Another area that many people are thoughtless about is those little RSVPs you see at the bottom of invitations. It stands for *répondez s'il vous plait*—please reply. It's considered the height of bad manners not to. If the invitation is for a sitdown dinner, it's extremely discourteous to delay replying. Never put someone in the position of having to phone you to see if you'll be attending their party after they've asked you to RSVP. Even if you verbally tell them you're coming, it's still good manners to send the card back. People sometimes forget whether you've accepted or not, and they count on those little cards to remind them.

    When it comes to special occasions like a wedding, where a great deal of time and money are being invested, it's a cardinal sin not to reply promptly! How lazy are you if you can't write your name on the RSVP card and mail the already stamped envelope?

- **Tipping:** Why is it necessary? It's a fact of life that most service people are deliberately paid lower salaries because it's expected that their income will be supplemented by tips. Cabdrivers, waitpersons, and hairstylists are all examples of people who should be tipped. But there also are others who should be financially rewarded, and you won't be remembered kindly if you don't. In a hotel, give the bellman who delivers your bags several dollars, usually $1 per bag. It's considered good manners to leave the maid who cleans your room a small gratuity, usually based on the number of nights you stay there. In a luxury hotel, about $5 per night is adequate. If you're staying in your basic Holiday Inn, $1 or $2 per night should suffice. In both cases, it's usually reimbursable on a business trip.

    When you're leaving a hotel, give the doorman a tip if he gets you a taxi, especially on a rainy night. A dollar is about right. In European hotels, it's expected that you give the concierge a gratuity, particularly if he's made dinner reservations or given you directions or maps of the city. In the hair salon, besides tipping your stylist and manicurist about 15 percent, don't forget the person who shampooed your hair, as well as the coat-check person. About $1 is fine for each.

- **Gossiping:** Be careful. This not only shows bad manners, it also can get you in trouble. Why be the one to spread someone's bad news—or even not so bad news—all over town? Some people indiscriminately repeat everything they hear (''Lynn's boyfriend stood her up last night. She's afraid he's seeing his ex again.'') Most people place a premium on privacy and view these kinds of gossipmongers as tacky and totally lacking in manners.

- **Putting on makeup in public:** This is a judgment call. We feel you shouldn't do it in a business situation. If you're in a restaurant with friends, it's okay to quickly reapply your lipstick. Any more than this becomes offensive. If your mascara's melting, or your blusher's blotching, fix it in the rest room.

- **Telling little white lies:** Never risk this in business. It'll definitely catch up with you and do you in, eventually. It's not viewed all that favorably in everyday life, either. People who continually tell little white lies are generally found out and are usually perceived as tricky and not to be trusted. There are some isolated occasions when a little white lie will spare someone's feelings. Then it's okay. Let's say you receive an invitation that you don't want to accept. Sometimes it's better to bow out by claiming a conflict. It's just too hurtful to say, ''No, I really don't want to go.'' At the same time, better make sure your fibs are foolproof. And don't overexplain or give too many details. That's when you get trapped. Say no more than ''I'm sorry, I can't make it. I have a previous engagement.''

- **Guesting overnight**: If you're a guest in the home of a friend's family, always offer to help when the opportunity presents itself. Some people don't want assistance in the kitchen, but you should make the attempt. This includes offering to serve the drinks, set the table, clear it, or put dishes and glasses in the dishwasher. It's also polite to ask what time you're expected for dinner; you don't want to be late. And it's just common courtesy to ask if you can take a soft drink, or whatever, out of the fridge. It's also very bad manners to abuse your host's telephone. A few local calls are fine, but anything long distance should either be put on your calling card or else you should reverse the charges. Even telling your hostess you'll be happy to pay for your phone calls is poor form. Sure, some hostesses may generously say "Don't bother," but you've made a lousy impression.

• And last, if you're staying with people who have household help, always check first before asking them to do something specific for you. One young guest assumed it was okay to ask the housekeeper to go to the drugstore and pick up some nail polish. This really annoyed her hostess, who needed the staffer at that time. Remember, you're not paying the housekeeper's salary. If you need or want anything, always go through your hostess, even if the household help volunteers to do it. Finally, always drop your friend's family a handwritten note thanking them for their hospitality.

Remember, courtesy goes far beyond knowing which fork to use. What it all boils down to, Gentle Reader, is the Golden Rule: "Do unto others as you would have them do unto you."

twenty

The Female Lair

Some women don't pay much attention to how their "single-girl" digs look. Instead, they choose to spend their money on clothes, join a fitness center, or maybe take a great trip. But we're certain that you, being both aware and ambitious, will make sure every facet of your life reflects your growing sense of self, including where and how you live.

Everything starts small—your job, your apartment, your wardrobe. And, as you climb up the career ladder, it's vital that all aspects of your life be headed in the same direction.

The way you live tells as much about you as the clothes you wear and the way you look. It's up to you to make sure your home expresses your taste and says the right things about you. It should be a warm, nurturing haven that you're proud to show off to co-workers, friends, and lovers.

Whether you realize it or not, your home affects you *mentally*. Subliminally, it can alter your mood, your confidence, and your self-image. It can make you feel as if you're able to conquer the world, or depress you so much you'd like to chuck it all and run away.

Grow Up!

There's little point in succeeding at work if you come home to drab, dreary surroundings that drag you down. After all, self-esteem is a twenty-four-hour-a-day thing. Home is haven, refuge, the place to kick off your shoes and unwind. It also reflects your personality, how you feel about yourself, and how you want others to perceive you.

Finding, funding, and furnishing the right place takes time, thought and single-mindedness. You have to know what you want, can afford, and the kind of statement you'd like to make. It's important to prove to yourself that you've grown-up, are ready to take responsibility for yourself, and that you've put your dorm days far behind you.

The Must-Haves

If you're just starting out and have zilch in the way of furniture, let's discuss the basics you have to buy right off the bat. Then, as soon as you get a little spare cash, there are some things you can add.

Bottom-Line Basics

- Bed and bedside table(s)
- Bureau
- Dining table (doubles as a desk)
- Two chairs to go with it

- Curtains—blinds—shades: take your pick
- Alarm clock
- TV
- Iron/ironing board or small, portable steamer
- Reading lamp
- Lamps for the living room
- A few plates and bowls
- Knives, forks, spoons
- Drinking glasses and coffee mugs
- Pots and pans
- Can opener, wine corkscrew
- Toaster oven
- Microwave
- Coffeemaker

Add-Ons

- Sofa
- Two side-tables for the lamps and phone
- Upholstered chair(s)
- Two more chairs for your dining table
- Set of matching china
- Set of matching flatware (knives, forks, spoons)
- Bookshelves
- CD player/radio
- Blender/food processor

- Vacuum cleaner—there are several models that cost anywhere between $70 and $100 that do a good job for the average apartment.

Cheap and Chic

Regardless of your income, the trick is to create an apartment that looks as if you're making a million, even though it didn't cost an arm and a leg to furnish. Here are a few tried-and-true tricks of decorating cheap but looking rich. They make your house a home, not just some impersonal place where all you do is sleep.

You can turn tin into gold. How? Recondition family castoffs. You can even dress up or camouflage a dreary sofa by draping a large, fringed, silky scarf over it. Don't forget thrift shops. As a rule, they only sell items that are in good condition. You can usually find lots of inexpensive, but interesting, things there. Don't pass up flea markets, tag and garage sales. If you're a do-it-yourselfer, buy unfinished furniture. With your three best friends—a staple gun, a glue gun, and velcro, plus a little paint—you can create magic. Leaf through decorating magazines beforehand to get ideas you can adapt inexpensively. The trick is to get pieces that look as if they belong together—coordinated colors and style.

Adrienne, a twenty-something artist living in New York City, made the most out of her tiny apartment by decorating on the cheap. She started by slipcovering an old sofa and chairs that she'd inherited from her mother. She found a zippy black-and-white-patterned fabric in an outlet store on New York's Lower East Side for $10 a yard. With the money Adrienne saved on the fabric, she was able to find a cut-rate upholsterer who made the slipcovers for her sofa and chairs. (There are also attractive, ready-made slipcovers available at home-furnishings stores.)

To fix her floors, which were kind of worn, Adrienne rented a sander and redid them. She then proceeded to bleach them white. She bought a few great-looking lamps and other accessories at a weekend flea market. Instead of curtains, she used some tortoiseshell window shades she found there. It took two years of searching until she spotted an affordable coffee table she liked. A closeout sale at a famous designer's showroom had the perfect piece, marked down to one-seventh of its original cost! When she needed a table to go next to a chair, she just piled up some coffee table–sized books and had a glass top made to cover them. You could do the same, or else buy pretty decorative boxes, about eleven by fourteen inches, and cover them with glass. For safety's sake, make sure the glass corners are rounded.

Adrienne hung good-looking prints that she found at street fairs and museum gift shops, where they sell for reasonable prices. She also recommends that you use only framed prints; they give a room a more finished look.

Her kitchen is minuscule, and since she uses her microwave for most of the cooking anyway, she bought a large cutting board and put it over the stove to give her additional counter space. Even though she claims cooking isn't her strong suit, Adrienne likes to give small dinner parties. "I have a drop-leaf table that I keep against the wall. When I'm having a party, I pull it out and, voilà!—there's a dining table that will seat eight."

The Four Steps

There are four basic steps in decorating your home:

- Determine your style.

- Choose a color scheme you can live with.

- Create a layout for your furniture.
- Accessorize as you can afford to.

Let's take them one by one.

What's My Look?

Step 1:

Before you begin to furnish your place, take the time to psych out your decorating personality. Determine your style. Do you see yourself as lacy, frilly, and ultrafeminine? Decorate accordingly. If you think of yourself as a New Age woman, opt for a sleek, spare, minimalist feeling. If you're into a dressed-down, country look, surround yourself with lots of bleached pine and hooked rugs. Conversely, the more formal and traditional woman usually goes for Queen Anne and Chippendale—authentic, if she can afford it, or repros if not.

If you don't know which type you are, look at pictures in magazines and see what attracts your eye to find the answer. Once you've determined your decorating personality, your apartment should reflect what you think you're all about—even if it's only as of this moment. You'll probably change as the years go by and your taste evolves. Mario Buatta, one of the country's most sought-after decorators, advises, "Never think that your home is completed. Think of it as a garden that grows with you as you go along in life."

Your True Colors

Step 2:

Psyching out the color scheme for your home is a uniquely personal exercise. At this point in your life, you probably know what colors look good on you and enhance your skin tones. Consider these shades as possibilities. Also focus on colors that make you feel good just by looking at them—that give you an instant "upper," or a feeling of warmth, comfort and/or serenity.

For more ideas on choosing a color scheme, flip through home-decorating books and magazines. Tear out or clip pages that show color schemes that appeal to you. Also, try to remember people's homes you've visited and liked. What were their color schemes?

Certain shades of soft blue or pale green are known to instill a sense of peace and tranquillity. If that's the feeling you want, then that's one way to go. Off-white or creamy beige are "safe" colors that go with virtually anything. They provide a neutral background for a wide range of fabrics, furniture styles, and any art you might want to hang.

At the other end of the spectrum, the late, great style-setter and *Vogue* magazine editor, Diana Vreeland, was well known for having an all-red apartment complete with lacquered crimson walls and screaming scarlet prints on the sofas and chairs. To top it off, she used leopard-print carpets throughout the rooms. Mrs. Vreeland compared her home to "a garden in Hell." Obviously, she had a well-developed sense of drama and the perfect personality to carry off this bold look.

While your color likes and dislikes are important, you have to factor in how any color you choose will work with the furniture you have on hand or hope to get in the near future. You also need to ask yourself what colors you can live with over time. For example, will you tire of passion pink, or pulsating purple walls after a few years? It's expensive to repaint and, needless to say, it discombobulates your life.

On the other hand, if you feel you really want a kicky color scheme, go for it. Just keep in mind our admonition that taste evolves over time. Special furniture that you bought or upholstered to match the walls also costs money. So, it pays to pick a color that you won't be tempted to change any time soon.

A word about wallpaper: While a bit expensive, wallpaper can give you a textured look that's impossible to get with painted walls. There are outlets where you can buy inexpensive wallpaper, or even overruns of better paper. If you can't afford to paper the living room, you can always transform a smaller space, like the bathroom or kitchen, into something special with wallpaper.

Tracy, one of our more outgoing friends, decided to paper every square inch of her studio apartment. She found a floral wallpaper print in her favorite color of the moment—hot pink. She used a matching fabric for drapes. She papered her bathroom walls—plus the ceiling—in a black-and-white zebra pattern with a nice sheen. She bought a matching shower curtain, coordinated the look with black and white towels, and hung a big print of a zebra on the wall. Her previously dull kitchen took on new life when she used shiny black wallpaper with big, beige mushrooms on it. All this wallpaper was a huge success and it made her somewhat ordinary apartment come alive. Her friends loved it and said it made them feel great just to be there.

Then Tracy married and moved to a new apartment; this time she chose a neutral beige background that set off her new furniture. After eight years of living with exuberant colors and patterns, her tastes changed, just as Mario B. predicts.

Always remember that whatever hues you choose, color has the power to uplift, depress, calm, or energize you.

Furniture Layout

Step 3:

As far as the layout of your living room is concerned, Mario Buatta suggests that your furniture be placed in groupings—a sofa flanked by two or three chairs, with side tables between them. "Visualize it as if the pieces were people, talking to each other. Sometimes the best way to figure out a room arrangement is to look at the furniture the day *after* a party. You can readily see how your friends rearranged the chairs so they could talk to each other more comfortably."

Most apartment buildings give you a floor plan when you move in. If no such plan exists, just do a rough sketch of the shape of the rooms, drawing in windows and doors. Then cut out tiny squares and circles representing the sofa, chairs, coffee table, bed, bureau, nightstands, etc. This will give you a basic blueprint for the furniture you need to buy.

There are reasonably priced computer packages you can purchase that can help you to lay out your room, determine where to place the furniture, and then illustrate it all in 3-D. You can play with all sorts of different arrangements until you've created the "virtual room" that appeals to you.

Accessorize with Room Charmers

Step 4:

Although accessories are not necessities, they're the charmers that give a room personality. Mario B. says you should fill your rooms with objects that express your feelings and dreams. For example, find some pretty, decorative plates that reflect your love of animals, flowers, the Orient, whatever. Prop them on little easels or hang them on the wall.

Candles are also one of the most effective accessories available, and they don't cost much. They come in all shapes, sizes, scents, and colors. Candles add a friendly, homey touch to your room. Use them! An afghan, also known as a throw, looks comfy, cozy, and colorful tossed over the side of a chair or couch. It makes people feel they can kick off their shoes and snuggle up. "Edible accessories"—like candy wrapped in gold foil—are also terrific. A glass bowl or box filled with M&M's or mixed nuts makes your home more hospitable.

Accessorize your side tables with lots of photos. For frames, you can use fabric, leather, brass, Lucite, or wood. For the maximum effect, use only one kind of frame in the same setting. When you mix them together, it looks disjointed. For the biggest splash, try silver-toned frames. They radiate success and good taste. Silver-plated frames come in a no-polish finish and look great.

Listen to the Pros

According to Betty Sherrill, president of Mc-Millen, Inc., one of the country's oldest and most prestigious decorating firms, "An easy way to add instant warmth to a room is to fill it with living things—a crackling fire, fresh flowers or plants, or even a bowl of fruit." When we reminded Betty that flowers are expensive, she gave us this tip: "Just put them in the fridge during the day—in water, of course—and take them out when you come home. This keeps them fresh for at least a week."

If posies are still too pricey, buy bunches of green leaves. Shiny red apples or a pyramid of big yellow lemons look great in a bowl.

Not only are they less expensive than flowers, but you can eat them, too! Plus, they're real. Death to fake flowers! They're too obvious and make people think you don't know any better. Dried flowers are a good alternative. They're natural—and permanent. Lots of plants, especially flowering ones, like a colorful gloxinia, also add a terrific touch. But, for heaven's sake, don't nurse decrepit, worn-out plants until they're yellow and limp. Spend a few dollars and replace them with lush, fertile ones. You can give inexpensive plants instant panache by placing them in good-looking containers—attractive baskets, real clay pots, etc. Anything's better than those ugly, green plastic containers plants come in. For extra drama, light your tall plants or trees with an inexpensive, floor-model "up-lighter." It creates wonderful patterns on the walls and ceilings when you turn the lights down low.

Remember, we said you need side tables to go next to the sofa—when you can afford them. One of the chicest touches you can get for your home—for the least amount of money—is a round table draped in a luxurious-looking fabric. It's a great look for the living room. All you need is an inexpensive round plywood top on a wooden base and some attractive material to cover it. Lots of catalogs like Horchow or Charles Keath sell them in an inexpensive kit. Try a pretty sheet with a floral or paisley design that reaches to the floor, or drape a velvet fringed shawl over a plain piece of fabric. Put a flannel blanket underneath as a liner (just make sure it's clean!). The blanket "poufs" the cover out and makes it look more expensive. Here's where you put one of the two lamps you're going to buy, plus a candy dish, framed photos, or pretty art books with beautiful covers and illustrations.

For example, Mary Louise Guertler, senior partner at McMillen, Inc., advises beginners always to remember that details make the difference between the ordinary and the special. A few of her hints include buying classic shapes for lamps, such as temple jars or a ball-shaped lamp in solid colors or white. When accessorizing a table, she says to keep taller things at the back, and always leave space for someone to rest a drink. Be careful not to overdo. Too many accessories can create a look of chaos.

More Success Statements

Don't skimp on the carpeting and throw pillows. An oriental rug adds a warm, rich touch that can "anchor" your living room. It doesn't matter if it's a fake, as long as it looks good. It's the effect that counts. Throw pillows—in needlepoint, cotton, or chintz—also convey a sense of the upscale life you'll have when you're at the top of the heap. If you're handy with a needle, make the pillows yourself. Just be sure they're coordinated, and don't use too many. If you put a big bunch of pillows on a couch, there's no room to sit—or lie down, as the case may be.

Books add a lot to the look of a room, as well as to your mind. Have at least one piece of furniture you can display them in. Plus, people are always interested in your choice of reading matter. You can make any impression you like by the books you display—from sexy to spiritual. Alice, a young ad executive, had a well-stocked bookcase filled with Shakespeare, Shelley, and Tolstoy. When one of her more pompous dates asked her, "What books do you read?" she pointed casually to her impressive collection of classics. (Quick save, as she hadn't gotten around to reading all of them yet.)

A Bedtime Story

Do *real* men sleep in frilly beds? According to dear Mario B.—"Of course they do! Men are attracted to soft, feminine women who wear pink and blue—not lumber jackets." That's why men find women's beds far more irresistible than their own. Don't let the chance pass to make yours supersensual. Get the fluffiest pillows you can find. Make sure the sheets smell sweet from fabric softener or a spray of your favorite cologne.

Buy all-cotton sheets with the highest thread count you can afford; they'll feel softer to the skin. This is not the time to use Mickey Mouse prints or some dark and dreary color. Best to go for white and lacy, with a soft embroidered trim. Mario tells the story of a couple whose bedroom he decorated with a frilly, canopied, all-white bed. He added lots of lace, ruffles, and trimmings. Initially, the husband was concerned that the style was too feminine and not somewhere a "real man" would sleep. Finally, he climbed into the bed—and was so comfortable, he refused to get out for two days!

An Anal-Retentive Apartment

So what if you're hyper about insisting that your home be maintained in superclean condition? Having order in your life always makes you feel better about yourself and the world in general. Going home to a disorganized apartment makes you feel out of control—and that can spill over into the rest of your life.

The most elegantly decorated digs don't impress anyone if they're not neat and clean. Keeping it littered like a pigsty makes you come across as if you haven't quite grown up yet. Don't fail to vacuum and dust at least once in a while. It's a drag, but worth it. A clean apartment speaks volumes about you and your standards. Besides, an energetic cleaning session is a great way to lose weight. And, don't forget, a tidy bathroom is a must. A dirty john is the biggest turnoff there is. A sink full of hair, a grimy tub, and, worst of all, ring-around-the-toilet, are just plain disgusting.

Don't be a pack rat. Set aside one day to de-clutter your apartment of unnecessary junk—like six month-old magazines that you haven't gotten around to reading, last year's Christmas cards, old letters, and shopping bags full of shopping bags. You also should unclutter your closets. If you can't decide which clothes to throw away, just put the possible discards in a shopping bag at the back of the closet. If you find you haven't worn them after a few months, chuck them. (Okay, you can wait a little longer, but not much!)

EVERYDAY NO-NO'S

Take a few minutes every morning to make sure you haven't left things lying around that you don't particularly want others to see—especially if that certain someone comes by unexpectedly. A few uh-uhs:

- An unmade bed
- Underwear and stockings hanging on the shower stall
- Last night's leftovers on the kitchen counter
- Ashtrays filled with cigarette butts
- Breakfast dishes on the table
- Razors lying on the bathroom sink
- Personal hygiene items scattered about (stow them away in a drawer)

Learn from the Best

The preceding pages are just a basic blueprint to get you started in the art of living a beautiful life. Like anything else, you have to educate yourself when it comes to decorating. Here are a few suggestions to get you started:

Learn from the experts. Look at interior-design magazines (see list at end of chapter). Haunt bookstores! Most have a section devoted to home furnishings. You'll find some great do-it-yourself ideas that range from somewhat complicated to really simple.

Check out upscale stores. Go to better department and home-furnishing stores and learn from their model rooms; it'll improve your taste. Zero in on the details. You can try to replicate the styles you like by hitting flea markets, garage sales, and inexpensive or discount stores for important pieces and accessories.

Visit museums, auctions, and decorator show houses. Anyplace where good design is on display is worth your while. You'll soon learn to recognize quality when you see it.

Okay—now go for it! You may make a few mistakes along the way, but it's the price you pay for trying to educate your eye. Money alone won't make your surroundings perfect. There are wealthy folks out there whose homes scream money and little else. As long as you care about your environment and are willing to invest the time, your place can and will give off the right vibes about you and your taste.

Wrap-Up

- Make sure your home reflects your sense of self.

- Your surroundings affect you mentally, for better or worse.

- Psych out your decorating personality.

- Get going on the basics.

- Make sure your bedroom is irresistible.

- Remember, the finishing touches make all the difference.

- Educate yourself about the basics of decorating.

- Expect your taste to change over time.

Decorating Sources

- √ Museum stores
- √ Thrift shops
- √ Flea markets
- √ The family basement
- √ Garage and tag sales

Home-Furnishings Outlets

- √ Bed Bath & Beyond: No 800 number. Corporate office: (201) 379-1520
- √ The Bombay Company: (800) 829-7789
- √ Calico Corners: (800) 213-6366
- √ Crate & Barrel: (800) 323-5461
- √ Ikea: (800) 434-4532
- √ Pier 1: (800) 447-4371 for Store Locator
- √ Pottery Barn: (800) 922-5507

Manufacturers' outlets: Found in discount malls across the country, they carry overruns (and sometimes slightly imperfect) merchandise from top-name designers.

Interior-Design Magazines

- √ *Architectural Digest*
- √ *Better Homes and Gardens*
- √ *Country Living*
- √ *Elle Decor*

√ *House Beautiful*

√ *House and Garden*

√ *Martha Stewart Living*

√ *Metropolitan Home*

√ *Southern Accents*

√ *Traditional Home*

√ *Veranda*

Decorating Books

√ *Chic, Simple Home*, by Kim Johnson and Jeff Stone (Knopf)

√ *Shortcuts to Great Decorating*, by Mary Gilliatt (Little, Brown)

√ *Complete Home Decorating Book*, by Nicholas Barnard (Dorling-Kindersley)

twenty-one

Solo or Share?

It's no secret that rents are sky-high these days. It used to be a rule of thumb that your rent shouldn't exceed one week's salary. Today, you're lucky if you can get a decent place to live for twice that amount. It's no wonder that most recent grads go roommate shopping even before they look for a place to live.

Just a word about where you live: Every city has its most and least-desirable areas. It all depends on your pocketbook. But try for some basic elements: security, especially in large cities like New York, Chicago, or Los Angeles; accessibility, whether by car or public transportation; and a decent neighborhood. Before you sign any lease, check out the neighborhood at night. If it's desolate—or if the street life makes you uneasy—keep shopping for a place to live.

Once you've found the right abode, you're up for the big question: solo or share? Some people prefer the companionship of a same-sex roommate; some opt for living with their Significant Other or a male friend. Either way, it means deciding who pays what. Obviously, having a roommate should save money and provide live-in company, but be forewarned—not every situation has a happy ending.

Take Laurie. When her roommate married and left, Laurie invited Julia, a longtime business associate, to move in. She was sure she knew what Julia was all about. She was 100 percent wrong. Julia kept telling Laurie she'd pay her share of the rent "next week." After a few months of excuses, Laurie finally realized that she'd been too trusting and that "next week" would never come. Julia even ran up huge phone bills which Laurie had to pay because the phone was in her name. After six months, without seeing a penny from Julia, Laurie asked her to leave. She immediately resolved to take these important steps to avoid another financial fiasco:

1. Insist on a month's rent in advance, as well as prompt payment every month.

2. Ask her roommate to have her own phone installed so that there would be two separate phone bills.

3. Make sure both names are on the lease so that responsibility for the rent is shared.

Pet Peeves

How do you find out if you and your roommate-to-be are a perfect pair or a disastrous duo? One way to help you decide is to take the time to sit down and talk out your pet peeves with your prospective roommate *before* you decide to live together. Our friend Victoria did just that. She and her friend, Brooke, let it all hang out when they drew up their personal Pet Peeves list. Vicki listed a few things that drive her crazy—the smell of cigarette smoke in the early A.M.; clothes scattered everywhere; even her fixation for having the toilet paper hang from the top, not underneath. (Believe it or not, people make a big issue over the tissue! Ann Landers received a record volume of mail when she asked readers for their preference on this very subject.)

Remember, while you may enjoy being with someone socially or professionally, living with that person is a whole new ball game.

Roommate-from-Hell stories are legion. Caitlin says that she had a series of roommates she'd like to forget forever. One was a slob beyond belief, who not only dropped everything she wore on the floor until it formed its own little clothes mountain, but also had a habit of hardly ever taking a bath. Although Caitlin's next roommate was cleaner, she had another kind of problem—a case of sticky fingers. She got her kicks by stealing and didn't hesitate to lift Caitlin's jewelry, clothes, and even her underwear!

The woods are full of stories of roommates who seemed to be perfect for each other but were classic mismatches. Take the example of Cara and Alison, who had been fast friends since their high school days in Cincinnati. Their friendship continued through college—and when they both landed jobs at a New York ad agency after graduation, they decided to share an apartment.

It was a disaster.

To put it in Cara's words, Alison was a total slob—clothes on the living-room couch, dirty dishes piled up in the kitchen sink, her bed perpetually unmade.

On the other hand, Alison complained that she hadn't realized how selfish and inconsiderate Cara could be. She frequently commandeered their one bedroom with a succession of sleep-over dates, and Alison had to make do on the living-room sofa. Not surprisingly, the former best friends wound up not speaking to each other and eventually went their separate ways.

As great as it may sound, even platonic male/female apartment-sharing can be difficult. In Angela's case, she felt it was not only practical, but very sophisticated to move in with her brother's friend, Allen, a would-be actor/model, working temporarily as a waiter. Gregarious and fun-loving (that was why Angela wanted to be his roommate), Allen would often invite his pals—perhaps a dozen of them—to "stop by for a drink." Around midnight, when Angela felt she'd fall over if she didn't get some sleep, the party would still be going strong.

Everything else was just fine. Allen paid his share of the expenses, and always on time. He was neat and tidy; after his friends finally left, he always cleaned up the mess. But Angela's home— her haven, her refuge from the pressures of daily life—didn't exist anymore. Reluctantly, she found another roommate.

Even if you have to swing the rent and expenses on your own for a month, it's better than living with the proverbial Roommate from Hell. Follow our guidelines, learn from these examples, and you'll find the right housemate.

Setting Ground Rules

There's an important message here: With roommates, just as in marriage, you never really know a person until you live with him or her. It's vital to set ground rules with a prospective roommate before signing the lease.

Some suggested stipulations:

- If you're both clean freaks, your rule could be: You mess it, you clean it. Now!

- If you're both on the sloppy side, you've found your perfect mate!

- Declare an off-limits area that's always to be kept neat and tidy, no matter what—like the living room.

- Rent or maintenance charges to be split down the middle. Ditto electricity bills. Long-distance calls paid for by the caller. All bills to be paid on time—no excuses.

- If you have only one bedroom, you each get your fair share of overnight ''guests'' as long as there's advance notice.

- Pet(s) only with the roomate's approval. Some people are allergic to, or just don't like, our furry friends.

- No parties without agreement. And if you don't include your roommate, you can cause hurt feelings.

- Discuss if you're a day or night person. If your roommate likes to get up with the birds and you don't, you'll have to make some compromises.

- No eating or drinking of food or beverages the other roommate has paid for.

- No borrowing clothes, jewelry, etc., without prior approval. Even with permission, it's considerate to offer to have the dress or suit cleaned after you've worn it.

- Discuss any personal habits that bug either of you—smacking gum, walking around naked, heavy perfume, etc.

Living in Harmony

For goodness sake, be cooperative and responsible. Do your equal share of apartment cleaning—vacuuming, dusting, cleaning the kitchen, etc. Ditto shopping for food.

Little things do mean a lot when it comes to keeping peace. Don't hog the TV if there's only one set. It's better to have two, anyway. If not, try the "Okay, you watch *The X-Files* tonight, I get *Ellen* next week" approach. It usually works. If you have a VCR, you can tape one program and watch the other.

Also, be sensitive to each other's personal problems. If your roommate is trying desperately to diet, don't stock the fridge with Häagen-Dazs. And when it comes to keeping your hands off your roommate's food, our friend Duane came up with a suggestion worthy of the UN. She says she drew an imaginary line down the middle of the fridge and the freezer. Everything on the right side was hers; stuff on the left belonged to her roommate—and they never crossed the line.

As for your roommate's phone calls, always, but always, be

responsible. Take a message and make sure your roommate gets it. A bulletin board for phone calls is usually a good idea. And even though it's difficult in a small apartment, try to give your roommate and her date some privacy. Don't be a fifth wheel whenever he's there. And, of course, we don't have to tell you not to get too cozy or to even think about coming on to him. All is not always fair in love—and this could start a war!

And speaking of no-no's, don't ever be late with your monthly rent check. You can damage your credit rating, as well as your roommate's, in no time flat. Prospective employers often run a credit check before hiring. A late-payment history can give off signals that you're careless and irresponsible about meeting deadlines. It rings a little bell in their heads that you might be a risky employee choice.

YOUR OWN SPACE

Finally, know yourself. If you really enjoy the company of another, in close quarters—and he or she meets your standards—go for it. But if you're basically a person who wants to do it your way, in your own space, sacrifice a little and get an apartment by yourself.

Furry Friends

So, let's assume you've finally got your own apartment and decorated it beautifully, yet you still feel something is missing. What to do? What you really want is a warm body, lots of kisses, someone who listens adoringly, loves your cooking, and is always eager to see you. Where-oh-where can you find it?

Get a pet! A furry friend is the best ammunition you can have against loneliness. It's a heartbeat to come home to. If you're worried about the responsibilities involved, don't despair. In most cities, you can find plenty of dog-walkers or cat-sitters. It's a good after-school source of income for young people, and you can also barter pet care with a friend or neighbor. They'll walk and feed Fido if you're out of town, and you'll find a way to reciprocate.

When you're single there's nothing like coming home to an adoring pup or a purring pussycat. It feels wonderful to have someone love you so much, and just as great to be able to return the love. Plus, they give great good-morning kisses—and don't snore!

Besides the fact that you love your pets, they can be a divining rod when it comes to Mr. Right or Wrong. You can tell a lot about a man by his reaction to animals. Almost invariably, a gentle, kind man responds well to a pet. Many animal experts think these four-footed friends are intuitive. Dogs, especially, seem to know who the good guys are. If your pet snubs your man, watch out. The Pet Patrol has given you fair warning.

Getting It Together

Whether solo or share, having your home life in order is just as important as the way you look and dress. To walk in and see what you've done—with your own taste and sense of style—is one of the most satisfying self-esteem builders you can have. Whether you open the door to a roommate, a lover, a pet, or just your very own digs, make sure your home says and is all the things you want it to be.

QUICK CAPSULE: ROOMMATE TIPS

- If you plan to share, make sure you know the other person is responsible about money.
- Set ground rules for each other.
- Longtime friends don't always make compatible roommates.
- Do your share of all household chores, no matter how grubby.
- Don't risk your credit rating by paying bills late.
- Give your roommate the same consideration you want for yourself.

twenty-two

The Care and Feeding of Your Social Life

Hitting the Party Circuit

When you go to a party, are you so shy and ill at ease that you'd rather crouch in a corner than try to talk to strangers? Such awkward behavior is not only self-defeating, it certainly won't put you on anyone's "Most Wanted" guest list. Developing your social IQ is one of the most important things you can do for yourself. Why? Believe it or not, the very same skills you use as a guest at a cocktail or dinner party are the ones you also need in order to succeed in business. Learning how to work a room—mingling with anyone and everyone, perfecting the art of cocktail conversation, and even overcoming your fear of talking to strangers—spills directly over into other parts of your life.

Outgoing people (and you can *learn* to be outgoing) are invariably the most effective and compelling speakers at business meetings. They not only communicate their ideas well, but they know how to deal with people effectively at the same time. So here's how to revamp your party persona and acquire some guest appeal.

Overcoming "Fear of Guesting"

Let's say you're invited to a party (social or business), and you're flying solo. The very idea of walking into a room primarily populated with strangers is giving you the queasies. How to deal with this everyday but anxiety-producing affliction?

Regardless of what kind of affair it is, many people—no matter how confident they seem—get nervous before going to a gathering. Especially if they're arriving alone. We don't want you to lose any sleep over this, so here's how to handle it.

One obvious solution is to ask the host if you can bring a friend or date. Having a pal on hand definitely eases those first awkward moments. But, let's assume you've got to go it alone.

Before you set off for the party, psych yourself up—and also take the time to look your best. It's worth it. Knowing you're sharply turned out can pump up your self-confidence. Remind yourself that you're probably not the only unaccompanied person who'll be there, so shed the "me against the world" attitude. When you walk in the door, hold your head high—and smile. You're not going to the guillotine, just a party. Once inside—find your host as soon as possible. If he or she is smart, you'll be introduced to a few other guests right off the bat.

If you're left at loose ends, scan the room for a familiar face. When the party is strangers-only, approach a person or group that looks appealing and introduce yourself.

The best way to get conversation started is to establish a point of commonality. "Are you a friend of Cindy's? Do you work with her at Mega-Fax Micro-Chip?" There's got to be something in common that brought you all together. Use that something to get the ball rolling.

Most business events use name tags. They may look tacky but

they provide great information—not only names but also company, title, and department. In that respect, they're a great tool. Use them!

When meeting new people, always remember this: There is virtually no one, male or female, who won't respond to your interest in them. People love talking about themselves. Giving them the opportunity to do so is the world's greatest ice-breaker.

If you want to get to know people, don't stand around with your arms folded and a glum look on your face. You'll seem stiff and unapproachable. What your body language is saying is "Leave me alone!" Instead, put a smile on your face, uncross your arms, and relax a little. It helps to hold a "prop" in your hand, like a drink, a plate of food, whatever.

The Ideal Guest

Becoming an ideal guest is a reasonable goal within anyone's reach. The rewards are terrific—you'll not only be welcome everywhere—you'll also be considered an asset to any party. The art of "guesting," however, takes a little work. A great guest realizes that she can't just sit back and expect to be entertained. Even if she's a shy soul way down deep, she makes an effort to be friendly and talk with everyone. She introduces herself to people she hasn't met and works at remembering everybody's name. She's developed an easy line of chatter ("Isn't this a terrific view?" or "You remind me so much of a professor I had in college. Are you a Shakespearean scholar, too?") And she wouldn't dream of bringing up potentially explosive topics, like negative remarks about someone's politics or religion.

When she's at a seated dinner, she divides her time equally between the person on her left and her right. She realizes it's poor manners to ignore either side, even if she's mesmerized by one of her seatmates and bored by the other. She's a good listener, as well as an equally good conversationalist.

Hosts love this kind of guest because she doesn't require constant attention and can take care of herself. Plus, she's helping to keep the party going. By being proactive, she's achieved "special guest" status. You can, too.

GUESTING TIPS: Ready for Lesson 101? Here goes . . .

- It shows good guest manners to respond to an invitation promptly and arrive on time.

- While not absolutely necessary, it's a nice gesture to bring a little something—candy, a bottle of wine, a pretty book, or a flowering plant (not loose flowers—the hostess won't have time to find a vase or arrange them).

- Never be so gauche as to bring anyone to a party without first asking the host's permission. It's really rude, and people resent it.

- Always take the time to send a quick handwritten thank-you note, or call the next day to say how much you enjoyed the party. It's the kind of thoughtful touch that will loom large in your host's mind.

The same rules apply if your job requires you to attend business functions: answer the invitation as soon as you get it, try to arrive at the designated time, and send the host a thank-you note the next day.

Ducking Out

You feared the party was going to be a downer, and, sadly—you were right. There's not a soul in sight you want to spend five minutes with. Have a scenario ready to politely extricate yourself, like, "I'm so sorry, but I have to join some people for dinner," or "I've got an early meeting tomorrow."

If you're at a seated dinner, however, and there's a specific place for you, you're stuck. Grit your teeth, be as charming as possible, and leave as soon as it's acceptable to do so. Chalk it up to experience. Into each life some rain must fall. The odds are that the next party won't be a drizzler.

And by the way, it's the ultimate in rudeness to switch place cards. If you have a valid reason for not wanting to sit next to someone, explain it to your host and see if she'll agree to change your seat. Most dinner party hosts give a lot of time and thought to planning who sits next to whom, and they don't look kindly on guests who decide to do it their way. In fact, people who play the card-switching game are rarely invited back. After all, you're not only challenging the host's prerogative, you're trespassing on her turf.

Turning the Tables

These days there are more single women out there than ever before. Unfortunately, lots of them are languishing at home, waiting for the phone to ring and the invitations to pour in. Smart women, like you, know it doesn't work that way. Again, be proactive. Instead of waiting (and hoping) for good things to fall into your lap, you make them happen instead.

Turn the tables. You do the inviting and make your home the nucleus of social activities. Get known in your circle of friends as the catalyst who stirs things up.

But before you embark on your entertainment course, decide what you want to accomplish. Parties can achieve all sorts of wonderful things—like gathering your closest chums together for fun and games; paying back some of the people who've entertained you;

impressing your co-workers or even your boss; or taking your casual male friendships to a more intimate level. If you really want to get to know a particular someone, there's no better way than to ask him to *your* party, where you're the focus for the evening.

If you're single and ambitious, there are a million reasons why you should entertain and very few real excuses why you shouldn't. Don't tell yourself you can't because you haven't the time . . . or the ability . . . or the money . . . and your apartment is too small, you don't have enough glasses, plates, etc. Those are usually alibis that delay your launch into the Good Life. Remember, people don't expect to be entertained like royalty. They just want to relax and have a good time. Sure, the food and drinks count, but they alone don't guarantee a successful evening.

Concentrate on why you should give a party. Keep your eye focused on what it can do for your career, as well as your love/ social life in general. Those who are on their way up—as well as the lucky ones who are already there—know this instinctively. They take entertaining seriously and view it not only as a way to gather friends together but a bona fide opportunity to accomplish a goal. They work almost as hard at being a successful party-giver as they do at their jobs.

If you feel uneasy about throwing a party all by your lonesome—just join forces, and combine guest lists with a friend (or friends) and host it together. This will not only bolster your courage, it'll also cut costs and give you an opportunity to meet new people.

When You're the Host

If you want to be an unforgettable hostess, with people champing at the bit to be invited to your parties, do it with wit and style. Work on getting a reputation for giving great get-togethers. You're calling the shots when you play hostess, and you're starring in a role you can control. Giving a smashing performance requires laying basic groundwork as well as clever strategizing. Here are a few success secrets of some of the top party givers we know:

1. **Send out advance signals that yours is a can't-miss party.** How? Set the tone by sending out the most intriguing, colorful, and imaginative invitations you can. You might even create something fabulous and unique on your computer. Using plain old fill-in-the-blanks types you find in a stationery store are too ho-hum. Coming up with a memorable invitation is worth the effort because it sets the mood.

2. **Follow up your invitation with a phone call.** Although not mandatory, this is a good idea because you can emphasize to your guests how much you want them to come. It makes people feel special. Mention that you've asked some people whom you think they'll enjoy meeting. Everybody can use that little extra push.

3. **Invite the most interesting people possible.** The right guest list can do more for your image than a ton of caviar. Get together as eclectic a group as you can. Mix and mingle people of all ages, professions, and achievement levels. Feel free to reach outside the realm of your usual social and business friends. Inviting the same chums all the time is the path of least resistance. And it's boring. Always include new people, and continuously enlarge your circle. It doesn't matter if you don't know every invitee all that well. Even if you're not a bosom buddy, a lot of people will be glad to get your invitation.

4. **Make sure everyone gets to know one another pronto!** We can't emphasize this enough. Plunge right in and establish instant rapport among your guests. This will do more than break the ice, it'll really get the party cracking. When you introduce people, don't just reel off everyone's name. Point out whatever you think they may have in

common (political views, same section of the country), or something you feel the other person would enjoy knowing: "Tom, meet Barbara. She's an exercise freak like you and just ran in the New York City Marathon." Tom now knows a lot more about Barbara than her name.

Instead of using name tags, one hostess types up a humorous tip sheet, "Meet Your Party Mates," which she hands out to all her guests when they walk in. Besides the usual professional descriptions—"Gary is an investment banker at Ego & Greed Inc."—she always includes a funny or intriguing fact. If she doesn't know one, she makes it up. Although it requires a little effort on her part, guests are flattered and amused by her descriptions of them. It starts a little buzz, and one by one they begin going over to each other, saying things like, "Bill, the party sheet says you have a yellow Lab, and so do I. Shouldn't they meet?" You don't have to be a Rosie O'Donnell to put this tip sheet together. Even if it's just name, company and job, people appreciate anything that helps them get to know each other more easily.

5. **Create a mood**. Some parties have an aura that brings out the best in people. It's created by a lot of subtle things—bits and pieces that add up to either a roaring success or a ho-hum evening. One important element is something as simple as lighting. Bright lights—especially overheads—can kill a party early on. They make guests feel exposed, as if they're in a convention center. Bad lighting stifles conversation, eliminates any sense of intimacy, and exaggerates every blemish. People feel uncomfortable and don't even realize why. That fabled hostess, the Duchess of Windsor, always insisted on keeping the lights low.

Add to the ambiance by using as many candles as possible, especially low votives in clear-glass containers that twinkle away. One tip is to put them in front of mirrors where they'll sparkle like little jewels. There's something mesmerizing about all that flickering fire.

You don't have fancy candleholders? Not to worry! Scoop out some fruits and vegetables—apples or artichokes, for instance—set candles in them, and stand back for the applause. This is especially effective if you put them on green leaves, set on a mirrored tray.

EASY TIPS

- When you serve hors d'oeuvres, even a humble chunk of cheese takes on a touch of glamour if you set it in a pretty straw basket with a doily underneath, or on an inexpensive lacquered tray. Set it off with the head of a big flower— an African daisy, an oversized mum, a sunflower, or even a rose in full bloom are all perfect examples.
- Another great party starter is to create one special drink to serve when guests arrive. It sets a festive mood. Some good choices are margaritas, a big pitcher of sangria with lots of orange and lemon slices floating in it, or flutes filled with inexpensive champagne and big red strawberries. Lots of other unique drinks can be created by using ready-made cocktail mixes you can buy in the supermarket—like strawberry margaritas, banana daiquiris, whiskey sours, Tom Collinses, and piña coladas.
- Stem glasses—made of real glass, not plastic—are always the prettiest to serve anything in, even beer. If you want to get a little creative, tie each stem with a colorful ribbon.

---

6. **Manufacture excitement.** From the moment your guests arrive, make them glad they came. You can do that by creating a magical environment. Concentrate on the Three *S*s—**S**ound, **S**mell, and **S**ight. Here's how:

- Put on a CD that makes people want to mix and mingle. Anything with a Latino beat usually works, but don't play it so loudly that people can't hear one another talk.

- A sensational smell makes everyone feel good; delectable cooking aromas tickle the taste buds.

- A room full of delicately scented candles—pine, cy-
  prus, lemon—is equally irresistible. (Forget about
  those overpowering, super-sweet candles like strawberry, pineapple, etc. They're cheap and they smell it.
  Nix to incense, too, unless you're doing something il-
  legal or religious.)

- Color splashed all over your apartment catches the eye
  and puts people in the party mood. Fresh flowers are
  a nice touch. If you can't afford big bunches, an
  equally effective trick is to place single stems in small
  bud vases around the room. An inexpensive alternative
  to flowers is to string up big, colorful balloons. Tie
  them with bright curly ribbons. You can even write a
  personal message on the balloons with a soft felt-tip
  pen. Your food should be colorful too, like a rainbow.
  Coordinate it as carefully as if you were painting a
  picture. Yellow, red, and green food, placed on the
  same plate, seems to taste even better.

7. **Serve all-time favorites**. Why bother with exotic recipes
   when it works best to stick with the things everyone
   loves—Italian or all-American? Try lasagna, any gourmet
   pizza, or some kind of pasta. If you want to go the American route, chili or meat loaf are all-time favorites. All of
   these are easy to fix and consistent crowd-pleasers. Besides, you can prepare this kind of food beforehand, and
   it's not very expensive.

   When you're making meals like these, it doesn't cost
   that much more to fix extra portions in case any last-
   minute guests show up. It's always better to have too
   much than too little.

   Unless you're Julia Child, don't ever try a complicated new recipe when you entertain. When you're feeding
   a crowd, it's no time to experiment. You don't need any
   extra worries! For goodness sake, if you do want to play
   Julia and serve something new, prepare it at least once
   before the party. After all, you want it to be as good as
   you can make it. We've included the titles of some of the

most popular and easy-to-follow cookbooks at the end of this chapter to give you a few recipe ideas.

Not everyone likes to cook, or wants to. In that case, it's perfectly okay to serve take-out food. Certain cuisines are better than others for this, like Mexican, Italian, Chinese, or Thai. Just remove the food from its container and put it in your prettiest serving dish.

8. **Just Desserts.** If you're really worried about what kind of food to serve and can't decide, a surefire crowd-pleaser is a Desserts Only party. Serve only delicious, delectable desserts that no one can resist. Include something as all-American as blueberry cobbler or good old apple pie. There'll always be a few dieters, so bring out the low-fat cookies and also serve a big fruit salad full of every fruit or berry that's in season. You can throw in a few candied dates or figs for a gourmet touch. Remember, you don't have to prepare any of these desserts yourself. Just go to your favorite supermarket or bakery and shop to your heart's (and pocketbook's) content.

Bring Ben and Jerry into your house. Have a "Fix Your Own Sundae" party. Besides every flavor you can haul home (of course, include some fat-free ice cream and/ or frozen yogurt), you can go nuts with the toppings: hot fudge and butterscotch sauces, crushed M&M's, whipped cream, maraschino cherries, wet nuts, Heath-Bar crunch, Reese's Pieces, raisins, bananas, granola, and sprinkles: chocolate or multicolored. Yum!

For beverages, you can serve herbal tea or exotic coffees. A slightly sweet wine also works. Liqueurs and cordials like Amaretto, Grand Marnier, Drambuie, Cointreau, and/or Creme de Menthe are great over ice. They're also expensive and potent, so it's perfectly all right to stretch them with cold water.

Your invitation for this kind of party could say something like "Get Your Just Desserts," etc. Naturally, guests will be asked to come after the dinner hour, like 9.00 P.M. or so.

9. **Lookin' Good.** Even if your party invite says casual dress, you can—and should—wear something sensational. After all, you're the star and are allowed to dress any way you want. But save the safe little black number for another time—never wear just any old outfit.

10. **Entertain when no one else does.** Got the "January Postholiday Blues" or the "Will-This-Heat-Ever-End August Angst"? Everybody else probably does, too. Take advantage of it. Give a party. Who wouldn't welcome a lift like a lazy Sunday winter brunch or a casual cocktail party in the park on a sultry summer night?

   Take advantage of off-season downtime to entertain, because nothing else is happening. A savvy hostess knows people are yearning for something fun to do. If you're squeezed for space, or your apartment isn't up for entertaining, don't despair. There are lots of alternatives—like a picnic in the park, an ice skating party, or renting a meeting room at a club for a minimal fee. There are also historical sites or the beach. You might even borrow a friend's apartment, patio, or pool deck. Some apartment buildings have a communal space or rooftop you can use. The point is, it's far better to entertain than to make excuses why you can't.

11. **Celebrate Big Events.** Sports events, for instance, give you a great excuse to entertain. A Super Bowl party, with beer and chili, is a natural. Or you could invite people to watch the Grammy Awards or that perennial favorite, the Oscars. You can serve something as simple as peanuts, popcorn, and hotdogs, or have pizza delivered. Add the wine, beer, Diet Coke, etc.

12. **Create your own "Toberizer."** Serve one really irresistible item, and give it an equally memorable name. Barbara Tober, former editor of *Brides* magazine, is known for her Pecan Clouds, cookies that all her friends find absolutely delicious. They sure worked magic for Barbara! At a party several years ago, she met Donald: handsome, single, and very eligible. When she learned he was leaving

on a business trip, Barbara decided to make sure he'd call her when he returned. She baked a batch of Pecan Clouds and left them at his apartment building, along with a little note.

Yes, he called her, *yes,* they started dating, and *yes,* they got married, one year to the day of their first meeting. The cookie recipe is framed and hangs in a place of honor in their home, as a shining symbol of the Cookie Cupid that brought them together. Barbara's agreed to share it with you, and wishes you the best of luck.

PECAN CLOUDS

1 pound lightly salted butter, room temperature
10 tablespoons sugar or 8 tablespoons fructose
2 teaspoons vanilla
4 cups sifted all-purpose flour
4 cups very finely ground pecans
1 cup (or more) powdered sugar
80 to 100 pecan halves

Fit electric mixer with whisk, if available. Beat butter on high until creamy and almost white. Beat in sugar or fructose one tablespoon at a time. Add vanilla and stir to blend.

Resift flour and slowly blend into butter mixture. Mix in ground pecans 1 cup at a time. Continue beating on high until very fluffy, at least 3 to 5 minutes. Refrigerate dough for about an hour to make handling easier.

Preheat oven to 325°F. Form dough into balls the size of a small walnut and arrange in rows on baking sheet. Press pecan half into each cookie. Bake until golden brown, 15 to 20 minutes. Let cool slightly, then sift powdered sugar over top. Cool completely and store in airtight containers.

Makes about 8 dozen. Recipe can be halved, but you won't want to.

As valuable as these ideas are, none of them will work without the basics: organization, having your house in order, and a realistic approach. Take care of the following details and you've got it made:

Party Strategy Sheet:

√ **Write it down.** Make a party checklist, just as you would for a business project or meeting. Don't say—oh, sure I'll remember to do that. How could I forget? To be safe, write it down. See a sample checklist at the end of this chapter.

√ **Check your guests' calendars.** This is particularly important if you're planning a dinner party and you want to get certain people there. If it's a spur-of-the-moment plan, just phone everyone and hope that most of them can make it.

√ **Plan the menu.** Don't leave it for a few days before, even if you're having it catered or delivered by your neighborhood pizza palace.

√ **Make sure you have enough china, glasses, flatware, etc.** You can borrow them if you have to. Also, many discount chains and stationery stores sell great-looking plastic plates and paper napkins that coordinate. If you don't want to use plastic knives and forks, which are relatively expensive and hard to deal with anyway, these same stores also sell cheap, but good-looking glassware and cutlery.

√ **Stock up on wine, beer, and/or liquor.** But don't forget the go-alongs—tonic, soda, fruit juice, lemons, and limes. There's no rule, by the way, that says you have to serve hard liquor. Many hosts just offer wine and/or beer. Always have an assortment of nonalcoholic drinks on hand because not everyone imbibes. Perrier, iced tea or coffee, cranberry juice, and diet soda served with a slice of lime should do it.

√ **Spiff up your digs.** Along with getting organized, it's equally important to make sure your home is sparkling clean.

The most expensive food and flowers can't make up for tattered towels in the bathroom, dusty shelves, and smudges on the mirrors. Now's the time to throw out old magazines and vacuum the rugs. If your sofa or chairs look tired and worn, drape a bright piece of fabric over them. Even an oversized scarf or shawl will work. Another idea is to buy at least three large pots of colorful flowering plants that are in season and group them together. It adds a big splash of color and creates a great effect.

√ **Don't bite off more than you can chew.** If you have a studio apartment or a smallish living room, don't invite half the world. Sure, it's fun to be crowded but it's uncomfortable to be squashed together like sardines. People don't have a chance to get to know one another in an overcrowded, noisy setting.

√ **Be a good friend.** For the guest who's had one too many, offer to call a taxi or else ask someone to drop her or him home. Yes, it's a bit awkward, but it's not worth taking the chance of letting someone drive while under the influence.

√ **Don't go it alone.** Appoint a friend to be the official bartender. Lots of people love to do this. Besides, you need to mix and mingle with your guests and not lose time fixing drinks.

√ **Be early—not just on time for your party!** Plan to be all dressed, every hair in place, nail polish dry, apartment perfect, thirty minutes before your guests are scheduled to arrive. That way, if any little thing goes wrong at the last minute, you'll have time to take care of it. Even if everything is just as it should be, that half hour of simply sitting by yourself will help you to defrazzle.

The most successful hosts are the ones who are obviously enjoying themselves, because they've planned so well in advance that everything works as smoothly as a state dinner at the White House.

Finito

We hope this chapter will launch you on your party circuit career. Entertaining is another skill that gets better and easier the more you do it. Women who know how to entertain, even on a limited budget, become known for their flair and style. Everyone wants to be on their guest list because they know they'll have a wonderful time. Entertaining can be a key part of putting together The Right Life. If you don't start now, how can you get there?

Party Checklist

√ Purpose:

√ Date:

√ Time:

√ Place:

√ Budget:

√ Number of guests:

√ Invitations:

√ Kind of party:

√ Decorations:

√ Lighting:

√ Music:

√ Food:

√ Drinks:

Helpful Entertaining Books

- *Better Homes and Gardens Cook Book*, (Better Homes and Gardens Books). The best-selling cookbook of all time. Its expanded section on basics should be a big help to the Culinarily Challenged.

- *The Complete Party Book*, by Don Ernstein (Viking Studio). Step-by-step guide, plus recipes and ideas for parties of all sizes.

- *Joy of Cooking*, by Irma S. Rombauer and Marion Rombauer Becker (Bobbs-Merrill). Considered the grandmother of cookbooks, it contains classic recipes described in a very practical way.

- *The Kitchen Survival Guide*, by Lora Brody (Morrow). A ground-zero book for people who can't distinguish between a cleaver and a Cuisinart.

- Martha Stewart's *Collected Recipes for Every Day* (Clarkson Potter).

- *Now You're Cooking*, by Elaine Korn (Harlow & Ratner). An award-winning kitchen primer that starts with how to hold a kitchen knife.

- *Silver Palate Cookbooks*, any of them, by Julee Rosso and Sheila Lukens (Workman). Simple, readable recipes with flair.

And, if long lists of ingredients turn you off, here are two cookbooks that contain recipes with only three ingredients:

- *Recipes 1-2-3*, by Rozanne Gold (Viking Studio).

- *Cooking with Three Ingredients*, by Andrew Scholoss (HarperCollins).

Magazines

- *Gourmet*
- *Bon Appetit*
- *Martha Stewart Living*

All these publications feature scrumptious-looking photos and creative presentation ideas.

twenty-three

Max-ing Your Money

How Not to Get Shortchanged

Are you baffled by banking? Is trying to manage your money making you miserable? Does the mere idea of investing seem incomprehensible to you? Well, it's time to get your financial act together! Successful people carefully monitor their money from the day they start making it. And they don't stop even when they get to the top! You may not be bringing home that $100,000-plus paycheck yet, but you still want a taste of the good life. It isn't easy on a slim salary.

No matter what your income is, it's dumb to let any of it slip through your fingers. While we don't claim to be financial experts, we do know that learning how to manage money is the basis of every fortune that was ever made. Regardless of your income, you can make your dollars stretch further if you learn good financial habits early on. The lower your income, the more important it is that you make the most of what you've got. If you don't have the luxury of a big fat salary or a generous Christmas bonus to fall back on, it's more critical than ever.

Presumably, one of your reasons for working is to participate in the Good Life to come. While you don't have to have megabucks to do this, you do have to be willing to take control of your financial life. Taking control means you've got to pull yourself out of fiscal illiteracy and educate yourself in the ABC's of personal money management.

Everyday Rules

There are a few basic, everyday rules to follow if you want to hold on to your hard-earned cash. They may sound obvious, but you'd be surprised at how often people ignore them and get burned in the process.

The first rule is to figure out exactly how you're spending your money. A key part of financial planning is tracking, as well as reducing, spending. The simplest way to do this is to keep a daily spending diary for a month. Write down everything, even magazine or newspaper purchases. Then look over your outlays with a cold, hard eye to see what you could have done without and really wouldn't have missed. You'll be amazed at all the unnecessary extras you buy on impulse.

The second rule is to set up a monthly budget. Once you know where your money is going, decide where you can cut back. Obviously, expenditures like taxes, rent, medical/dental expenses (not covered by your health plan), student loan payments, car loan payments, and automobile insurance are nonnegotiable. Other expenses, such as telephone, utilities, food, transportation, etc., are flexible to a degree and can be trimmed. Putting these costs down on paper makes them easier to grasp. How do you know if you're spending too much? Easy. Compare your outgo with your income. If you come up with a negative number, you've got to move fast and make some tough choices.

Start with your flexible expenditures. Is your phone bill sky-high because of hour-long chats with your sister in Sacramento? Do you leave the lights and air-conditioning on all day, even when you're not there? Are you eating out several nights a week instead of cooking at home? Cutting back on these three items alone could save you a sizeable chunk of change.

On the other hand, let's say you're lucky enough to have a little money left each month. That's called your discretionary income. Some of this should be set aside for savings and emergencies; the rest is for items that are not absolutely vital—unnecessary clothing, trips, health club, entertainment, etc.

Tip: If you need budgeting help, there are numerous computer programs on the market to get you started. One of the newest is *Prosper*, from the well-known accounting firm Ernst & Young. This kit includes a software program, plus a book, *Personal Financial Planning Guide*, that's designed to help you set up a budget, calculate your 401(k) contribution (more on that later), and get you started on saving and investing. It costs about $70. (To order, call 1-800-225-5945.) Another program, *Quicken 5*, one of the world's best-selling personal finance software packages, also helps you organize your finances. It tracks your accounts, speeds bill paying, and helps you plan for the future. It sells for $39.95, plus shipping and handling. (Call 1-800-624-8742 to order.)

Here's some additional advice from financial planners:

- **House Rules**—Experts say you shouldn't spend more than 30 percent of your monthly take-home pay on rent. This may be hard to swing in big cities like New York, San Francisco, Miami, Los Angeles, or Chicago, unless you have someone to share expenses.

- **Savings Policy**—Like most young career professionals, you're probably not saving enough money to meet your future financial goals. Whatever it is you want, you've got to have a plan to get there. Experts advise that you try to save at least 10 percent of your take-home pay every month to build up your nest egg. The best way to do this is to have your company automatically deduct the money from your salary and deposit it into whatever account you designate. (More information to follow on the types of accounts you can choose from). This is a no-brainer, and an effortless way to build a financial cushion for the future, as well as for emergencies. Look at it this way: Whenever you save money, it's almost like getting a raise.

Finance 101

Lots of us don't know how to manage money because we were never taught how. Unfortunately, schools don't teach us the financial basics: how to earn, spend, and save money. To take charge of your financial well-being, you've got to understand basic money talk. Here's a quick course on your financial options:

- **Checking Accounts**—Many banks don't charge for checking if you maintain a minimum balance, which varies from bank to bank. If you can't maintain the minimum, the bank will charge you a monthly fee. You'll also be charged for each check you write. Scout around for the lowest-cost checking account you can find. Talk to friends, use the Yellow Pages, and call a few banks. Some of them allow you to combine your checking and savings accounts in order to meet their minimum balance requirement.

- **Savings Account**—This is the simplest and most conservative way to save money and earn interest on it.
  Advantage: You need very little cash to open one and it's liquid, meaning you can withdraw from it whenever you want to, with no penalty involved.
  Drawback: Banks tend to pay a very low rate of interest on your money. It's probably best to keep just enough in a savings account to qualify for free checking.

- **Certificates of Deposit (CDs)**—This is another savings product that pays a fixed interest rate if you keep your money invested in it for a specified period of time (known as the term of the CD.)

Advantage: CDs usually pay better rates than savings accounts. You make a one-time investment and earn interest until the term is complete.

Drawback: Your money isn't liquid. If you withdraw it before the end of the term, you get socked with a steep penalty. You're also stuck with the going interest rate determined at the time of purchase. This could be good or bad, depending on the fluctuation of interest rates.

- **Mutual Funds**—Once you have enough money in your bank account to qualify for free checking, some experts believe you should seriously consider mutual funds as a major part of your financial portfolio.

  What is a mutual fund? It's simply a type of investment that "pools" the money of thousands of people who then become shareholders of the fund. At the helm is a fund manager who determines how the money is to be invested. In effect, investing in mutual funds is an inexpensive way to hire a professional money manager. These funds are typically invested in stocks, bonds, and money market instruments, all known as securities.

  Advantage: You don't sink or swim, as you might if your money were invested in only one or two stocks. The term for this investment principle is diversification.

  Drawback: While generally regarded as safe, even mutual funds can be affected adversely by a catastrophic drop in the market. Also, there's no sure way to pick a winning mutual fund. Just because it performed fantastically last year doesn't mean it'll do the same this year.

  How do you select a mutual fund? Look in the financial section of your newspaper. Many publications rank mutual funds daily, based on their performance. You can call these funds directly for information. Should you decide to invest in a mutual fund, it's not necessary to go through a stockbroker. For more in-depth information, pick up a copy of the book *Get a Financial Life*, by Beth Kobliner, a writer for *Money* magazine. It's written especially for twenty- to thirty-year-olds. Ms. Kobliner tells you how to choose a mutual fund and even recommends a few worth considering because of their performance and low expense rate.

If you want to learn more than just the bottom-line basics outlined here, many colleges offer night and weekend courses in investments and money management, some targeted directly to women. You could also broaden your knowledge base by joining or starting an investment club. It works like this: each member contributes a set amount of money, which is then pooled and invested in securities recommended and approved by a majority of members. Along the way, you'll learn about the stock market and, with any luck, come out on top! There are also some suggested books at the end of this chapter to further your knowledge.

Money from Heaven

Now that you've learned something about the different money menus out there, let's zero in on what many people believe is the very best investment you can make for your future—your company's 401(k) Plan.

If your company has one—don't wait for the elevator—race up the stairs and sign on. A 401(k)—which sometimes is called a savings and investment plan, or retirement program—is the best financial deal you can make. For starters, most companies will match a portion of the amount you put into it. This means the company will contribute a set amount—say, fifty cents for every dollar you invest, up to a specified figure. That's an immediate 50 percent return on your money! It doesn't get much better than that.

Another big advantage of a 401(k) is that it's tax deferred—you don't pay taxes on the money you've invested until you withdraw it. In other words, if your salary is $30,000 and you invest $2,000 in the plan, you pay income tax on only $28,000.

Your contributions to the plan are automatically deducted from each salary check, leaving you no decisions to make. If you change jobs, you can usually roll the money over into your new company's 401(k). You still won't have to pay taxes on it unless you withdraw the money before you reach the age of 59 1/2.

Don't let anyone tell you you're too young to lock up your money in a 401(k). While it's true that you'd have to pay a penalty for early withdrawal, the tax-free growth of the plan could more than offset the penalty. Additionally, lots of companies allow employees to borrow against their 401(k). Another big benefit is that even if your firm folds, your money is protected.

The 401(k) is golden. Go for it!

Alternative: If you're not fortunate enough to work for a company that offers a 401(k) Plan, a good alternative is an IRA (Individual Retirement Account). You can invest up to $2,000 per year, and the tax advantages are very similar to those of a 401(k). The downside of an IRA versus a 401(k) Plan is that there are no matching contributions from your employer, and under current government regulations you can't borrow against it. Also, your contribution is limited to no more than $2,000 per year. Still, if you can afford it, it's a very good deal and one you shouldn't overlook.

How to Borrow Money

What if you don't have any discretionary income, or your investment in your company's 401(k) Plan has left you strapped for cash? You want to buy a new computer, upgrade your furniture, or take a special vacation. You need a few extra bucks, but the cupboard is bare. How do you handle it?

Easy. Just do what millions of other Americans do—get a bank loan. Most banks charge a relatively low rate of interest for a small personal loan, but it pays to shop around first. Besides providing the money you need, a bank loan also helps you establish a positive credit history, assuming, of course, that you pay it back on time. Taking out a loan is not all that complicated. In fact, banks are falling all over themselves to lend you money. They have simple applications and loan officers who are more than happy to meet with you. As long as you have a steady income, there should be no problem. Often you can get an on-the-spot decision.

Avoiding Rip-Offs

We've told you how to save, build, and borrow money. Here's how to hang on to what you've got and not get taken for a ride on the rip-off roadway.

- Always check your restaurant bill. If you find a discrepancy, speak up. Why should you pay for something you didn't have? Our friends Felice and Al were almost fleeced to the tune of $100 by a Manhattan restaurant where they were entertaining another couple for dinner. When the check came, Al thought it was a bit steep, since the whole table had only had two glasses of wine. When he double-checked the bill, Al discovered they'd been charged for two *bottles* of wine rather than the two *glasses* they'd actually ordered. When he pointed the mistake out to the waiter, it was corrected immediately.

- When you're in a restaurant, watch where you put your handbag. There are purse snatchers who specialize in stealing pocketbooks hanging on chair backs. Keep your purse on your lap or securely tucked between your feet. It's a real bummer to lose your cash, credit cards and checkbook in one fell swoop.

- Don't ever be talked into giving your credit card or telephone calling card numbers to strangers, especially on the phone. That's a favorite con man ploy. If you think it's a legitimate request, say you'll call them back. If it's a con job, odds are they'll hang up pronto or else give you a phony phone number.

- Don't count cash in public. And be especially careful when you're leaving an ATM. You just might inspire a passing thief to help himself to your wad.

- Don't ever allow workmen you don't know to have access to your apartment, especially when you're not there. That's how jewelry, VCRs, and other portable items suddenly turn up missing.

- Watch out for airport security checkpoints. The private security guards on duty are not police officers. They're hired to search for concealed weapons, drugs, or any other suspicious materials. Since they're not there to protect your belongings, refuse to put your purse on the rolling belt until you're able to follow it closely.

    If your handbag is going through and you're suddenly "beeped" and asked to walk through the metal detector again, announce loudly that you want your purse back immediately. Those few seconds—when your purse is sitting unattended on the other end of the belt—are all it takes for a quick-handed thief to rip you off.

- Don't put money, credit cards, or jewelry in luggage you're going to check. Hidden cameras have caught unscrupulous baggage handlers rummaging through every suitcase that comes on board.

- Never leave your purse, blank checks, jewelry, or cash in your office desk. It's no safer there than anyplace else, even if you lock your desk at night and when you go to lunch.

- Don't ever sign an agreement without reading it thoroughly. If you don't understand it, ask someone who's knowledge-able to explain it in layman's language. Also, don't be pressured into signing a contract on the spot just because you're told "Time is running out." Sez who? Lots of people make up phony deadlines. Any credible company will gladly give you a copy of the contract and time to study it before you sign.

Don't OD on ATMs

Those clever little automatic teller machines (ATMs) seem like a match made in heaven for Generation Xers. They offer easy access to your money, all day, all night. Although banks formerly didn't charge to use ATMs, beware! The free ride is virtually over. Today, you could pay up to $2 per transaction (sounds small, but it can multiply fast). To avoid these charges, check with your bank to see if there's a minimum balance required for free ATM use. Some banks impose an extra fee if you use the ATM for transactions other than simple withdrawals or deposits, such as transferring money or giving you your balance. They can also hit you with a fee if you use another bank's ATM.

The best policy is to limit yourself to a fixed number of ATM withdrawals a month, and then STICK to it. Using the machine say, once a week on a designated day, makes it easier to keep track of your money and can help you to discipline yourself at the same time. If you run out of cash, replenish it the old-fashioned way: go to the living, breathing teller at the bank where you do business. There's no charge for the service in most banks.

GENDER GOTCHAS

Why do most department stores alter men's clothing either for free or for a pittance? Alterations for women's clothing, on the other hand, not only cost you but also are usually quite pricey. Why do some dry cleaners charge more for cleaning a woman's suit than a man's? And while we're at it, why do women's haircuts cost an arm and a leg while a man's trim is much more reasonable?

What can you do about this? Speak up! Sometimes it works. In a department store we once overheard a woman customer going ballistic because her husband had paid zip to have his suit altered, but she was being charged plenty to have her dress hemmed and taken in. Guess what happened? The store reduced the charges. It often pays to complain.

Caution: Credit Cards Can Be Catastrophic

Isn't this great! The Bank of Ice Pack, Alaska, notifies you that you've been "preapproved" for their credit card! A week later it arrives, the newest addition to your collection of cards. Don't be flattered when companies send them your way. They're in it strictly for the bucks, and they're counting on getting yours.

Danger! Danger! Finding one more way to shop without paying cash immediately can be disastrous, especially if you're living from paycheck to paycheck.

Even though signing your name on those little credit card slips is so simple, this is not Monopoly Money. It's the Real Thing. If you get in over your head, you can end up owing a lot of money to a lot of people. That's why multiple cards can be a curse.

For example, if you're only making minimum monthly payments on your cards instead of paying the entire balance, just be aware that you're being charged interest on the *full* original amount. And, it's usually at an extremely high rate. Before you know it, your debt can be up to four figures or more!

Among other serious repercussions, credit card debt can even keep you from getting a job. Employers run checks to make sure prospective employees are credit-worthy. They frown on people who can't manage their own money. It makes them wonder if you'll be equally irresponsible on the job.

If you crawl into this Black Hole of debt, your credit rating will be shot to hell, your assets can be attached, and your salary garnished, meaning part of your pay can be legally taken by your creditor(s) until the debt is settled. This scenario could turn into a nightmare. If eventually you want to buy a high-ticket item—a dishwasher, a car, or a home—a bad credit rating can come back to haunt you, even years later.

Digging Out of Credit Card Hell

If you're in way over your head and owe lots of money to several different credit card companies, what do you do?

As much as it hurts—get out the scissors and destroy all but one or two cards. This way you can keep close tabs on what you're spending and what you owe. Sure, credit cards are convenient, but only if you remember you have to pay sooner or later for what you buy—and the sooner the better.

Besides cutting up your credit cards to prevent future damage, you could do one of several things. Consider contacting a credit card consultant to help you handle your problem. There are nonprofit consumer credit counselors who charge little or no fee. They will help you negotiate a realistic monthly payment and possibly reduce the rate of interest. One such organization is the Consumer Credit Counseling Service (CCCS). To locate an office near you, call 1-800-388-2227. This will get the credit card reps off your back. However, you'll still be on a severe debt diet—that's the cost of overindulging. We hope the relief you'll feel when you've shoveled your way out will keep you from similar binges in the future.

Credit Card Cure

Now that you're starting to see daylight, you don't want to return to your spendaholic ways. Assuming you need the convenience of a card, there's a fairly new system called a debit card you might consider. While it looks like a credit card, it doesn't act like one. A debit card is connected directly to your checking account. When you pay by debit card, the amount is automatically withdrawn from your checking account—it's just like writing a check. The beauty of a debit card is that it's as convenient as a credit card, but it doesn't tempt you to spend money you don't have. It's a great way to discipline your spending habits.

You may want to consider applying for a low-interest credit card. These companies charge appreciably smaller percentages than the name-brand cards, so you can save meaningful money. There are certain financial requirements for these cards and no guarantee that you'll be approved. It's worth a try, though! For lists of low-rate credit card issuers, send a request and $4 (check or money order) to Bankcard Holders of America, 524 Branch Drive, Salem, Virginia 24153, or call (703) 389-5445. Another source is RAM

Research's CARDTRAK, P.O. Box 1700, Frederick, Maryland 21702. The charge for this is $5.

Cash Control

Since so many of us find it difficult to live within our means, it's super-important to find ways to save on life's little everyday things. Although some of the following may sound almost elementary, you'll be surprised at how the savings can add up.

- Ask for an itemized bill, no matter what you're buying. Why should you be charged for six when you only bought five?

- Clip coupons from the Sunday newspaper. Fifty cents off here and there adds up.

- Sign up at supermarkets for their bonus club plans. It's another way to get things for less.

- Buy panty hose in bulk from the manufacturers, like the L'Eggs catalog, which offers big savings.

- Consider taking on part-time jobs—after-hours temping, baby-sitting, tutoring, dogwalking, etc. The extra money earned from a series of well-paid temp jobs enabled our friend Marie to buy a vacation home!

- Buy generic drugs whenever possible. They're generally just as good as name brands and cost half as much.

- Try to negotiate the sticker price whenever you can. In places like small gift shops, boutiques, flea markets, and street fairs, ask the vendor: ''Is this the best price you can give me?'' If you buy more than one of anything, ask for a volume discount.

- When you pay a small shop in cash or by check, instead of using a credit card, ask for a discount. Stores save money when you pay cash because credit card companies charge them a fee.

- Join the public library. You can get all the latest best-sellers, as well as the classics, for free. Plus, they have most current magazines, including business publications, as well as the daily newspapers.

- Sign up for an organization like Pet Privileges that will help you lower your vet bills and other pet-related expenses. For a modest annual fee—$49.95—you'll get discounts for vet bills and medication, coupons for food and other pet products, plus free access to their "ask-the-vet" hot line. Call 1-800-VIP-PETS.

- Save on airline costs. For the best possible price, call the airline and use the magic words: "I want the lowest price available." The airline is under obligation to give you all the alternatives, like special discount rates, thirty-day excursion fares, or weekday versus Saturday stay-over costs.

- To get a hotel room at the lowest rate, call them directly, not the chain's 800 number. They'll only give you the standard rate, never specials. Another way to save is to call the Hotel Reservation Network, a consortium that buys huge blocks of rooms at a discount and passes the savings on to you. Call 1-800-96-HOTEL.

- Eat on the cheap by getting yourself a dining card like the one offered by Transmedia Network, Inc. It offers big discounts at various restaurants around the country and can also be used at theaters, movies, spas, hotels, museum gift shops, department stores, even golf courses. To get the card, call 1-800-422-5090.

- If you buy an item in a department store and see it on sale a few weeks later, you can ask them to refund the difference. It's an automatic policy for most large department stores. Just make sure the price tags are still on the item or, if it's clothing you've worn, bring in your sales receipt to prove your point.

- Never let fast-talking telemarketing callers pressure you into buying anything. It's easy to make a mistake when you don't have all the facts in front of you. If you want to stop their sales pitch, simply say "I don't take telephone solicitations."

Extra Tip

If you really want to get rid of these pests, tell them firmly to take your name off their list. If they don't, you can either sue them in Small Claims Court or write your state's attorney general and complain. Keep a record of the date and time of the calls, along with the company's name and address as well as the caller's name.

- Take advantage of credit card companies' incentive programs—air mileage, hotel accommodations, and car rentals.

- Lights out! Turning lights on and off does not send your bill spiraling; leaving them on when you don't need them does. And—high-watt bulbs (150–200 kw) use much more power than you probably need or want to pay for.

The Professionals in Your Fiscal Life

At this stage of the game, there are two financial professionals you might find necessary: a lawyer, if the need should arise, and an accountant to do your taxes. What's the best way to ferret them out?

When you need a lawyer, start by asking family and friends for a recommendation. You not only want legal advice, you want it from someone who's respected in the field and has a reputation for integrity. You should look for an attorney who specializes in the particular area where you need help—i.e., accidents, divorce, discrimination/sexual harassment, housing, etc. To find a specialist, you can go to the public library and look through the *Martindale-Hubbell Law Directory*. It lists lawyers by city, state, education and specialty. It also rates them for performance. A similar list can be obtained from the American Bar Association.

Before retaining a lawyer, always ask up-front what the fee is. It can vary widely—from contingency (you don't pay unless you're awarded money) to huge hourly fees.

If your problem is relatively simple, you'd probably be better off with a small law firm. They're usually happy to have your business and will probably give you more attention. The bigger law firms often turn up their collective noses at anyone other than large corporations or the very rich, who have complicated holdings and estates.

Tax Time

War or peace, sun or snow—no matter what else is happening in the world, IT invariably comes—Income Tax Day. How do you get help?

Here are a few tips from New York's Albert M. Goldstein, who wears two hats—he's a tax attorney and a certified public accountant (CPA), the top professional credential in the field. Al advises:

1. Try to find a tax preparer who's an ex-IRS agent. He/she has been on the other side and generally knows the best ways to keep your tax payments as low as possible—legally of course.

2. Ask several friends and co-workers for the name of an accountant who falls into this category.

3. If your return is fairly simple, it's okay to use the large tax preparation chains. Their rates are fairly low—$150 to $200 per return.

4. If you have a more complicated return (you've won the lottery; are self-employed; received a large inheritance), you may want to find a CPA. Choose a large enough company so that the individual who prepares your return is usually available to you. Someone who works in a one- or two-person office is often so busy he/she might not always be there when you need them.

5. Try to find a company that tells you—in writing—that they'll accompany and advise you in the event of an IRS audit. Note, however, that some tax firms charge extra for this.

Good accountants can do more than just prepare your taxes. There's a whole litany of things they can advise you on—financial planning, renting, selling or buying real estate, and reviewing contracts of any nature.

THE FIVE BIGGEST MONEY MISTAKES MADE BY THE NEWLY EMPLOYED

1. She lives from paycheck to paycheck. In other words—she makes it, she spends it—all.

2. She doesn't create a budget or figure out where she can trim expenses.

3. She abuses her credit cards and is soon wallowing in a quicksand of debt.

4. She's an impulse buyer. She just can't resist the designer suit, Prada bag, or the latest CDs that she must have *right now*.

5. She doesn't bother to enroll in the company's 401(k) Plan or an IRA, using excuses like "Later," or "I'm too young to think about stuff like retirement plans."

Wrap-Up

Why is managing your money so important? The last thing you want is to invest blood, sweat, and tears in your career and have little to show for it. Where's your return? You owe it to yourself to be smart about the money you make, so you can track, monitor, save, and grow it. By max-ing your money, you'll be able to afford the little luxuries that make life so pleasant.

There's a whole world of options out there for making the most of your money. When you're ready to take control of your finances, then the perks and pleasures that only money can buy will soon be at your fingertips.

Feed Your Financial Know-How

The following books offer excellent grounding in the basics you should know about your money:

Get A Financial Life, by Beth Kobliner (A Fireside book, published by Simon & Schuster), a best-selling guide to help young people get a handle on money matters.

Personal Finance for Dummie$, by Eric Tyson (IDG Books Worldwide), a primer to get you started on all aspects of your financial life.

401(k) Take Charge of Your Future, by Eric Schurenberg (Warner Books), a detailed explanation of 401(k) plans and other investment options.

twenty-four

Psyching Yourself Up: Crisis Time

What are the things that can throw you into the pressure cooker faster than anything else? It's usually trouble on the job front; problems with husband, lover, family, friends; or money. In the worst-case scenario, both your career and personal life are in jeopardy at the same time.

Your nerves are frazzled, you can't make a decision, you're confused and desperate. You feel helpless and literally don't know where to turn. This is the time to realize that you can't go it alone. You need help.

There are various options available to you. They run the gamut from your best girlfriend's advice to highly specialized professionals in the mental health field. Some people find it helpful to pursue alternative methods, such as meditation and yoga. They feel these therapies not only ''center'' them, but also enable them to work through stressful situations. Are they effective? Plenty of people think so. If, on the other hand, you feel you need to talk through your problems, there are various people trained to do just that.

In today's frenetic world, you don't have to feel embarrassed or ashamed to seek help if you can't solve your problems yourself. If you feel so paralyzed you can't think your way through them, outside advice can provide both the sounding board and emotional support you need.

Free Advice

Sometimes you can unload on friends, parents, relatives, and other so-called armchair psychiatrists. You could, indeed, get surprisingly good advice—as long as it's fairly balanced. Mommy means well, of course, but her love is blind. Her telling you that your Significant Other was lucky to have you—after he's just dumped you—isn't really very helpful. You need more objective advice from someone you can trust to keep your confidence and to whom you can turn on a regular basis.

Confidentiality is very important. Even close friends are sometimes unable to resist telling others the deep, dark secret you've revealed. (Under most circumstances, trained professionals are obligated not to disclose anything you've told them in session.) Dr. Harry Levinson, an industrial psychologist, goes even further: "Well-meaning friends often give worthless advice. A suggestion to 'cheer up' may actually make you feel worse. During times of prolonged distress or painful interpersonal problems, professional therapists offer decided advantages: They've been trained to make diagnoses . . . they won't make you feel guilty, as you would with friends, in taking up too much of their time . . . and they won't get discouraged if you don't show immediate improvement."

More Free Advice

Other ways to soothe your psyche include highly respected self-help groups such as Alcoholics Anonymous (AA) and Alanon. AA is a free, group-support organization that helps people stop drinking and/or taking drugs, through its twelve-step program. AA welcomes everyone who thinks they have a chemical addiction. Listed in every phone book in the country, as well as overseas, AA will tell you when and where meetings are being held in your city. You can even find meetings where most members are in your age group. Alanon, closely allied with AA, is a support group for families and friends of the chemically addicted. If Alanon isn't listed in your phone book, call AA and they'll be able to guide you to a group in your area.

There are other twelve-step programs that offer help for virtually any compulsion. They're also free. Overweight? Try Overeaters Anonymous. In hock up to your eyeballs? We know a woman who goes to DA—Debtors Anonymous. Spending too much time and money at the racetrack? Gamblers Anonymous or Gam-A-Non can help. Usually, these programs work even better in conjunction with therapy. It's a double boost.

Self-help books have flooded the bookstores in the last twenty years. They can be useful; however, some are like popcorn—full of air. No matter how great some of them are, books can't talk to you in the deep dark of the night when you feel as if you're falling apart.

When something like this happens, you need a shoulder to lean on. Don't forget the old reliable sources—your priest, minister, or rabbi. You don't have to be particularly religious to take advantage of their compassion and wisdom. However, if these customary ways of overcoming problems don't work, you may want to fork over the cash to see a therapist.

Are You Losing It?

There are people who still equate the need for therapy with severe mental illness. They are definitely out of touch with reality. Do you have to be crazy to see a therapist? Absolutely not!

Talking out your feelings with a *licensed*—and we stress that word—professional can be one of the best investments of your life.

However, you should know a few of the basics. Never forget—not all therapists are equal. Some are brilliant, some merely mediocre. Unfortunately, a few are just plain frauds. But there are ways to tell the difference.

How to Find Help

The search for a therapist who's right for you should not be taken lightly. Discuss it first with your own physician. Tell him or her the general nature of your problem and ask for a recommendation of a competent therapist. Later, we'll discuss the different kinds of professionals who are available to help.

When making an appointment with a therapist, don't be afraid to mention price. Just a simple "What's your fee?" will do. The cost of therapy fluctuates widely. Some professionals charge on a sliding scale, depending on your ability to pay. You should find the very best you can afford. Therapists will usually suggest an initial meeting to determine if there's a "fit." Most of them charge a fee for this. Your first few visits will be exploratory. He or she will be trying to find out about your problems and how you deal with them. Most therapists will attempt to assess honestly whether or not you need treatment and if he/she can help.

Just remember: It takes two to tango. You, too, will be exploring to determine if there's a match. The relationship with a therapist is a delicate one. If you don't feel the chemistry is right after one or two visits, say good-bye. Don't waste time or money thinking it will get better. Responsible therapists won't try to intimidate you into staying in treatment with them if you've decided otherwise. There are greedy, unscrupulous practitioners in every field, and you shouldn't have to pay the price when it comes to your mental well-being.

Who Does What?

Basically, there are three kinds of professionals who are trained to work in the mental health field: psychiatrists, psychologists, and social workers.

What's the difference between a psychiatrist and a psychologist? They sound so similar, but there are differences. According to Dr. Clarice Kestenbaum, Clinical Professor of Psychiatry at New York's Columbia University, training and education form the dividing line between the two.

A *psychiatrist* is a medical doctor (M.D.) who has completed four years of general medical training, plus a one-year medical internship, and has spent three years in specialized training in psychiatry. Just as any physician, he or she can carry out diagnostic evaluations and prescribe medication. Specifically, psychiatrists are trained to work therapeutically with you. And remember, they are *licensed* to practice—very important!

Psychologists are licensed professionals who have completed two years of postgraduate work for an M.A. (or Masters), and may or may not have a Ph.D. Only if they have the latter can they be called Doctor. Don't confuse this kind of academic doctorate with the medical kind. Psychologists cannot prescribe medication.

Additionally, there is another group of counselors called social workers. They have a Masters in Social Work and usually work therapeutically with individuals, families, or groups. Like psychologists, they cannot prescribe medicine. Because their academic training is less extensive, their fees are generally lower.

And there's always group therapy. This is where various patients gather, under the supervision of a therapist, and talk out their problems. It costs less and it's obviously not one-on-one therapy. Each person has to wait his/her turn to share problems. Sometimes the hour ticks away before you can utter a word. The idea, though, is that you'll learn from the others.

For those who cannot afford therapy, Dr. Kestenbaum suggested some alternatives: "Most hospitals have clinics or can refer you to mental health centers where fees are based on ability to pay. You should also check out your health insurance plan because many of them now cover some type of psychotherapeutic treatment."

Formerly, employees were hesitant about seeking reimbursement for therapy from their company's health plan. They didn't want anyone to consider their emotional problems as indicative of weakness and possible instability that could affect their job performance. This trend appears to be changing, as more and more enlightened companies view therapy as an acceptable way to handle emotional problems.

If you need professional help, get it. However, it's smart to keep your personal problems undiscussed and undisclosed in the workplace. This is private information, and you certainly don't want it circulated on the office grapevine or used against you in any way.

Frauds Not Freudians

It's shocking, but *anyone* can hang out a shingle and call himself a therapist or "lay analyst." Believe it or not, there's also no legal restriction on the use of the term *psychotherapist*. In other words, there's no agency policing the field. Caveat emptor! Let the buyer beware!

It's up to you to find out if a therapist is licensed—whether as a psychiatrist, psychologist or social worker. Their certificate is usually framed and hung on the wall. If it isn't there, don't hesitate to ask to see it. A license may not fully guard against incompetence, but it's a big step in the right direction.

THERAPY NO-NO'S

- Don't try to make your therapist part of your social life—inviting him or her to parties or out to dinner. It could be awkward for both of you.
- Under no circumstances should there be sexual innuendos or physical contact between you and your therapist. It's not only unethical but against the law.

It's easy enough to talk about a problem; changing your behavior is when the real work begins. If you're willing to be open and honest and try to put what you've learned into practice, it can improve your life in umpteen ways.

This subject could be endlessly explored, but that's another book. Be careful with your psyche—it's the only one you've got!

Head Tips

- Don't feel embarrassed if you need help to cope with personal problems.

- Armchair psychiatrists—friends and family—can help in certain cases.

- Self-help or twelve-step programs have high success rates.

- Seek professional help if necessary.

- Ask your doctor to refer you to an accredited therapist.

- Never consult with a therapist who isn't licensed.

- If you don't feel comfortable with your counselor, leave!

- Changing your behavior is hard work, but you can do it.

twenty-five

What's Up, Doc?

The Care and Comfort of Your Bod

What does your health have to do with your job, your man, your life? Everything! What if you're due to make an important business presentation and you wake up with a migraine headache so blinding you can't see straight? What if you have a hot date and your stomach is cramping like crazy? What if you're planning a party and your allergies act up so badly you can barely breathe? You can't afford to let health problems get the best of you. Take charge! Learn how to be a well-informed medical consumer so you can find the best possible medical care when you're under the weather. Then you can zip back to business and get on with your life.

First of all, there are lots of good doctors out there. You just have to know how to find them. And, if you ask the right questions, you'll get the right answers.

Med Alert: The time to find the right doctor is when you don't need one. If you're sick and under the gun to find someone fast, you could make exactly the wrong choice.

Doctors Aren't Gods

Even though they bear responsibility for matters of life and death, doctors are only human—the same as you and me. They can have a variety of personality quirks, some of which may turn you off. Regardless of what your doctor is like, you're still entitled to five key things:

1. **Competent care**—This means the physician you pick must have the proper professional credentials, including education, residency training, and board certification. Find out where a doctor went to school and served a residency. There are two books, available in most libraries, that list information about doctors' credentials: the American Board of Medical Specialities' *Compendium of Certified Medical Specialists*, and Marquis's *Directory of Medical Specialists*.

   Although it's certainly a plus if a physician went to a prestigious medical school, it doesn't necessarily tell you about his/her skills as a doctor.

   By the way, board certification indicates that after graduation from medical school, a doctor has gone on to complete a residency, anywhere from two to four years, and has passed an intensive examination in his/her chosen specialty.

2. **Professional reputation**—There are physicians who have blue-ribbon credentials but are not necessarily good practitioners. Although their reputation may be outstanding, it could be based on research, for instance, not patient care. Why bother going to a doctor who's not particularly interested in working with people?

3. **A personable bedside manner**—A cold, brusque physician may be a terrific technician—but you're a human being, not a car in need of a mechanic. A report by Towers Perrin, the management consulting firm, states that "after

reputation, communications skills are the most important factor sought in doctors. Patients want sensitive and caring doctors who listen carefully and demonstrate their concern.'' If a doctor doesn't take the time to listen carefully to you, how can he properly evaluate your condition?

4. **Availability when necessary**—No doctor is so busy, regardless of caseloads, that he or she can't at least return your phone calls.

5. **An efficient, pleasant, and *sanitary* office**—You're entitled to staff and surroundings that make you feel the patient is important, respected, and understood.

Competency Checks

So, how do you determine a physician's competency? First ask his staff if he has a ''hospital appointment'' or admitting privileges to a well-respected facility, such as a teaching hospital. This type of hospital is connected with a medical school or research facility and is known for two critical factors: high-quality nursing staffs as well as effective infection control. Because teaching hospitals are on the cutting edge in terms of technology and medical information, they're able to attract the best doctors. In effect, they've actually done the prescreening for you.

If your doctor isn't affiliated with a top hospital, you probably should switch. Watch out if you discover your doctor isn't associated with any hospital at all. Without such an appointment, he won't be able to act as your primary physician, should you have to be hospitalized. A different doctor, not necessarily familiar with your case, will be in charge of your care.

According to Robert Arnot, M.D., in his book, *The Best Medicine*, ''Your hospital can be even more important than your doctor. Studies have found that by the end of the hospital stay, only 20 percent of an operation's outcome can be attributed to the surgeon. The hospital is responsible for the remaining 80 percent.'' Some may argue with this figure, but we've heard enough horror stories about mistakes made in hospitals to give it some credence.

Med Alert: If you ever need hospitalization, try to bring an ''advocate'' with you, a friend or relative who can intercede with doctors and nurses to make sure you're getting the proper and correct care. It's important!

The New Medicine

Medical care has changed dramatically in the last few years. It's gone from straight health insurance to various forms of managed care. Company health plans usually fall into two categories: a fee-for-service (FFS) arrangement or a managed-care plan. Health Maintenance Organizations (HMOs) are the best-known form of managed care.

The key differences between the two types have to do with cost and the freedom to have the physician of your choice. FFS plans offer the option of seeing any physician you choose and the right to visit specialists if needed. These plans are on the costly side and require you to pay a deductible before the insurance kicks in. HMOs, which are more predominant than fee-for-service arrangements, cost less and require you to use a list of participating physicians. If you're not satisfied with the treatment you receive from your assigned HMO doctor, complain. Tell the plan administrator and ask for an alternative physician. Even though you're in a managed-care plan,

try to make sure you get the same attention as you would from a
physician in private practice.

Fee for Service

If you're free to choose your own doctor, your first
step is to find an internist, otherwise known as a general practitioner.
An internist is trained to treat the entire body. He or she should be
your primary care physician, responsible for your overall health. An
internist is like the conductor of an orchestra, determining when and
if a specialist should come into play and directing you to one of
them for a particular skill.

To find a good internist, you should get recommendations from
a number of sources. You can ask a few friends whose opinions you
respect. However, always ask *why* they recommend him/her. It could
be the physician's low fees, affable manner, or willingness to make
house calls. While these are valid considerations, they should *not* be
the main reasons for choosing a doctor. That choice should be based
first on his/her credentials: education, residency training, board certification, and hospital affiliation.

You can also ask around in the medical community for recommendations. For example, your dentist, eye doctor, or psychiatrist
can be great sources of information. Nurses are often very knowl-
edgeable resources, too, as they tend to know the inside story. If
you've just arrived in a city, you can check back with your hometown physician for names of competent doctors. Alternatively, you
can call a major hospital and ask the Department of Internal Medicine for several recommendations. Make sure you call a top-rated
hospital to get this information, since medical institutions recommend only their own staff physicians. You could also contact the
County Medical Society for at least three names. Presumably, they
will match the ones you've already gotten.

Even if you've done your best to check out a physician's reputation, remember that not all doctors are created equal. There's a wide range of competence in the medical world, just as in any profession. Our friend Wendy told us a chilling story about Dr.Q., for whom she had worked as office manager. Dr. Q. graduated from a leading university, attended a top medical school, was board certified, but he was a disaster as a physician.

Extremely disorganized, Dr Q. used to leave blood samples lying around, forgetting to tell his office staff which patients they belonged to! Since the samples weren't properly processed, they couldn't be sent to the lab for testing. He was also famous for his "wallet biopsies"—unnecessary tests to bring in additional income. To top it off, Dr. Q. liked to gargle in the office a lot, except that his "mouthwash" was pure scotch. Shockingly, Dr Q. is still in practice.

If you ever have the slightest suspicion that you're in the hands of a quack, find someone else immediately. And, if you question your doctor's diagnosis, get a second opinion. A qualified physician should not feel threatened when you suggest this. A second opinion that confirms your own doctor's analysis should give you greater confidence in him or her. If, on the other hand, the second physician gives you an entirely different opinion, it can be confusing. Medicine, however, is not an exact science, so if you can't decide what to do, seek a third opinion.

The Initial Interview

Take plenty of time to choose your primary care doctor. It's a little like marriage: look before you leap. The best way to sense what a particular physician is all about is to request an exploratory interview with him. This is an opportunity for you to sit down face-to-face with a doctor and, in effect, determine if you want to "hire" him/her to care for your health. Don't be intimidated by the idea of checking out a physician. It's an accepted medical practice. You'll probably be charged for this, but it's worth it in the long run.

When you schedule this meeting, ask the staff what the charge will be and inquire about the doctor's credentials—education, training, board certification, and hospital affiliation. You also should ask about office hours.

The reason for this initial meeting is to determine if there is positive chemistry between you and the doctor. Are you comfortable with the physician's style? Is he/she pleasant and interested in you? Do you get the feeling that this is a person you can trust? Do you feel the physician will allow you sufficient time to discuss your concerns or is he/she in a rush?

Here are some of the basic questions you should ask during the initial interview:

- If I get sick in the middle of the night, can I reach you?

- Which hospitals do you send your patients to?

- Who is your office manager, in case I have a question about procedures or billing?

- Who covers for you when you are away? Can I meet her or him?

- Do you make house calls if needed? (That'll give them their chuckle for the day!)

If you choose to combine this initial interview with a physical examination, always make it clear that you want a brief face-to-face meeting before your examination, while you're still dressed. It will be a more businesslike interview if you're fully clothed rather than in a flimsy paper gown, which no one can ever keep closed.

Office Criterion

W hen choosing a physician, another important factor is a friendly and professional staff—from the person who makes your appointment, to the nurse who assists the doctor, to the answering service personnel who pick up the phone after five o'clock. It really makes a difference. Never put up with shabby treatment from anyone on the doctor's staff. If this should happen, complain to their boss, the doctor. The staff members who assist a physician are service providers and should behave accordingly. Besides, you're paying dearly for it.

A well-organized office begins with an efficient receptionist, who takes your call promptly and doesn't overbook patients. If a doctor's time is properly organized, you shouldn't have to sit in the waiting room very long. Ask for the best time to make an appointment to avoid waiting; usually the first one of the day works best. And when the doctor meets with you, he or she should give you his or her full attention and take sufficient time to answer all your questions thoroughly.

Around-the-Clock Service

A physician's office should work smoothly, day and night. If you ever need to speak to the doctor after hours— whether it's an emergency or not—the answering service should be as helpful as the daytime staff, putting you in touch with your physician as soon as possible. If you're in pain or discomfort and don't hear back from the doctor within a reasonable length of time, call again and ask if your message was delivered. Unfortunately, answering services have been known to "lose" or "misplace" messages. If the message was delivered, however, a responsible physician will call back within the hour. If he doesn't, and you're still doubled over in pain, don't hesitate to call again. You're not being pushy; you need help, and it's your doctor's job to see that you get it.

Your Legal Rights

Doctors are legally bound to tell you about the medicines they prescribe—instructions and side effects. Never hesitate to ask your physician about any medicine you'll be taking. Some doctors get their information regarding drugs from the *Physicians' Desk Reference* (PDR). This two-thousand-page book is a comprehensive listing of all available prescription drugs, side-effects and potential risks. The same publisher puts out a layman's version, *The Family Guide to Prescription Drugs*. It's well worth buying. You can also ask your local pharmacist about your prescription. They've had at least five years' study in the preparation, use, and effects of drugs. Pharmacists are very accessible to customers and a treasure trove of information. Recent studies rank pharmacists as the most trusted of all medical professionals.

Doctors Can Be Duds, Too

Even though there are thousands of caring, competent physicians, there are a few we could all do without, like the **Doctor Icebergs** of the world. These kinds of medicos practically give you frostbite when they enter the room. No matter how many times you've been there, they act as if they hardly know you, much less remember your name. They give you minimal eye contact and discuss your medical problems in such a distant manner you can't wait to get out of the office. If this kind of icy demeanor describes your physician, you can feel perfectly justified in "firing" him or her and finding another. Going to the doctor is stressful enough without having to put up with cold, impersonal treatment. The skilled physician, who is truly interested in your health and well-being, can speed up the healing process.

We'd also never miss **The Authoritarian**. This arrogant breed implies that their opinion and judgment is final. When he or she gives you a diagnosis, you don't dare question it. You're made to feel stupid, as if you're wasting their time when you ask for a more detailed explanation. This kind of doctor does little to allay your fears, and much to keep you mystified about the cause of your problem.

Equally expendable is **Doctor Mumbo-Jumbo**, who has trouble making himself or herself understood. This kind of physician just can't seem to explain things clearly, no matter how many times you ask to have the diagnosis repeated. Always remember, it's a doctor's obligation to tell you what's going on in terms you can understand. Some doctors can't—or won't—explain things in an easy-to-follow manner. Realize it's their problem, not yours.

When Dr. Mumbo-Jumbo says, "You have an imbalanced strabismus. Next patient!"—ask him to please drop the medical jargon. You want to hear in plain English exactly what the problem is. After all, you didn't go to medical school. Sometimes asking for a visual explanation will help. Maybe seeing your X rays will make it clearer. Some doctors will even draw simple sketches of the body to explain a patient's problem. You should never leave a physician's office wondering what he or she said. It's important that you understand what's wrong with you and how to handle it. And, if you happen to be the kind of person who becomes anxious when you're talking to a doctor, it's perfectly all right to take notes during your session so you can review them later.

Another kind of physician we'd all like to avoid is **Doctor**

Surprise! Surprise! He or she specializes in keeping you in the dark and never bothers to tell you what's going to happen during the exam. They suddenly stick needles in you, poke around and do tests without telling you beforehand that you might feel some pain. The best doctors take it slowly and tell you what they're going to do before they do it, and what you'll feel while they're doing it. Even when it's a routine examination, they take great care to go over every little detail. When you know what to expect, you can handle things a lot better. Even for something as simple as a Pap smear, good doctors will give you a step-by-step explanation of the procedure. If your doctor doesn't do this, tell him/her you'd appreciate having it done.

Patient, Heal Thyself!

The old adages—adequate sleep, a well-balanced diet, exercise, and the right vitamins—still apply. Have regular medical checkups and gynecological exams. Ditto for the dentist. Neglected teeth can cause a host of seemingly unrelated medical problems. The body is a temple—your temple. Keep it fit with first-rate preventive care. And when you do have a problem, remember that you're entitled to top-notch, compassionate medical assistance.

Quick Capsule: Getting Through the Medical Maze

- Find a doctor while you're healthy, not sick.

- Doctors aren't gods.

- Demand competence, proper credentials, and hospital affiliations.

- Look for a doctor with a good bedside manner.

- Make sure your doctor is available when you need him.

- You're entitled to a clean, well-organized doctor's office.

- An internist is mandatory for primary care.

- Ask for physician referrals from others within the medical community—nurses, dentists, and of course, other doctors.

- Get a second opinion if you're in doubt about the diagnosis.

- Set up an exploratory interview before you become a patient.

- Ask your physician to explain all tests and treatments.

Resources:

– *The Best Medicine*, by Robert Arnot, M.D. (Addison Wesley). A guide designed to help you choose the top doctors, hospitals, and treatment.

– *The Consumer's Legal Guide to Today's Health Care*, by Stephen L. Isaacs, J. D. Swartz, and Ava C. Swartz, M.P.H. (Houghton Mifflin). Details your medical rights, how to assert them, and where to turn for help.

– *The Family Guide to Prescription Drugs*. (Medical Economics Data). A comprehensive encyclopedia of information on prescription drugs.

twenty-six

The Good Life Express

All aboard! Getting a seat on the *Good Life Express*, with the Right Job, the Right Man, and the Right Life, isn't easy. But you'll have a first-class ticket when your self-esteem is in hand. It's the fuel that powers the Express. It can take you anywhere, anytime you want to go.

Self-confidence affects everything—your job, your personal relationships, the way you live. When life throws you a curve ball or two, a strong sense of self helps you hang on tight. It's no accident that self-esteem is the dominant thread that runs through this book.

One of the biggest challenges you'll ever face is keeping your self-esteem in high gear. You may begin with a bang but freeze like a rabbit as soon as your self-confidence is attacked. Take heart. Most people have had more failures than they'll ever admit. The Express doesn't necessarily run smoothly or on schedule for every passenger. Into each life some rain must fall. There are unplanned stops, jolts, and maybe a derailment or two. It's how you handle those unexpected setbacks that matters. When you reach an impasse and doubt the sun will shine tomorrow, we hope you'll pull out your ''Success Bible'' for encouragement and direction.

When you're starting out, it's particularly important that you don't let life *happen* to you. It's so easy to be swept along like a leaf in the wind. Hold fast to your dreams and believe they'll come true. Others may try to discourage you, but don't let them stop you from having high hopes. The women profiled in this book had the kind of strong inner belief that helped them realize their ambitions, despite the fact that few of them had a cheering section.

Josie Natori, for one, had so much faith in the idea of starting her own business that she quit a lucrative job on Wall Street to follow her dream. Her friends thought she was foolish to give up a successful career in finance. She did, anyway, and built a multi-million-dollar fashion empire.

Kay Koplovitz had the vision, perseverance, and self-confidence to turn her early understanding of satellite technology into a business bonanza. People told her that the idea of a woman running a cable TV network was a crazy concept. Good thing she didn't listen, as her company is now one of the country's most successful cable network operations.

Muriel ''Mickie'' Siebert always knew deep down that she had what it takes to become the first woman in history to hold a seat on the New York Stock Exchange. She can't remember a single, solitary soul who encouraged her to go for the brass ring.

No one sprinkled fairy dust on these women and magically turned their fantasies into reality. Instead, each of them had the courage to march to the beat of her own drummer. They made life happen *for* them, instead of *to* them. Getting on the *Good Life Express* wasn't easy. Even now, they face daily obstacles and career crises that could terrify women with less self-esteem. If you follow their lead, along with the advice in this book, you, too, will have the self-confidence to hang in there.

Understand, though, no book—not even ours—can give you what only *you* can give yourself: a belief in your own talents and inner worth. When you feel undermined and unsure of yourself, just remember that what seems hopeless at night is never as bad in the light of day. Put self-doubt in the back of your mind and pull self-esteem to the front. Self-respect is such a fragile commodity that it needs constant reenforcement in order to flourish. It may be nurtured by others, but it must be rooted deep inside you if it's to remain alive and growing.

Does a seat on the *Good Life Express* mean having it all? It depends on what "all" is to you. If it means having a terrific job, finding a great guy, and savoring your lifestyle, yes, it's possible. But there are always compromises to be made. For example, juggling a demanding career and your personal life often requires a balancing act that would make the Flying Wallendas wobble. It's a constant challenge to find fulfillment in all aspects of your life, without feeling you're shortchanging one of them.

Part and parcel of having it all is a close involvement with a Significant Other, and mutual respect is the glue that holds it together. Please don't get exasperated, but you'll have to work at these relationships every day of your life. There is no vacation!

Does taking a trip on the *Good Life Express* mean you've got it made? No way! Some people will be green with envy that you're on board and they're not. Thankfully, there are others who'll be just the opposite—supportive and proud of your achievements. Your challenge, however, will be to fill your life with the good guys and to keep from becoming an easy target for the bad ones. You can do a few basic things to help. Don't flaunt your success. Modesty is a trait everyone admires. Be kind to everyone, especially those who can't fight back. Be generous with your heart and spirit. It will always come back to you.

Learn to count your blessings. Our friend Oprah Winfrey once said she continues to keep a "gratitude journal," where she lists all the good things that happen to her every day—especially the kind acts of others. Smugness and complacency can be your worst enemies. Always take time to sniff the roses and enjoy the view, even while you're striving ever upward.

Never think you know it all or that there aren't any more lessons to be learned. An openness to new knowledge, experiences, and challenges will keep you fresh, young at heart, and evergrowing. Plus, you'll be that much more interesting as a human being.

Last, when you get that seat on the *Good Life Express*, take someone with you. Reach your hand out and pull others aboard to share in your good fortune. Like so many other things in life, you'll find the ride even more exhilarating when it's shared.

About the Authors

TINA SANTI FLAHERTY was the first woman ever to be named a vice president at three of America's largest companies—Colgate-Palmolive, GTE, and Grey Advertising. A former radio-TV newscaster in her hometown of Memphis, Tennessee, she has authored books for various corporations and has been published in *Advertising Age*, *Dun's Review*, and *Ladies Home Journal*. Described by *Business Week* as one of America's top corporate women, she also is a much-sought-after speaker by universities, corporations, and women's organizations. She lives in Manhattan, the Hamptons, and Palm Beach, Florida, with her husband, William E. Flaherty.

KAY ISELIN GILMAN was born in New Jersey and started her writing career at the *Asbury Park* (N.J.) *Press*. She then became the first woman sports columnist for the *New York Daily News* and *Vogue* magazine. She is the author of a book about professional football, *Inside the Pressure Cooker: A Season in the Life of the New York Jets*. In the 1980s, she became a partner in Hemming and Gilman, a New York City–based special events firm. She has three sons and lives in New Jersey and Manhattan with her husband, Bjorn Ahlstrom.